A THEORY OF THE STATE

ECONOMIC RIGHTS, LEGAL RIGHTS, AND THE SCOPE OF THE STATE

This book models the emergence of the state and the forces that shape it. State creation is bound to protection needs. A specialized protector-ruler is efficient, but is also self-seeking. Individuals are expected to install rulers only after they have created mechanisms to control them. Among the off-shoots of the organized protection are a legal system and decision-making procedures that include voting. The initial "state of nature," then, may gradually evolve into a rule-of-law state.

The state endows individuals with rights by delineating what it will protect. Enforcement, however, is never perfect. People also use other third parties, such as firms, to enforce agreements. The mix of the actually chosen enforcement methods determines the size and character of the state.

As commodities become standardized, scale economies to contracting increase. We expect the state to expand its contract-enforcement territory by treaty or by conquest in order to exploit the economies of within-state enforcement. The desire to expand the contract-enforcement territory may also explain the creation of rule-of-law empires.

Yoram Barzel received his education at the Hebrew University and at the University of Chicago and has been at the University of Washington since 1961, where he is a professor of economics. His research encompasses applied price theory, the economics of property rights, and, most recently, political economy. His most recent research is on the emergence of the state, applying his model to medieval England and France. He has published extensively in the main economics journals, and in 1995 his essays were reprinted in Edward Elgar's series *Economists of the 20th Century*. His *Economic Analysis of Property Rights* (Cambridge University Press) is in its second edition. Professor Barzel is president of the Western Economic Association.

POLITICAL ECONOMY OF INSTITUTIONS AND DECISIONS

Series Editors

Randall Calvert, Washington University, St. Louis
Thráinn Eggertsson, Max Planck Institute, Germany, and University of Iceland

Founding Editors

James E. Alt, Harvard University
Douglass C. North, Washington University, St. Louis

Other Books in the Series

Alberto Alesina and Howard Rosenthal, *Partisan Politics, Divided
Government, and the Economy*
Lee J. Alston, Thráinn Eggertsson, and Douglass C. North, eds., *Empirical
Studies in Institutional Change*
Lee J. Alston and Joseph P. Ferrie, *Southern Paternalism and the Rise of the
American Welfare State: Economics, Politics, and Institutions, 1865–1965*
James E. Alt and Kenneth Shepsle, eds., *Perspectives on Positive
Political Economy*
Jeffrey S. Banks and Eric A. Hanushek, eds., *Modern Political Economy:
Old Topics, New Directions*
Yoram Barzel, *Economic Analysis of Property Rights* (2nd edition)
Robert Bates, *Beyond the Miracle of the Market: The Political Economy
of Agrarian Development in Kenya*
Peter F. Cowhey and Mathew McCubbins, eds., *Structure and Policy in Japan
and the United States*
Gary W. Cox, *The Efficient Secret: The Cabinet and the Development of
Political Parties in Victorian England*
Gary W. Cox, *Making Votes Count: Strategic Coordination in the World's
Electoral Systems*
Jean Ensminger, *Making a Market: The Institutional Transformation of
an African Society*
David Epstein and Sharyn O'Halloran, *Delegating Powers: A Transaction Cost
Politics Approach to Policy Making under Separate Powers*
Kathryn Firmin-Sellers, *The Transformation of Property Rights in the Gold
Coast: An Empirical Analysis Applying Rational Choice Theory*
Clark C. Gibson, *Politics and Poachers: The Political Economy of Wildlife
Policy in Africa*

Continued on page following index

A THEORY OF THE STATE

*Economic Rights, Legal Rights,
and the Scope of the State*

YORAM BARZEL
University of Washington

CAMBRIDGE
UNIVERSITY PRESS

PUBLISHED BY THE PRESS SYNDICATE OF THE UNIVERSITY OF CAMBRIDGE
The Pitt Building, Trumpington Street, Cambridge, United Kingdom

CAMBRIDGE UNIVERSITY PRESS
The Edinburgh Building, Cambridge CB2 2RU, UK
40 West 20th Street, New York, NY 10011-4211, USA
10 Stamford Road, Oakleigh, VIC 3166, Australia
Ruiz de Alarcón 13, 28014 Madrid, Spain
Dock House, The Waterfront, Cape Town 8001, South Africa

http://www.cambridge.org

First published 2002

Printed in the United States of America

Typeface Sabon 10/13 pt.   *System* QuarkXPress [BTS]

A catalog record for this book is available from the British Library.

Library of Congress Cataloging in Publication Data
Barzel, Yoram.
   A theory of the state: economic rights, legal rights, and the scope of the state /
Yoram Barzel.
      p. cm. – (Political economy of institutions and decisions)
   Includes bibliographical references and index.
   ISBN 0-521-80605-4 – ISBN 0-521-00064-5 (pb.)
   1. State, The. I. Title. II. Series.
JC11 .B385 2001
320.1 – dc21   2001025951

ISBN   0 521 80605 4   hardback
ISBN   0 521 00064 5   paperback

To Dina

Contents

ix

Contents

Preface

In the fall of 1995 I was visiting New College at Oxford University as a guest of Michael Hechter. At that time, I was working on a paper on the nature of the state, and I asked Michael to read it. Once he asked "Why don't you make it a book?" it became clear to me that that was where I was heading, and there was no going back. Michael, who is now back at the University of Washington, has been a constant source of advice and encouragement ever since.

A major theme of this book concerns agreements, their enforcement, and control of the force-using enforcer. The enforcement organization the state employs specializes in the use of violence. People, however, can use other third parties, such as religious institutions or private firms, for enforcement, or they may engage in self-enforcement. In fact, they frequently use more than one enforcer to enforce individual agreements. The approach in this book differs from other approaches concerned with the state, such as those of Olson and North (as well as Hobbes), by focusing on how enforcers are chosen and how those force-using enforcers are prevented from becoming dictators. An analysis of the enforcement of agreements and the choice of enforcers is shown to require the tools of conventional price theory and of game theory. For that reason, in spite of its non-conventional subject, this book uses tools from the economist's tool-bag.

The price theory used here is directed primarily toward the analysis of property rights and the cost of transacting. A major distinguishing characteristic of this analysis is the absence of absolutes. Acquisition of information is costly, and knowledge of economic entities is never complete. What people own and what they trade are not fully known. Thus property rights are not fully delineated, and opportunities for theft, capture, and other forms of transfer are ever present. No aspect of the material world is "first best," or Pareto optimal. Maximization requires that we take into account such "imperfections" (relative to conditions in the classic, Walrasian model) in the world in which we live. This is what the transaction-cost approach adopted here attempts to achieve.

My training in the game theory and contract theory needed for this project was acquired on the job, in the process of attempting to solve problems as I ran into them. I believe that aspects of the strength as well as the weakness of this book are due to my attempt to discover on my own the needed applications. Because I have not been constrained by the straitjacket that game theorists impose on themselves, I have been able to probe questions that more conventionally trained researchers are unlikely to ask.

In addition, as mentioned earlier, I may have expanded the scope of the theory by avoiding the assumption that any kind of knowledge is freely available. Statements such as "The principal knows that . . ." are common in the literature. I adopt the notion that what one knows is always costly to obtain and is subject to error. The more productive notion, in my view, is this: "At a cost, the principal can acquire information about X, and the cost of perfect information is always prohibitive." Errors thus remain, and their existence is accounted for in the model. The weakness of my operating mode comes from having, figuratively, to reinvent the wheel, which results in increased chances for error and awkwardness.

On many occasions, Fahad Khalil and Jacques Lawarreé patiently and graciously steered me out of trouble, corrected my mistakes, and apprised me of hidden assumptions I was making. My warmest thanks to both. I did not consult with them on every issue, however, and probably did not carry out their instructions to the letter. Thus they bear no responsibility for the errors and ambiguities that undoubtedly remain. I would be gratified if game theorists (or anyone else) should find my assertions challenging enough to explore their properties more deeply than I have been able and (after correcting my remaining errors) should delineate and extend the applications of my propositions.

This book suffers from meager scholarship. I am a slow reader, and the relevant literature is vast. I have no doubt that I have failed to examine important materials whose study would have made the book better. In any case, I apologize to those authors whose work I failed to cite; the oversight is not intentional.

My approach is positivistic. In spite of occasionally straying, being carried away with notions that may not have any empirical counterpart,

I attempt to be operational. I seldom test the predictions I make, however. The historical material serves primarily to indicate that the issues I deal with are not entirely imaginary. In my mind, at least, several propositions are actually tested. Because it would be difficult to convince the reader that I obtained the evidence after forming the hypothesis, I refrain from formal hypothesis testing. It is only proper that others do that.

The material in this book was presented to three cohorts of students. The interaction with the students was most stimulating to me, and hopefully that was mutual. Timothy Dittmer was especially insightful in his comments, criticisms, and elaborations. Materials from Chapters 3 and 5 were presented in a number of seminars, and these chapters were improved greatly as a result of the discussion. An earlier version of Chapter 3 has been published (Barzel, 2000b). John Wallis read an early version of the entire book as well as parts of newer versions. I thank him for the excellence of his extensive comments. I have also benefited from comments made by Douglas Allen, Scott Cameron, Paul David, Robert Ellickson, Edgar Kiser, Margaret Levi, Dean Lueck, Fred McChesney, Haideh Salehi-Estefani, and Dick Startz, as well as comments by an anonymous reader for Cambridge University Press. I had innumerable conversations with Levis Kochin in which he provided great insight into issues we discussed and pertinent empirical observations. Thanks to Karen Russell for drawing my attention to the citation at the opening of the book.

My wife, Dina, contributed significantly to the style and presentation of the material in the book. Early on she was exposed to every wild idea I had along the way. Somewhat reluctantly (being *ezer kenegdo*) she forced me to retract some of them and to rethink and reformulate most of the others. The book is immeasurably better for that experience.

I

Introduction

ואמר שמואל . . . זה יהיה משפט המלך אשר
ימלך עליכם . . . את שדותיכם ואת כרמיכם
וזיתיכם הטובים יקח . . . ואתם תהיו לו לעבדים

Samuel said "These will be the ways of the king who will reign over you
. . . he will take the best of your fields and vineyards and olive orchards . . . and
you shall be his slaves."

Samuel I, 8, 10–17.

This book attempts to explain how "the state" first emerged and to
describe the forces that have shaped it over time. Relying heavily on
property-rights tools, I propose a unique angle from which to view the
state. The book focuses on the paths taken by states that came to be governed by the rule of law. The model I use starts at a time just prior to
the advent of socializing by individuals, before any social trappings
existed. Although the findings are illustrated by numerous examples that
span much of history, my model does not take historical faithfulness as
its starting point. Rather, the building blocks of my model consist of particular aspects of the most basic conditions of early human life.

In this model, the creation and functioning of the state are tightly
bound up with the protection needs of individuals (and, later on, groups).
The mechanism that individuals must create in order to make good use
of such protection proves to play a major role in the formation of institutions. This is especially evident in the creation of rule-of-law institutions, which is the focus here. It will be shown that one of the offshoots
of institutions that provide organized protection is a legal system that
delineates and enforces legal rights.

The model I use reveals that the enforcement of agreements is a
basic feature of the state, but that the state is not the only enforcer of

agreements. The distinction between agreements enforced by the state and those enforced by other third parties, such as firms or religious institutions, determines the scope of the state. Moreover, I show that the nature of enforcement varies sharply between rule-of-law states and dictatorships. It emerges that the study of the state should be concerned not only with conventional political issues, such as voting, but also with conventional economic issues, such as contract choice and vertical integration. The property-rights angle adopted here for study of the state makes it clear that it is imperative to explore certain fundamental features of the state that have largely been overlooked in earlier studies.

My approach is Hobbesian (1991 [1651]), with Umbeck (1981) as a contemporary forerunner. The initial state of affairs considered here roughly corresponds to what Hobbes called a "state of nature." Individuals use their resources, including their ability to employ violence, to become better off. As in Hobbes, individuals here willingly install a specialist in the use of violence – a ruler resembling Hobbes's king – in order to constrain their predatory inclinations and to protect themselves from one another. In contrast, and echoing Samuel, I do not view the ruler as benign. Like everybody else, here the ruler is deemed self-seeking (what others sometimes characterize as "predatory"); he uses his power to make himself better off, whether others gain from his actions or not. The ruler may gain by confiscating subjects' wealth, including their wealth gained from specializing and from dealing with him.[1]

Hobbes gives a wealth-maximizing reason for the existence of monarchies, but he does not ask how they, or institutions in general, arose. Going beyond Hobbes, I propose that, given the opportunity, individuals will install a ruler to protect them *only after* they have created a collective-action mechanism. This mechanism will reduce the chance that the ruler will use his protection organization to confiscate their property. In Chapter 7, the creation and maintenance of such a mechanism emerge as fundamental features in the operation of the state governed by a rule of law.[2]

---

[1] Sened (1997, p. 15) similarly notes that, "a central flaw in this [Hobbesian] argument is that it assumes a benevolent sovereign who protects the right of his or her subjects, instead of explaining the motivation of the sovereign to do so."

[2] Popper (1962, vol. 1, pp. 124–5) recognizes the threat posed by the ruler to his subjects. He strongly asserts that to cope with the problem, institutions with the power to dismiss the ruler must be created. He states that the specific mechanism for effecting dismissal is "social-traditions." He recognizes that a mechanism using social traditions may be flawed, but does not explain how it operates.

Besides curbing the ruler, the collective-action mechanism delineates, partly through legislation, the rights it wishes the protection organizations to protect. If individuals fail to create such a mechanism before they allow protection to become a specialty, a protection specialist may quickly become a dictator. By the model here, individuals take elaborate and costly steps to avoid being governed by dictators. When they are successful, the state will delineate rights and encourage contract trade (i.e., market transactions), along with the standards that facilitate such trade. It will also attempt, by treaty or by conquest, to expand the territory over which contracts are enforced.

The state enforces agreements by the threat of or use of violence. Violence, however, is not invariably the most efficient means of enforcement. Third parties that do not use violence have a comparative advantage, primarily in enforcing agreements regarding the provision of various services (as distinct from commodities) and intellectual properties, as well as agreements among individuals residing in different states. When the information the parties use for enforcement is subjective, self-enforcement has an edge. Throughout this book, and especially in Chapter 4, we explore reasons for the existence of diverse third-party enforcers and conditions under which different enforcers tend to flourish.

Many of the more prominent theories of the state are normative.[3] The model developed here, relying on the Coasean property-rights (or transaction-cost) framework and spiked with elements of game theory, belongs to the more recent trend that strives toward operationality. Such a framework also underlies, to a substantial degree, studies of the state and state institutions by other scholars, including Olson (1965, 1982, 2000), Umbeck (1981), and North (1981, 1990), as well as Greif (1989, 1994), Levi (1988), Weingast (1994), and Williamson (1999).[4] The present study emphasizes a neglected issue: the mechanisms that people must create if they are to control their violence-wielding protectors. In addition, it is argued that the methods chosen to enforce the diverse exchange agreements determine the size and character of the state.

In order to prevent being taken over by the protector, individuals in rule-of-law states will not relinquish control of their means for

---

[3] The authors of these theories wish, among other things, to bring "the greatest happiness to the greatest number" or "provide a legal context for good will and respect for people." Hobbes's theory itself, although offering a rationale for the institution of royalty, is also largely normative.

[4] Buchanan and Tullock (1962), terming their pathbreaking work as "normative," have also provided much positive analysis.

collective action after the state is erected; rather, they will form institutions that will continuously protect their interests. In that, the present model diverges from, for instance, that of Olson (1965, 1982, 2000) and that of North (1981, 1990). Indeed, the individuals who decide on the rules of the game may change those rules to prevent the protectors they employ from confiscating their wealth.

Although some of the historical events and features of institutions I use for illustration are contemporary, the model's development stops short of reaching the present in at least one important respect. The services supplied by the modeled state include external and internal protection, legal services, and services that facilitate contracts, such as the formation of standards and the provision of currency. But the state in this model does not supply social services, nor does it provide services such as education or mail. Such limited government seems to have characterized much of Europe from the feudal period until the nineteenth century, but it does not seem to have continued beyond that period.

A model that is built in order to discover what people *actually do* must be operational. The state, then, has to be defined in such a way that pertinent competing theories can be tested. Because the literature does not provide a consensual definition of the state, and I find none of the existing ones satisfactory, I propose my own definition here.

Definition. *The **state** consists of (1) a set of individuals who are subject to a single ultimate third party who uses violence for enforcement and (2) a territory where these individuals reside, demarcated by the reach of the enforcer's power.*

Note that I am making the simplifying assumption that the ultimate third party is treated here as a single entity, even though it may consist of many individuals. I shall briefly elaborate on this issue later. The state is commonly viewed as having exclusive control over the use of violence, and it is sometimes defined by such exclusive control. I, too, define the state by the use of violence. However, I argue that such control need not be exclusive – and my definition does not require it.

In Chapter 2, the definition of the state is reiterated, and its features, including its scope, are discussed in detail. Chapter 3 addresses third-party enforcement and the scale economies unique to the use of violence for enforcement. The relationships between the state and third parties and the jurisdictions of the various third parties are discussed in Chapters 4–6.

In the model proposed here, as individuals begin to cooperate they specialize in production, but not in protection, and they form a collective-action mechanism to commit themselves to cooperate with one another. Only then will individuals allow specialization in protection. As discussed in Chapter 7, individuals acting collectively will constrain the specialized protectors and their organizations in order to reduce the chance that any of the protectors will take over.

What initially is a "state of nature," then, may gradually evolve into a rule-of-law state. The process consists of a series of self-enforced inter-actions, crucial among them being the creation of a collective-action mechanism.

As stated, I treat the state as a single entity, almost as a single person. All but the tiniest states, however, use the services of many individuals. I expect each of these individuals to do the best he can for himself, rather than fully catering to the state.[5] Only in two cases do I discuss the state's harnessing of individuals' motivations in order to attain its own goals. Both cases are discussed in Chapter 7, in connection with individuals' control over their protectors. One case concerns the way in which individuals are induced to participate in the collective action needed to prevent a specialized protector from taking over. The other case concerns the creation of multiple, partly independent, military forces. The desire of individual commanders not to fall prey to the others is exploited for its potential to prevent any of them from becoming a dictator.

In rule-of-law states the clients of the protection specialist are also his employers. Such clients face a trade-off between the probability that the specialist will take over and the efficiency of his operation (thus, its cost to them). Clients will prevent protectors from amassing the wealth nec-essary for a takeover by rewarding the protectors primarily by a wage. Clients will also constrain their protectors' actions in order to reduce the protectors' ability to gain full control of the protection resources. A pro-tector's incentive to perform is weakened, however, when his reward is less than his full contribution to the outcome. To reduce shirking, clients will supervise protectors and supplement their wages with a partial resid-ual claim to the protection outcome. Constraints imposed on protectors and inducements given to them are the focus of Chapter 8.

---

[5] Hechter (1987, ch. 7) discusses in detail the agency issues that arise as a result of the state not being a single person.

The balance of power between clients and protectors is subject to shocks both from natural disasters and from the invasion of a state by an enemy. The more severe the shock, the more costly it becomes for protector and clients to collect information about each other. Disputes between protector and clients will be more likely, and their behavior will be more "arbitrary." When the opportunity arises, I expect protectors to gain at their clients' expense. Ensuring that dictatorships could *never* arise would be prohibitively costly, and thus dictators sometimes will emerge. The larger the shock, the greater the chance that a protector (or a set of them) will take over and become dictator. The evolution toward the rule of law, then, may be interrupted by a dictator's takeover. Dictatorship is the historically dominant form of regime, seemingly because such takeovers are not easily reversible.

The distinction between economic rights and legal rights is of fundamental importance to this analysis. As defined here, economic rights reflect individuals' ability to consume or exchange commodities. These rights may exist in the absence of legal rights, though the latter tend to enhance the former. Legal rights are rights delineated by the state. The state, as a rule, chooses to enforce the rights it delineates. The means of enforcing economic rights that are not backed by legal rights include long-term relations. Both economic rights and, by the present model, legal rights are the consequences of maximizing behavior. Individuals will spend resources to create and increase these rights only when, net of the cost of the enhancement, the enhanced rights will increase their wealth (or utility, when it diverges from wealth).

The state must delineate what it agrees to protect. Providing protection, therefore, entails the legal delineation of rights. In Chapters 3 and 8–10 I argue that the state, with its power-backed adjudication mechanism, is best suited for contract exchange that relies on comprehensive specification of the exchanged commodities and services.[6] Rule-of-law states (in contrast to dictatorships) will encourage such trade. The state's enforcement serves to delineate the rights stipulated in contracts by individuals. Because the state tends to provide legal services at no marginal charge, I predict that it will restrict the scope of contracts in order to prevent excessive use of its services.

Two types of scale economies can affect, in part, the size of the state (Chapter 11). One category includes the scale economies that arise in assembling the power needed for protection. The other is associated with

---

[6] The term "contract" is used here exclusively for agreements enforced by the state.

contract trade. The trade of commodities requires territorial contiguity (or sea lanes), as does the use of force for contract enforcement. The larger the territory controlled by a state, the greater the gains from trade by contract. I conjecture that trading empires were created to take advantage of these economies.

The scale economies to the size of the state are tempered by individuals' efforts to constrain the state's protection power and by the intensification of incentive problems associated with larger states. These problems can be alleviated, in part, by enhancing local autonomy. As the state expands, subjects will encourage the protector to spin off some of his operations. This serves to reduce the concentration of power as well as the cost of bureaucracy, providing, among other things, for more local independence, making the state less of a leviathan (Chapter 12).

The agreements enforced by the state constitute what are usually considered market exchanges. These tend to be more impersonal than agreements enforced by other means. The latter types include agreements, or parts of them, supported by long-term relations and enforced by groups' various collective-action mechanisms. They also include the agreements taking place within organizations such as families and, most importantly in recent times, firms. Vertical operations within firms are one form of such activities. The interaction between contracts and merger is discussed in Chapter 5. Provisions enforced by a power-backed third party often accompany enforcement within organizations. Questions regarding when the exchange will take place in the market and when it will be within organizations, or will be backed by a brand name, are standard fare for economists. It emerges, then, that at least in part the study of the state falls squarely within the domain of economics.

The paths a dictatorial state may take are discussed here only peripherally. Elsewhere (Barzel, 2000a) I argue that as a dictatorial regime gains stability, the dictator can enrich himself by curbing *his own* confiscatory ability. One method of restraining himself is to form rule-of-law and voting institutions. A threat from the outside may induce him to do so.

In Chapter 15 I consider some of the attributes of dictatorship and compare dictatorial states with those governed by the rule of law. A dictator is more of a residual claimant to his own action than is an employed protector. A dictator, then, is not subject to the incentive problems of the employed protector. On the other hand, he has reason to fear rebellion and will take steps to avert it. One obvious measure in this direction that a new dictator will take is to dismantle or at least weaken the collective-action mechanisms that have been operating in his territory.

I hypothesize that this weakening will reduce the level of non-state third-party-enforced agreements and that of all the agreements made in dictatorial regimes, the ratio of power-backed third-party-enforced agreements to all agreements will exceed that seen in rule-of-law regimes.

Of all the work on the state during the past few decades, mine may seem to resemble most closely that of Olson (1965, 1982, 2000). The resemblance, however, is only superficial, and actually there is almost no overlap between us. If anything, my work is complementary to that of Olson. It is useful, then, to point out the nature of the differences.

The most basic of these is with regard to institutions. By and large, Olson takes them as a given. He analyzes the problems that arise in the production of public goods and the need for collective action in order to resolve them. Whereas small groups may be able to take such action, large groups cannot voluntarily do so. Large groups need the coercive power of the (already existing) state. Olson also probes the difference in behavior between what he calls a roving bandit and a sedentary one, showing how the encompassing interests of the latter lead to non-confiscatory taxes and to the sharing of the fruits of public goods with subjects. The tools he uses are drawn primarily from traditional public finance and linear taxes. The fascinating discussion of the Soviet Union in *Power and Prosperity* (2000), Olson's posthumously published book, brings up non-linear taxes as well as some property-rights notions. These, however, seem to be afterthoughts and are not integrated into the earlier analysis.

In contrast, my starting point is the absence of institutions, and, correspondingly, the absence of legal rights. I explore how institutions emerge and the actions that individuals undertake to preserve them. In my model, constraining the protector from becoming a dictator (here one with exploitative powers) is a continuing concern to any rule-of-law society. A trade-off exists between specializing, especially in protection, and takeover by the protector. Depending on the prevailing conditions, people choose their preferred position. Many of the actions taken by such a society should be interpreted in this vein. Indeed, both the prevention of dictatorship and the creation of institutions are collective-action problems that I address explicitly. Olson, at best, addressed these issues only implicitly.

The costliness of information implies that neither legal rights nor economic rights are ever fully delineated. Enforcing agreements is costly, and the state has a comparative advantage in enforcement only under certain circumstances. The scope of the state, defined as the ratio of state-enforced agreements to all agreements (Chapter 2), then, is less than 100%. Olson and most other students of the state seem oblivious to the notion of the state's scope and to the possibility that it could be anything other than 100%.

I share with North (1981, 1990) the view that institutions are at the heart of the state. My view, however, differs from that of North in one important respect. North claims that some societies adopt wealth-enhancing institutions, whereas others adopt wealth-destroying ones. He does not show why a nation will adopt "bad" institutions. In my analysis, institutions emerge as a result of the actions of wealth-maximizing individuals. Subject to the costs of transacting, these individuals will always create institutions that will maximize wealth.

PART I

The Emergence of Protection and Third-Party Enforcement

2

The State and the Enforcement of Agreements

A BEGINNING

The model developed here attempts to capture the emergence of social interactions. What should be its starting point? Knowing what is cause and what is effect is essential, and if one attempts to start at a relatively advanced stage of human development, disentangling effects and causes is exceedingly difficult. It is difficult to know which of the forces that might affect political institutions are exogenous and which are endogenous. Were it possible to go back in time to observe the sequence of development of such forces, this problem might be overcome. But at its dawn, coming out of the "primordial soup," society left behind no social record. A social record is a by-product of social order, which did not exist at that early stage. It is not possible, then, to reconstruct faithfully the early conditions of human life. Instead, we must develop a model for that purpose.[1] This is a problem similar to that of the origin of life, and Dennett's solution seems appropriate here also. Dennett (1995, p. 454) theorized about how life originated: "Since the relevant period was prehistoric, and since he [the evolutionist] had no fossil record to consult, his story would have to be rational reconstruction."

What could constitute *the* model or at least *a* model of the beginning? A candidate for one of the starting assumptions is that humans socialized and cooperated with one another from the outset. To proceed, however, we must have answers to questions such as these: Were they

---

[1] Rousseau (1761) portrays the beginning in a similar fashion. However, he does not seriously pursue the subsequent evolution. Rather, he explores what he views as some of its consequences. His main conclusion is that the levels of human freedom and happiness quickly went downhill with the development of society and the emergence of property rights.

then ruled autocratically, democratically, or in some other way? How specialized were individuals within groups? Were the groups small or large? No a priori way to come up with answers seems available. This, then, is not a useful starting point. I assume, instead, that at the beginning individuals operated independently. That beginning preceded socializing, and the model to be adopted must accommodate all interactions among individuals.

I make one exception, however, in asserting sexual interaction, rather than deriving conditions for it. Given sexual reproduction, survival for any length of time would have been inconsistent with individuals operating completely independently. Mating and the raising of the young must have occurred early. I take it as given that such had taken place. I abstract, however, from whatever effects such interactions may have on the operation of the model.[2] I now proceed with the other assumptions and their setting.

The basic assumptions are simple: At the beginning, individuals are independent of each other. They are diverse, differing in talent and in ability to use violence.[3] They are distributed over non-uniform space. Most importantly, each maximizes his utility, which is primarily a function of physical and human wealth and of personal safety, but not necessarily of the well-being of other humans. Such a beginning conforms to Hobbes's "state of nature."

Individuals use their skills and power to acquire assets and to defend themselves against others by whatever means they see fit. They will interact whenever they expect to gain from the interaction. As is obvious, at this point no institutions yet exist.[4] Therefore, we must guard against

---

[2] It seems plausible that successful integration of family formation and of the relationships within the family with the rest of the model will yield substantial returns. Among the questions that can be explored are those regarding the opportunities for long-term relationships among mates, among siblings, and between parents and their offspring. The relationship between parents and offspring is a component of the all-important continuity of long-term relations.

[3] Umbeck (1981) assumes that individuals are homogeneous.

[4] North (1981) makes a distinction between institutions and organizations. He defines institutions as the rules of the game, and organizations as the players. Here I attempt to show how the players will derive the rules of the game, and what rules they will derive. As will become clear in the course of the discussion, the distinction between institutions and organizations tends to be blurred. North (1990) seems to come close to this view. He discusses (p. 127) the "interplay of . . . economies of scale associated with a growing volume of trade . . . and the development of improved enforcement mechanism" and continues on to say that "surely the causation ran both ways."

using results that are derived from models that rely on the existence of institutions. Consider the market, for example. Whether the term means an organized exchange, as used for trading futures, or a medieval meeting place, individuals can exchange in either type of market only because an elaborate enforcement mechanism has already been put in place. It is improper to assume that individuals can trade in such markets before the appropriate institutions have been created.[5]

ECONOMIC RIGHTS

Initially, individuals have no legal rights over the assets they acquire, as no legal institutions exist. They do have, at least partially by might, "economic rights," akin to Hobbes's "natural rights," over these assets.[6] Economic rights, which I now define, pertain to what individuals *can* do with assets. The concept of "rights" here is strictly positive, carrying no normative connotation.

> **Definition.** *Economic rights: an individual's ability, in expected terms, to directly consume the services of an asset, or consume it indirectly through exchange.*[7]

This definition, like that of cost or of demand, is forward-looking: You own today the apples that will mature on your tree tomorrow. Indeed, you own today even the apples you intend to steal from your neighbor's tree tomorrow. Because the chance is positive that assets will be captured or stolen, assets that may appear fully owned are owned only in part. The probability that an asset will be stolen (or captured), as well as the level of its protection, will depend on its value. As the probability of theft increases, the ability to enjoy it declines, whereas the expense of

---

[5] The statement in the text may seem to belabor the obvious. Nevertheless, the current economic literature is replete with instances where the problem has been overlooked. This is especially true in much of the contemporary modeling of the predatory state. These models seem invariably to adopt some Walrasian ingredients. Such ingredients, however, are obtained under the assumption of costless delineation of rights. In such a world, the Coase theorem applies, and predatory behavior that transfers wealth at a resource cost must be absent.

[6] I use the terms "goods" and "commodities" interchangeably, and both largely interchangeably with "assets."

[7] The definition follows that by Cheung (1970), Alchian and Allen (1977, p. 114), and Alchian (1987). See also Allen (1991b). Allen's definition of transaction costs, which I use, is closely related to that of economic rights. It is as follows: *"Transaction costs are the resources used to establish and maintain property (i.e., economic) rights."*

protection is likely to increase. The ability to enjoy an asset varies, then, as its value varies. What individuals maximize (subject to their personal safety) is the value of their *economic rights*. Economic rights can exist in the absence of legal rights. Legal rights, which I define and discuss in Chapter 9, tend to enhance economic rights.

Individuals can acquire economic rights over new assets and protect their rights over existing ones by the use of violence in conjunction with other talents and skills, such as cunning and the ability to plan ahead. They invest in their own skills, including their physical power. For instance, they make weapons and learn to use them; they enhance their physical skills and build up stamina. They continue to invest as long as the net return is positive. I assume that a balance of power exists when all are simultaneously at their self-enforced individual equilibria.[8] Because each devotes to developing a capability in physical power the amount of resources he deems optimal, an equilibrium that our model predicts to prevail seems to exist. The existence of a balance does not require equality of power. As long as a strong (and clever) person does not think it profitable to take action against a weaker (and duller) one, because the latter is, say, hard to reach or well protected, there is a balance of power between them. The assets that individuals retain, including their own bodies, are those that others would find too expensive to capture. The less powerful (and cunning) an individual is, the fewer the assets he has. In addition, individuals can be enslaved, that is, can lose command and economic rights over (much of) their human resources.

INTERACTION AND INFORMATION

Individuals may interact by cooperating, especially through trade, or by capturing others' assets. Theft, with or without the use of violence, is a form of capture. Capture also occurs under conditions of moral hazard, adverse selection, and shirking, as well as when queuing and "excessive" picking and choosing take place.

Information is an essential ingredient in the interaction decisions. Both trade and capture activities require information about what each party possesses and thus what is available to trade and to capture. Individuals

---

[8] Prior to the emergence of cooperation, violence seems to have been the main means of capture. Cooperation opens the door for various forms of capture that do not necessarily use violence.

need information to form estimates of the outcome, or distribution of outcomes, of the action. Information on the relative powers of the actors is needed to make decisions on aggression and resistance to it. Finally, information on the parties' behavior patterns that are conducive to self-enforcement of agreements is needed to make decisions on trade.

Independent individuals first become acquainted with, and gradually accumulate information on, each other's operations. In the process of accumulating information, individuals discover, and take advantage of, opportunities for aggression. The information about patterns of behavior that is needed for cooperation seems very demanding and likely will emerge only slowly. Therefore, early on, the interactions between people are expected to consist primarily of acts of aggression and resistance to them. At that stage, then, individuals engage in production, self-protection, and theft. As time passes, the information they accumulate also enables them eventually to identify and act on exchange opportunities. Exchange can emerge only with individuals' repeated observations of each other. Exchange will take place if it is perceived that the opportunities will continue to be sufficiently profitable in the future that the parties cannot gain more by reneging on agreements in the present.[9]

The accumulation of information is one of only two forces for change here. The other, discussed in a later chapter, is the force of random shocks.[10] The accumulated information may exert its effects indefinitely provided the information and the investments it leads to are not destroyed. Given its public-good nature, information such as that on the pattern of an individual's actions, which is costly to collect, is likely to be of use to more than one person. Individuals, then, are expected to cooperate in sharing the information, rewarding its producers, and preserving it by developing means such as writing.

THE CONCEPT OF POWER

The term "power," as conventionally used, is not free of ambiguity. Power, especially in the context of the state, is usually viewed as the ability to inflict physical harm. The police and the military are the primary state institutions wielding power. Others, such as thieves and

[9] See Tirole (1988), especially pp. 246–7, and his citations.
[10] To a country, the threat from a newly emerging imperialist power may be a random event. In a more general setting, such emergence is endogenous.

marauders, usually have and often use such power. Although physical power is routinely used to enforce adjudication decisions, the more fundamental enforcement requirement is the ability to punish and impose costs. Physical power is only one of the means used for that purpose. The dictionary definition of "power" alerts us to the broader meanings of the term, including, besides "force," such notions as "authority" and "ability to impose one's will." People can impose costs in a variety of ways, including rolling a boulder into one's path, alienation of affection, and cutting off trade routes, as well as the use of spiritual power (ostracism), and even putting a hex on. The substantial amount of power, seemingly spiritual, that the pope had during the Middle Ages in countries beyond the borders of the Vatican is an example of power not involving force.[11] It does not seem appropriate, then, to equate "power" with ability to use violence.[12] The definition I adopt is in this spirit.

Definition. *Power is the ability to impose cost.*

Power is most useful to its owner when the threat of its use suffices to achieve the desired end. Imposing costs uses up resources. The wielder of power and his target will do well if they can come to terms and avoid the actual imposition of cost. If they estimate each other's power accurately, they know who has the edge, and by how much. They can then also assess the costs the aggressor and the victim will incur if the latter chooses to resist. They are aware, then, of a range of terms that will make both of them better off than if they actually use their power.

Reaching agreement is difficult because of the need to divide the cost savings between the parties, although the severity of the problem is reduced when power and resistance to it apply marginally. A more fundamental problem is that the power of each must be estimated, and such estimates are subject to error. When, between them, the two err in the direction of excessive optimism regarding their relative powers, they may choose to deploy their power.[13] In addition, if the two are to reach an agreement, the winner must commit not to renege after receiving his payment. I argue later that it is significantly easier for those using long-

---

[11] Stalin, who purportedly made the sarcastic comment "How many divisions does the pope have?" nevertheless suppressed and persecuted organized religion in Russia.

[12] It is commonly asserted that employers have power over employees (the master/servant relationship, in Coase's terms), and landlords over tenants, even though they seldom use violence.

[13] In Chapters 3 and 15, I discuss factors that lead to the use of force.

term relations to make such commitments than for those imposing costs by the use of violence.

Both violence and long-term relations can be used for the enforcement of agreements. Because these powers can also be used for capture, the clients for enforcement services may wish to constrain the enforcers, but constraining is also costly. Whereas individuals may choose not to constrain enforcers that impose costs by using long-term relations, they are unlikely to employ enforcers that impose costs by violence unless they can constrain the latter. The collective-action mechanism, discussed in Chapter 7, may be used to effect such constraining.

The problem of the ability or, more to the point, inability to commit is also at the root of theft and some wars. As stated, the aggressor and the victim can achieve a superior outcome between them if the actual use of violence can be avoided. Consider, say, a marauder. As a rule, he can overpower his victims by surprising them, even though they might have been able to deter his aggression if they had had sufficient warning. In spite of its potentially higher value, the marauder is unlikely to agree to negotiate a peaceful settlement. With the removal of the element of surprise, to which the marauder would have to commit, he would no longer be the more powerful side. He would require a commitment from the would-be victims, but the latter could not readily commit not to renege. Even within the narrower setting of an ongoing assault, the damage could be reduced if the marauder could make a firm commitment – say, not to murder a person if he gives up his hidden treasure – but such commitments are seldom enforceable. History is replete with incidents such as that of a general promising safe passage to the people in a city under siege provided they lay down their arms, and then promptly slaughtering them after they accept the terms offered.

As a last point regarding the avoidance of the use of power, consider its observability. The ability to come to terms will depend on the sides' estimates of their relative powers. There are various reasons to conceal one's power, or to exaggerate it, or to display it, or to restrict its size. Concealment is useful when the holder of power wishes to surprise his adversary. Exaggeration is used when the holder attempts to persuade his adversary to concede without putting up a fight. If the sides are able to come to terms, they may commit to display their powers. Because such a display will reduce the chance that power will be used, the parties will gain from the commitment. Indeed, if they can commit, they may be able to spend less capital on their power in the first place.

THE EXCLUSIVE-POWER DEFINITION OF THE STATE

The state is commonly defined in terms of its exclusive control of power. By Weber's pioneering definition (1968 [1922]), the state has a monopoly on the "legitimate" (by subjects' judgment) use of violence. According to Nozick, who provides a variation on Weber's definition, a necessary condition for the state is that "only it may decide who may use force and under what conditions ..." (1974, p. 23). The exclusive-power condition in these definitions, however, is too strong to be useful. It diverts attention from other essential features that the definition should capture.

As the state is conventionally perceived, its actual control over power is never complete. Numerous individuals and organizations not viewed as states have power too. Parents have power over their small children. Individuals who own weapons, legally or otherwise, have some power. Criminal organizations have a great deal of power and use force to commit crimes.[14] Indeed, if the state truly had such a monopoly, then, among other things, policemen would not have to fear criminals.

Even what constitutes the geographic jurisdiction of the state, that is, the area over which the state is presumed to have exclusive power, is not clear. The power that states have is not always confined to their "accepted" boundaries. For instance, for the past several decades, Israeli and irregular Lebanese forces have been able to operate sporadically inside each other's territory.

Exclusive power seems to imply a unified control of that power, sometimes in the hands of one person. If we fudge about the extent of "exclusivity," the exclusive-power definition may apply to despotic states in which the despot is the sole controller of power. In some rule-of-law states, however, a "separation of powers" prevails. Consider a territory in which individuals with collective power employ their protector. An essential feature of the conditions underlying the agreement between the two parties is that *neither* of them has exclusive power; rather, each set has some power, and there is a balance of power between the two.[15] The

---

[14] The fact that criminal power exists within all states (as conventionally perceived) either contradicts Nozick or, at best, makes the actual set of states that conform to his definition empty. The existence of criminal power does not contradict Weber, but then it seems that nothing does. Later on, however, I connect the notions of state power and legitimacy.

[15] Medieval England, where both the king and the nobility had power, provides an example of such separation. The Magna Carta (1216) emerged as a result of the

reason for the existence of a balance of power between clients and protector, as elaborated later, is that the former will enter into an agreement with the latter only after they assure themselves that he will not be able to overpower them. Clients may form several organizations, each with some power, to provide different forms of protection, thus reducing the chance that they could be overpowered. More importantly here, the power that the collective-action mechanism controls is not usually viewed as part of the state's power.[16] The exclusivity definition seems incapable of coping with the simultaneous existence of several power centers.[17] It is not useful to define the state in terms of *the* locus of power if such a locus does not necessarily exist.

DEFINING THE STATE

Given that power is an essential ingredient of the state, but that assignment of exclusive power does not provide a satisfactory basis for an operational model, what factors should the definition cover? Anticipating the state's role in power-backed third-party enforcement, the definition should allow for a classification of activities into two categories: (1) activities that altogether eschew exchange (fixing one's car, growing one's own vegetables), those involving self-enforced exchange (many of the activities within families), and those for which means other than violence are used for third-party enforcement (church-sponsored activities); (2) activities enforced by a violence-using third party (exchange by contract). In addition, the definition should accommodate the separability of powers and the non-exclusivity of power.

The definition should also take account of certain general conditions. To be useful, the definition must relate to observable magnitudes. It must therefore shun phenomena that are not readily measurable, even if they seem pertinent. In particular, the difficulty of measuring the effects of the

---

English nobility flexing its muscle to oppose King John's attempt to concentrate power in his hands. Both before that revolt and after it, a balance of power between the two seems to have prevailed.

[16] It is plausible that Weber would not have considered dictators with exclusive control of power as legitimate. Still, rule-of-law regimes, presumably legitimate, practice the separation of power.

[17] Wittfogel (1957) is clearly aware of the two major points made here: first, that the state does not have exclusive power even under despotism; second, that constraints on the use of power must be imposed for constitutional states to exist. The enforcement of the constraints also requires power. He does not, however, offer a definition of the state.

activities of illegal organizations may dictate their exclusion from the measure of the state, even if such organizations play a significant role *vis-à-vis* the state.[18] In addition, except for the presence of a random factor, two states with the same measured attributes should be equivalent for the purpose at hand.

At the heart of the definition of the state that I offer is the notion of power-backed third-party enforcement. The definition focuses on enforcement that relies on violence, but leaves open the question of its exclusivity and its character. In the next section I define the state's scope, in an attempt to capture the depth of third-party enforcement.

> **Definition.** *The **state** consists of (1) a set of individuals who are subject to a single ultimate third party who uses violence for enforcement and (2) a territory where these individuals reside, demarcated by the reach of the enforcer's power.*

In the remainder of this chapter, I discuss the nature of the state as defined here and explore, among other things, the state's geographic dimensions and its relationships with other organizations.

To better appreciate the geographic component of the definition, consider the following scenario. Locate on the map all the individuals who were residing at a particular time in pre–Common Market Western Europe. Draw a straight line between any two individuals who had an agreement subject to power-backed third-party enforcement, and note the identity of the enforcer. Assign to each of the enforcers operating in the area a distinct color, and color all the lines accordingly. The map, then, will contain many colored lines. By the definition here, and abstracting from the rest of the world, the area traversed by the set of all lines of a given color will constitute a state's territory. When lines of different colors do not mix, each third party is in control of an exclusive territory,[19] and the boundaries between the colors are the state borders.[20] I argue later that unless states form agreements to cede to each other some of their jurisdiction, the color lines of "legitimate" states are

---

[18] This is not to imply that illegal organizations are ignored here. They are explicitly discussed, and implications related to them are derived.

[19] The requirement that the lines be straight is too strong. It is sufficient that those of one state can be drawn without crossing those of others, which allows, for instance, for U-shaped states.

[20] Taiwan, by the definition here, is unambiguously a separate state, rather than being part of mainland China, in spite of the latter's contrary assertion.

unlikely to cross. Where illegal organizations operate, however, the colors are bound to mix.

THE SCOPE OF THE STATE

Definition. *The **scope of the state** is the ratio of the value of all violence-backed third-party-enforced agreements to the value of the gross product, inclusive of the imputed product, within the boundaries of the state.*

The state uses its third-party power to enforce certain agreements, called contracts here. Later I show that it delineates rights in the process. The rights the state delineates are designated "legal rights." Economic rights not backed by legal rights are not part of the scope of the state.[21]

I have one caveat before proceeding. Criminal organizations use violence to enforce agreements and thus might be said to meet the definition of a state. It is not likely, however, that we would observe the agreements that they enforce. Therefore, they are excluded from the numerator in the ratio that defines the scope of the state. By the same token, it does not seem that data could be obtained that would allow one to divide the value of the gross product between the legitimate state and the criminal organizations.

It is useful to consider the numerical values that the scope of the state can take, even though I make no attempt to calculate them. In an economy with no market exchange, the entire product consists of the imputed value. In such a state there are no power-backed third-party-enforced agreements, so the value of the ratio is zero. The lower the level of vertical integration in a market economy, the higher the value of the ratio.[22] To see this, consider a numerical example showing how the value of the ratio changes as an operation becomes more vertically integrated. Suppose person B buys $10 worth of raw materials, adds to that $20 of labor and capital services, and contracts to sell his product to person C for $30. In turn, C, contributes $30 of labor and capital services to the $30 of purchased materials and contracts to sell his product to others

---

[21] Some primitive tribes do not have specialized protectors (Taylor, 1982) and do not use violence for enforcement. Such tribes are not "states," as their scope would be zero.

[22] Vertical integration is defined and extensively discussed in Chapter 5.

for $60. The sum of the two values added is $20 + $30 = $50. The sum of the dollar amounts of the two exchange contracts, which are what the state enforces, is $30 + $60 = $90. The ratio of the latter to the former – the scope – is $90/$50 = 1.8. Had the two individuals merged into a single vertically integrated firm, the value added still would have been $50, but the $30 transaction between them would have become a within-firm transfer, and the dollar amount of the exchange contract would be only $60, giving a ratio of $60/$50 = 1.2. In general, vertical integration lowers the numerator but leaves the denominator unchanged, so it must lower the ratio. Here it would have fallen from 1.8 to 1.2. The greater the extent of contract exchange in a state, the higher the ratio, and the greater the scope of that state.

SELF-ENFORCEMENT AND THIRD-PARTY ENFORCEMENT OF AGREEMENTS

The state enforces contractual agreements, but not other forms of agreement. The geographic distribution of individuals who can gain from trade by contract, then, can affect the size of the state. Similarly, the advantages and disadvantages of different forms of agreements within a territory can affect the scope of the state. In this section I discuss the nature of the different forms of interaction.

Although interactions vary in purpose and mode, they can be handled within a common framework. This is achieved by treating all interactions as "agreements," including those involving capture. Agreements have to be enforced. Each individual will make agreements using the enforcement method that will yield him the greatest increase in wealth. Individuals' interactions can be self-enforced or enforced by a third party, with various alternatives within each category. Because the state provides third-party enforcement that uses force, but not other enforcement forms, individuals' choices of enforcement methods will determine the scope of the state.

As is obvious, the joint value of the outcomes of collaborative relationships that are enforced through long-term relations is higher than that from interactions in which one directly captures from another or protects against capture by another. The latter can take place only when the formation of long-term relations is subject to (relatively) high cost. I predict that as the cost of forming long-term relations falls, less theft will occur. We expect, for instance, more long-term relations among sedentary individuals than among nomads, because forming long-term relations among the latter is costlier than among the former. We expect, then, that as groups of nomads settle down, theft among them will decline.

Long-term relationships can be used directly for enforcement. They can also be used to form third-party-enforced agreements. Third-party enforcement is attractive in that subsets of directly interacting parties that make use of it are freed from the need to form long-term relationships between themselves. By relying on the third party, the transactors may be able, among other things, to execute exchanges with positive net present value even if the value of the relationship to one of them will become negative during the life of the agreement. This, for example, is the case with "pure" loans. Loans not accompanied by other relations cannot be self-enforced. The borrower would always be better off reneging once he had received the loan, and thus the loan would not be granted. A third party, however, may be able to enforce the terms of the loan, thus making both parties better off.

Third-party enforcement requires, besides the power to enforce, the commitment to enforce and the ability to adjudicate. Enforcers tend to differ in their ability to adjudicate. The need for adjudication and, more broadly, for assigning credit and blame suggests that self-enforcement has an edge over third-party enforcement in situations in which insiders can easily infer what their transacting partners have done but others cannot easily observe those actions.

The costs of applying different means of enforcement will differ according to circumstances, and the scale economies in applying them can vary widely. Each such means, then, may have a comparative advantage under different circumstances, and no single means is likely to be preferable to all the others all the time. For instance, excommunication cannot be effective if the transactors do not belong to the same community in the first place, and physical force will not be useful if the transactors are located far from the enforcer. The nature of the interaction can determine which form of enforcement will be used.

Scale economies to enforcement depend on a large number of factors, such as the ease of delineation, the existence of standards, population density, the nature and density of physical barriers, weapons technology, the nature of the communication technology, and the numbers and locations of adherents to different creeds. One important distinction here is between interactions for production purposes and interactions for protection or for capture. The reason, as stated earlier, is that those possessing skills for protection can also use them for extortion. The demanders of protective services are expected also to take measures to prevent extortion.

Individuals, whether singly or in cooperation with one another, initiate the third-party enforcement that they use for their agreements. One effect of enforcement is to reduce the wealth of some of the enforced. Enforcement will be ineffective unless all of the enforced (and organized subsets of them) perceive that resistance would not be worthwhile. If enforcement is by physical force, the enforcer must have more of it than the enforced. If enforcement is by excommunication, the enforcer must be able to persuade the members of the community to adhere to the ruling even as the excommunicated attempts to get the members to violate it. This condition also applies to a trading ban, or any other form of enforcement an enforcer may employ.

CONSTRAINING THE PROTECTOR

Because enforcers possess sufficient power to overcome clients' resistance, they can also use it to confiscate individual clients' assets. As argued in detail in the next chapter, a force-using enforcer, unlike other enforcers, can confiscate the assets of one client without increasing the cost of confiscating the assets of all others. At least some of the time, his return from doing that likely will exceed the return he could have from acting on behalf of his clients.

North (1990) views this as a dilemma for the theory of the state: "Third-party enforcement means the development of the state as a coercive force. If the state has coercive force, then those who run the state will use that force in their own interests at the expense of the rest of society." He sees no way out of this dilemma. He seems doubtful about Madison's proposed solution in the Federalist papers and Ostrom's (1971) elaboration thereof.[23] He sides with Riker's (1976) skepticism about that solution. I share that skepticism. In my view, however, the problem does have a solution. In Chapter 7, I attempt to demonstrate that *prior* creation of a collective-action mechanism constitutes a way out of the dilemma. Briefly, when clients perceive that the would-be enforcer's net return from confiscation would be positive, they will not empower him until after they have erected a mechanism to constrain him.

---

[23] One should bear in mind that the constituent units [i.e., the states that Madison (and Ostrom) were concerned with] were governed by rule of law. Individuals, then, had a great deal of freedom and did not have to fear repression by the state.

A collective-action mechanism that has the ability to prevent individuals from taking a free ride on others' action can also be used for that purpose. However, maintaining such mechanisms is expensive, and eventually substitutes for them may be developed, as also discussed in Chapter 7. Some of the time, however, these mechanisms or their substitutes will fail.

Suppose a third-party enforcer is able to overcome the collective-action mechanism that was erected to control him. I predict that he will take over, become a dictator, and confiscate some of his subjects' assets. The other existing collective-action mechanisms, however, pose a threat to him. Although these cannot exert physical force, and thus their threat is not immediate, they can use their organization to acquire such force and may try to unseat the current power-wielding enforcer. For that reason, I predict that when the force-using enforcer becomes a dictator, he not only will confiscate clients' properties but also will dismantle the other existing collective-action mechanisms. The more successful he is in doing that, the lower the chance that he will be toppled by an organized revolt. On the other hand, when individuals continue to control the force-wielding third party, they can be expected to allow some other third parties to operate in their domain. This difference between dictatorships and regimes controlled by subjects, as discussed in a later chapter, provides a rationale for the suggested definition of the state.

It is useful now to bring up a distinction between contracts and agreements and to introduce certain property-rights terms. The term "agreement" is used in its conventional sense. The term "contract" is restricted to agreements enforced by the state.[24] Thus contract trade is enforced by the state, and the exchanging parties' rights to the exchanged entities are delineated by the state as legal rights. All other agreements concern economic rights that are not backed by legal rights. I argue later that rule-of-law states will encourage contract trade (i.e., trade agreements enforced by the state), whereas dictatorships will tend to discourage contract trade. Nevertheless, as the current discussion implies, I predict that contract trade will constitute a larger fraction of all agreements in dictatorial states than in rule-of-law states, because the former will discourage even more forcefully any exchanges enforced by other third parties. In a dictatorship, then, the ratio of legal rights to all rights is predicted to be higher than in a state governed by the rule of law.

---

[24] Masten (1999) seems to have been the first to use the term "contract" as I do in the text and to have clearly made the distinction I am making.

THE STATE'S JURISDICTION AND NON-STATE THIRD-PARTY ENFORCEMENT

Besides the conventional state, various distinct organizations offer third-party adjudication and enforcement. These include, among others, families, firms, religious organizations, local governments, and criminal organizations. Such organizations may be in opposition to the "legitimate" power-backed third-party enforcer, independent of him, or subordinate to him. Those in the first category are characterized as criminal, or insurgent. Those in the other categories are either endorsed or at least tolerated by the power-backed third-party enforcer. Which, if any, of these organizations meets the definition of a state?

The definition stipulates that the enforcer must be "ultimate." Because the enforcer of an organization that is subordinate to another organization is not ultimate, such an organization cannot be a state. Eliminated as candidates for statehood, then, are organizations determined to be "nested" within others. In addition, organizations that use enforcement means other than physical power do not meet the definition of a state. These may be subordinate to the state, as in the case of chartered corporations. Others may operate at the fringe of the state, as with families that are not legally constituted and thus are governed entirely by their own self-enforcement or by non-state third-party enforcement. Finally, some may be independent of the state, as is the case for the Catholic church and certain organized ethnic groups.

The capabilities for imposing costs are diverse, and the enforcers' enforcement costs will differ from one application to another. Therefore, the most efficient means of enforcement for some relationships will differ from those for others. Consider the family. The traditional family is clearly nested within a larger state. It is subject, or subordinate, to state jurisdiction in that the marriage contract is enforced by the state. The family itself has some features of a state, in that parents can police, adjudicate, and use force to enforce relationships between underage children. Still, it operates "under the shadow" of the state. Indeed, the state can intervene in cases such as child abuse, revealing that, rather than the parents, it is the ultimate enforcer. Parents take charge of enforcing certain decisions regarding their young children, seemingly because their enforcement cost in these cases is less than the state's. The state could, conceivably, enhance its exclusivity in the use of force for enforcement by banning parents' enforcement, but it does so only on rare occasions (e.g., child abuse). The jurisdiction of the state relative to that of parents is not constant, however. For instance, parents' advantage seems to be greater at home than out of it, such as in schools, in kindergartens, and in day-care centers. We expect state enforcement to increase as children spend more time out of the home. Similarly, as children grow older, the physical power that the specialized protector has becomes more appropriate for enforcement, and outsiders in general may find the information needed for enforcement easier to obtain. Thus, it is expected that the enforcement role of the parents will decline as children grow older. This change is explicitly acknowledged by statutes declaring children legally independent when they reach a certain age.

Not all families operate under state tutelage. Consider the families formed by Catholic priests or the case of separated couples. These familial relationships are not necessarily governed by states that endorse Catholic doctrine; they are not nested within the state jurisdiction. Parents and superiors in these families sometimes use force for enforcement. Although the size of such families relative to the states in which they operate is minuscule, nevertheless they meet the criteria of being states.

The corporation is another type of organization operating within the state. Corporations engage in policing, adjudication (by management or by ombudsmen), and enforcement. However, they are incorporated under state law, and they do not use physical power to resolve disputes. The corporation, then, does not constitute a state. Does a sport league such as the National Football League constitute a state? This league has the power to impose various penalties on players, functionaries, and team owners. But like the corporation, it cannot use physical force for enforcement, and it is nested within the state's jurisdiction.[25] Like the family, local government can use physical force to enforce its adjudication decisions. By its very nature, however, local government is always subordinate to the central government, and thus does not constitute a state.[26] In secular states, religious organizations are not necessarily subordinate to the state, and some operate in more than one state. These organizations are not states as long as they do not use physical force for

---

[25] The difference in comparative advantage among third-party enforcers is illustrated by the attempt to reduce drug use. Both the state and sport leagues impose bans on drugs. They operate, however, on different enforcement margins. The state enforces the prohibition on the possession and trade of drugs. Sport leagues enforce the prohibition on actual use by their athletes. Quite clearly, neither has a comparative advantage in the other's line of enforcement.

[26] I discuss local autonomy in detail in Chapter 12.

enforcement. However, they become states when they take up arms to oppose existing regimes.

Certain organizations, although satisfying the definition of a state, are outlawed by the "legitimate" power-backed third-party enforcer and are labeled as criminal or as insurgent organizations. Later, in Chapter 13, we discuss why one state is defined as "legitimate" and another as "illegitimate." Organizations such as the Mafia and the Basque separatist movement possess the means for power-backed third-party enforcement, and they use such power to enforce agreements among individuals. The Mafia, for instance, uses force to ensure performance on exchange agreements involving smuggled goods. It obviously lies outside the jurisdiction of the legitimate state. By the definition here, then, it is a "state."

In terms of the appearance of the map described earlier in this chapter, colors will overlap where such organizations operate side by side with the legitimate state. Within the territorial overlap, neither has the exclusive control of power. The scope of each, then, is less than 100%. This scope is not geographically uniform. For example, Spain's scope is less in "Basque country" than within the rest of its conventional boundaries. Typically the scope of "legitimate" states is close to 100%. Because of the difficulty of measuring the scope of the state, we ignore illegitimate states when doing so. In the case of a civil war, or where a criminal organization seems to prevail, the difficulty of measuring the state's scope reflects the ambiguity of its power under those conditions.

Until relatively recently, a ship at sea constituted an interesting, somewhat exotic, example of a state. In the era preceding radio communications and air power, ships met the definition of a state. While at sea, the captain was the ultimate enforcer, applying force as needed, although perhaps somewhat constrained by the authority he would encounter in the ports he contemplated visiting. Whenever a ship entered a port controlled by a conventional state, the ship came under the jurisdiction of that state. Thus, ships, except for pirate ships, flip-flopped in their status as states.

Given the existence of numerous third-party enforcers, it might appear that a broader definition would serve us better: one in which the operations under *any* third-party enforcer would constitute a "state." But such a definition, besides diverging from common usage, would be unworkable. Moreover, as will become apparent in subsequent chapters, a third party that uses force has features that single it out from other enforcers. Still, it is important to recognize that something is being sacrificed by the use of the narrower definition. This can be illustrated by briefly considering the Catholic church and the German Hansa, two organizations neither of which seriously relied on physical force but nevertheless exercised a great deal of power for protracted time periods.

The Catholic church has its headquarters in the Vatican. For a long time, the armed forces of the Vatican have consisted of a small but potent Swiss Guard.[27] Since the unification of Italy, however, the Swiss Guard has provided the Vatican with enforcement power confined, at most, to its tiny enclave in Rome. This force obviously is not very useful in inducing compliance among the vast number of Catholics outside the Vatican. Nevertheless, numerous adherents comply with Catholic restrictions, such as not divorcing without the church's permission, even if their state of residence permits divorce.[28] Given that the definition of the state adopted here requires enforcement using physical force, the Catholic church is not a state. It resembles a state, however, in the extent of its power of enforcement, and thus we might consider it a state, with an asterisk.[29]

The German Hansa, too, had a great deal of influence, while lacking military power.[30] By A.D. 1300 some 180 German cities joined forces in the Hanseatic League to collectively defend their commercial interests in their foreign trade. The organization lasted more than three centuries and exercised a tremendous amount of power. However, it kept its own members in line not by physical force but rather by the seldom-acted-on threat of exclusion from its commerce treaties with other states. Against outsiders, a few times only, it did use force, consisting of the armies of its members. The organization's main weapon against outsiders was the commercial blockade, which proved effective most of the time. The German Hansa, then, does not qualify as a state either, but it, too, merits an asterisk.[31]

---

[27] The name is a relic from the Renaissance era, when the Swiss were major suppliers of mercenaries.

[28] Conventional states also exert influence on individuals beyond their borders (though seldom adjudicating their disputes). Israel, for example, exerts influence through religion and Zionist ideology on Jews abroad, and Soviet Russia exerted influence on individuals in the West through Communist ideology.

[29] It also resembles a state, in that it, too, may have to deal with "criminal" organizations, namely, those that flout its authority, usually termed "heretical."

[30] The information on the German Hansa is from Dollinger (1970).

[31] The European Union is another case that may deserve an asterisk. This union by now has a parliament, a vast bureaucracy, and other features that make it look like a state, especially in the ability to induce its members to comply with its decisions. Still, compliance seems to be strictly through long-term relations.

THE STATE AND THE MARKET

What is the relationship between the state and the market? We shall explore this relationship, starting with two definitions.

> **Definitions.** *Contract exchange: exchange enforced by the state, where the associated transfers constitute the legal transfer of ownership.*
> *Market: the interface between individuals or organizations engaged in contract exchange.*

Given my definition of "market," all contract exchange between individuals or organizations is in the market, but exchanges within organizations are not. In later chapters I shall elaborate on the usefulness of this definition of the market.

Contract exchange requires agreement, but not all exchange agreements are contracts. As I indicate later, the state's third-party enforcement facilitates low-cost transferability. The lower the cost of transferring legal ownership, the greater the number of transfers that can be expected, and with that the higher the scope of the state.

The change in women's participation in the labor force in the United States during the past half-century illustrates the enhanced role of markets. A "homemaker" (i.e., a woman supplying labor services within the family) is legally protected by the marriage contract and by various laws. The state, however, enforces only a small part of the agreement between husband and wife. The agreement regarding the amount and quality of homemaking services the husband expects from his wife, and the reward she expects for them, are largely self-enforced. They are also enforced to a moderate degree by non-state institutions such as the church. Short of divorce, disputes regarding the terms of the agreement tend to be resolved within the household (or by the church); the courts seldom intervene in resolving them.

The situation regarding labor services exchanged in the market is different. Suppliers of labor services in the market are usually bound by a reasonably detailed contract. Today we are seeing a wide range of disputes between women in the labor market and their employers regarding the contractual terms of employment, and those disputes are subject to court adjudication. During the past half-century, most women of labor-force age switched from being primarily homemakers to becoming primarily participants in the labor force. By the definition here, then, the scope of the state has expanded during that period. In Chapter 4 and beyond, I elaborate on the application of the definition of the state, in order to distinguish between power-backed third-party-enforced agreements and those otherwise enforced, and to evaluate their effectiveness.

CONCLUSIONS

This chapter offers a preliminary discussion of some distinct features of the state. Power (i.e., the ability to impose costs) can be exercised by the use of violence or by other means. The state is defined by its use of violence to enforce agreements and resolve disputes. Agreements, however, can also be self-enforced or can be enforced by other third-party enforcers. The scope of the state is defined as the fraction of the transactions it enforces relative to all transactions within its territory.

The state emerges with the specialized use of violence. In general, specialists are more efficient than generalists. Specialists in the use of violence, however, also have the power to confiscate. Individuals can control the violence specialist by prior creation of a collective-action mechanism. The tension between the need to constrain the specialists and the need for efficient protection is a major problem that people have to address, and it occupies much of the discussion in this study.

3

Third-Party Enforcement and the State

INTRODUCTION

Realizing the gains to be had from specialization requires exchange, and exchange agreements must be enforced. The parties themselves may enforce the agreements. Self-enforcement, however, works well only for some agreements. Third-party enforcement often works better, because third parties are able to provide the principals to an agreement an altered set of incentives such that their net gains from interacting will exceed those they could attain under self-enforcement. Third-party enforcement, however, is costly and will not be used in all cases.

Third-party enforcers impose costs, either by the use of violence or through long-term relations. The distinction between the two types of enforcers is fundamental to the theory of the state, because there are differences between the kinds of agreements they can enforce, as well as differences in their capacities to abuse their own power.

In this chapter I first argue that many different individuals and organizations, each with their comparative advantages, can supply third-party enforcement services. Third parties can follow one of two radically different sets of measures for imposing costs. One set imposes costs by limiting or reducing the extent of valuable long-term relationships between the enforced party and its outside trading partners. The ability to do so requires that the enforcer and the enforced maintain a long-term relationship. The other set of measures is used where there are no enduring direct relationships between the enforcers and the enforced

An earlier version of this chapter has been published as "The State and the Diversity of Third-Party Enforcers," in *Institutions, Contracts and Organizations*, ed. Claude Ménard, pp. 211–33. Cheltenham, UK: Edward Elgar, 2000. Reprinted by permission of the editor and of the publisher.

parties. In this case the enforcers impose costs by inflicting harm. This latter enforcement form is at the heart of the state.

I continue by exploring two central themes: the nature of third-party enforcement and the commonality and differences between the two third-party enforcement modes described. Chapters 4 and 5 will elaborate on the scope of self-enforcement versus third-party enforcement and, within the latter category, on the scope of enforcement with and without violence. They will also bring out the relationship between the state and anonymous trade.

Following are the definitions of the central terms used in this chapter.

> **Definitions.** *Economic rights: the ability to enjoy (directly or indirectly) the services of assets.*
>
> *Dispute: the simultaneous expenditures of resources by multiple individuals to claim the same assets.*
>
> *Power: the ability to impose costs.*
>
> *Enforcement: the credible threat to induce compliance.*
>
> *Violence: impersonal means of imposing costs (i.e., by individuals who do not form enduring relationships with the enforced).*[1]
>
> *Theft: taking assets, sometimes by use of violence* (as just defined).
>
> *Extortion: extracting payment by the threat of imposing costs* (whether by using violence *or* by other means).

THE DIVERSITY OF DISPUTE-RESOLVING ENFORCEMENT FORMS

A useful unifying theme here is that of dispute and its resolution. Any interaction among individuals either is a dispute or has the potential for becoming one. A fistfight over a material good is obviously a dispute. So is plain theft, because one individual spends resources to retain a good, and another to take it away. Less obvious are cases in which there is no charge for a good whose supply is limited. These are disputes in which consumers compete with one another by spending resources – by waiting in line, for example – to the point that their marginal valuation of the good becomes zero. What methods can parties employ to avert and to resolve disputes?

---

[1] Thanks to Paul Heyne and to Fahad Khalil for helping to elucidate this concept.

Individuals can interact on a one-time basis, with no continuation, or on a long-term basis. In the absence of third parties, a large fraction, if not all, of one-time interactions will consist of capture or transfer at a resource cost. As a rule, one individual expects to gain, and one to lose, and because of the costs involved, the joint value of the interaction is negative. In long-term interactions, on the other hand, both parties expect to gain. Such interactions require an investment in reputation and incur costs in policing the relationships. Direct long-term interactions, however, will not accommodate all jointly valued projects even when these requirements are met.

Consider ventures that have a positive present value at their inception. Such ventures may be negatively valued to one party or the other at different points in time. The greater a party's belief that the value of the venture will become negative, the greater the advantage of third-party enforcement over self-enforcement.[2] A loan agreement is the most prominent type of agreement that is certain to become negatively valued during its life. As is well known from the literature on sovereign debt, lending agreements are definitely not self-enforced, as the borrower is sure to renege once the loan is granted.[3] The parties can gain from the assistance of a third party in ensuring that the ventures will be undertaken.

Before proceeding, the primacy of self-enforced relationships must be made clear. In an early society at the onset of interactions, all agreements must be self-enforced, because no external organization yet exists to offer third-party enforcement. Indeed, ultimately, all agreements in any setting must be self-enforced. Third-party enforcement, including that by the state, can be embedded within self-enforced agreements. Being a bootstrap operation, third-party enforcement requires agreements between clients and the would-be third-party enforcers. These agreements must also be self-enforced. In their relationships with one another, then, the third parties and their clients must perceive, individually or collectively, that the gain from maintaining their relationships in the future will exceed whatever gains they could reap from reneging on their agreements in the present.

---

[2] Even a small probability of reneging can turn an otherwise highly profitable project into an unprofitable one and thus prevent the undertaking of jointly profitable projects.

[3] The borrower will not renege immediately only if he expects the lender to be foolish enough to increase the loan at a later time by an amount exceeding, in present-value terms, the interim payback.

Proceeding with the main theme: The third party induces the principals to perform in cases in which the value of the project may become negative to one or the other principal during the life of the agreement. It is well understood that under such circumstances a party will perform even when his direct gain becomes negative. The reason for this is simply that he is unwilling to incur the even greater penalty that the third party would impose if he did not perform. It is also well understood that third parties sometimes incur enforcement costs that are lower than those incurred by parties enforcing their own agreements.

Seemingly not recognized is the fact that the third party can induce performance in an entirely different fashion: by offering the principals incentives to perform in a way that will generate a higher joint wealth than they could achieve on their own. Probably the most prominent activity of this kind, but one not usually viewed as falling under third-party enforcement, is turning self-employment into wage employment.

Consider a specialist whose output is another specialist's input. When the two operate independently, the latter buys the product of the former. The exchange itself consumes resources. For instance, the product may be heterogeneous and expensive to measure and to sort into uniform groups. The seller may then try to convince the buyer that the quality of the product is higher than it actually is, and the buyer may claim that it is lower. They may resolve the problem directly by engaging in excessive (compared with joint maximizing) measurement.[4] This problem may become less acute if, instead of operating independently, they are both hired by an entrepreneur who rewards them with wage payments. Although they then could gain by shirking, their gain from excessive measurement would be reduced. The entrepreneur here is a third party to his employees. The more costly is the measurement of the (intermediate) output relative to that of the factor inputs, the more attractive is the employment relationship.

The discussion to this point suggests that in spite of its unusual character, third-party enforcement is a service that is subject to demand and supply forces. I proceed by discussing various aspects of the "market" for these services. Among these are the amount of power that third parties acquire, the clients' choice among providers, the constraints that

---

[4] Barzel (1982). An alternative scenario with the same implication as here is that one or the other may capture quasi rents associated with resources specialized to the venture at hand (Williamson, 1975; Klein, Crawford, and Alchian, 1979).

clients impose on the providers, and the special role of violence. Although violence plays a central role in the theory of the state, it cannot be understood without a proper understanding of third-party enforcement. The analysis of such enforcement partly precedes and partly is mingled with the elucidation of the role of violence.

THIRD-PARTY ENFORCEMENT AND THE NATURE OF ENFORCEMENT COSTS

The contract-theory literature concerning individuals' behavior in the presence of a third party usually takes for granted the latter's existence and readiness to enforce agreements. Moreover, it routinely assumes, though usually not explicitly, that third-party enforcement relies only on (the threat of) violence.[5] The state, as I define it, uses violence for enforcement. Third-party-enforced agreements and state-enforced contracts are not the same things, however. The nature of the third party and its mode of operation are not as straightforward as the conventional thinking implies, and they call for careful scrutiny.

As stated in Chapter 2, the essence of enforcement power is in the enforcer's ability to punish (i.e., to impose costs).[6] Those costs can be imposed both by the use of violence and by other means. Enforcers who use violence for enforcement usually lack the long-term relationships that could also be used to impose costs. Although enforcers who rely on long-term relationships may use physical power, they do not seem to have a comparative advantage in it. I argue that the use of violence for enforcement differs from other enforcement means in three respects: It is often cheaper; it is more threatening of confiscation; and it has an edge in enforcing contract (market) exchanges. I elaborate on these differences later in the section on the prevention of confiscation.

---

[5] A major exception is discussed by Milgrom, North, and Weingast (1990). They recognize (and offer an explanation for) why third-party enforcement does not require the use of the state's power-backed mechanism. They describe the operation of the "law merchant" whereby agreements between merchants from different states were enforced without recourse to physical power. They then construct a model to show how transactors who transact with each other only sporadically, but are connected to a network, can form a dispute-resolving mechanism in spite of the absence of state enforcement.

[6] Milgrom et al. (1990) use the term "enforce" only in conjunction with the state's police power. While I have no disagreement with their analysis, I adopt a wider interpretation of the term.

Everyone is endowed with some ability to impose costs. The absolute and relative amounts of the cost-imposing abilities will vary across individuals. These abilities are valuable to their possessors. Their owners can threaten to use them in order to engage in extortion as long as others cannot resist them easily. Given such value, and provided that some investment in such abilities is worthwhile, individuals can be expected to invest in them to the point where one dollar invested in them will yield one dollar in extra revenue from extortion. Individuals will also invest in their abilities to reduce the costs inflicted on them by others.

Third parties are diverse, variously consisting of independent individuals such as tribal elders or operating as (parts of) organizations. Contemporary organized third parties include, among others, the legal system of the state, firms, the Catholic church, the World Trade Organization, and the International Tennis Federation. Such third parties differ in terms of comparative advantage. For example, the World Trade Organization's advantage seems to be in inducing sovereign states to reduce trade barriers, whereas that of the Catholic church lies, in part, in family matters.

Different third parties impose costs by different means. The state imposes costs through use of the physical force of the police, and the Catholic church through excommunication and the prospect of purgatory. As is evident from these illustrations, the ability to impose costs does not necessitate the use of physical force, nor does it require a formal organization. I now show that without the deliberate erection of an organization, third parties can emerge as by-products of collaboration among individuals. Next I discuss enforcement without the use of physical force.

Consider *any* profitable self-enforced (long-running) cooperative venture undertaken by three or more individuals. The value of the contribution of each individual must exceed his potential contribution in alternative employment, and his reward, too, must exceed his reward elsewhere. Except for individuals who just break even, all of the participants in a cooperative venture share in the gains. By withholding his services, each is able to impose costs on the others who share in the gain. Every member of the group, then, has enforcement power. When two individuals bicker with each other, the third may demand that they "clean up their act." The third-party enforcement here, which is a by-product of a straightforward cooperative venture, is embedded within the overall self-enforced relationship among the three. The one posing a threat is a third party to the other two. In addition, individuals may take advantage of others' enforcement power to extend their activities to areas where self-enforcement was not economical.[7]

To underline the assertion that physical power is not necessary for enforcement, and to anticipate the notion of the optimizing level of power, consider what seems a plausible scenario regarding elders who are not their tribes' military leaders. These elders lack the physical power for enforcement; their enforcement power resides in their ability to tarnish the reputations of individuals who do not abide by their decisions. Tribe members rely on elders to resolve disputes. The members compensate the elders with gifts. The "elder" status is not acquired merely by becoming old; not every old individual is an elder. It is implausible that early in their lives individuals would have been effective in resolving disputes. A young person's judgment in a dispute would be unlikely to be heeded. The loser could easily claim bribery, and there would be no prior reason to support the claim of either. Individuals invest in their reputations, and the ones with a comparative advantage in acquiring names for themselves presumably are the ones who will eventually become the "elders." The more a would-be elder invests in his reputation, the more credible he becomes relative to others. We would expect him to be less challenged then. He acquires the ability, then, to adjudicate without having to spend much on enforcement.

Not only clients, but elders too, must perceive that they will become net losers if they break their agreements. Clients are induced to abide by the elders' decisions because otherwise the elders would tarnish the clients' reputations, and thus reduce their ability to form agreements in the future. Elders, too, may break agreements, and instead accept bribes and engage in extortion. Given the gain from concealment and the background noise in the system, not every act of extortion or bribery would be detected. To a degree, however, the elders are self-policed. The more they abuse their power, the greater the chance they will be detected. If detected and exposed, they will lose their clients and thus their expected enforcement income.

As stated, enforcement power can be based either on long-term relations between the enforcer and the enforced or on violence. Long-term relations, as in the case of an elder and his tribe, are of value to the

---

[7] The discussion in the text suggests that the demarcation between self-enforcement and third-party enforcement is not sharp.

enforcer. The potential loss of that value tends to restrain him from confiscating the gains that his enforcement facilitates. The situation regarding the enforcer using violence is very different. Long-term relations do
not bind this enforcer to his individual clients. If not constrained, he is
likely to benefit from confiscating the gains that his enforcement will
have helped to generate.

Clients cannot avoid the abuse ex post. However, they may be able
to avert it ex ante. They can cooperate with one another to form a
collective-action mechanism capable of controlling a third party. When
he is under their control, they can make him commit not to confiscate.[8]
The power that the collective-action mechanism can exercise is likely to
be dispersed and unspecialized. Still, when mobilized, it must exceed the
power that the violence specialist possesses. By using a collective-action
mechanism to control the specialist, individuals' fears of abuse are
abated.

How does the fact that dictators are not limited by a collective-action
mechanism affect their ability to enforce agreements? It seems appropriate to define an *absolute* dictator as one whose relationship with his
subjects is maintained *solely* by violence. Such a dictator will seize everything in sight. An absolute dictator obviously possesses enforcement
power. He is likely to enforce his own rules. In this sense, he is definitely
an "enforcer" of sorts. Having that power, however, is not sufficient to
make him an enforcer in the sense we are discussing. What third parties
enforce are *agreements* among individuals. Agreements are relationships
that individuals are free to form or not to form. Individuals who perceive the potential for a profitable agreement among themselves will ask
a third party to enforce it if they expect to gain from it. These expecta-
tions depend not only on the nature of the agreement but also on the
expected conduct of the third party. In particular, the principals will not
seek the service of a third party who would seem inclined to confiscate
their gains.[9] Absent error and unanticipated changes in conditions,
then, those who actually become third parties will not perceive that
confiscating the gains from the agreements they will enforce would be
profitable.[10]

---

[8] Self-constraint is considered elsewhere (Barzel, 2000a).

[9] Anybody with power, especially physical power, may attempt to confiscate the
(current and past) gains from agreements, regardless of who the enforcers are. Confiscation, however, requires knowledge of what there is to confiscate; an actual
enforcer has an advantage there.

[10] It would be prohibitively costly to prevent all errors and to anticipate all changes.
Situations are bound to occur such that enforcers will choose to renege on their

A dictator who does not commit not to confiscate is deprived, then, of the potential income that third-party enforcement services may generate. Making such a commitment, however, would require him to give up some of his dictatorial power, and he would cease to be absolute. In reality, of course, no dictator is truly absolute. A dictator must form long-term relationships with at least some of his subjects to secure their cooperation.

DIRECT AND INDIRECT ENFORCEMENT POWER

Third-party enforcement services are diverse and are costly to provide. In the next few sections we inquire into the nature of the interactions between the enforcer and the enforced.

A third party must be able to impose costs in order to induce each of the principals to an agreement to make one-way transfers to the other. The enforcer induces the parties to an agreement to perform in situations in which they would not be inclined to perform on their own. He does so by threatening to impose costs on them. The amount of cost-imposing power that a third party possesses sets a limit on what he can enforce.

Parties making an agreement subject to third-party enforcement will comply only if they think that the enforcer is able and willing to impose a cost at least as large as the required transfer. Individuals who wish to form agreements that will benefit from third-party enforcement will favor third parties who have sufficient power to effectively enforce their relationships.

The cost imposed by enforcers who use violence is direct. Imposing it does not require long-term relationships, neither between the principals and the enforcer nor among the principals themselves. It consists in the threat of physical punishment, which can include incarceration and seizure of property. The cost is indirect when it takes the form of curtailing long-term relations. The indirect enforcer threatens to deprive the enforced of benefits from future interactions with other individuals. That threat will be effective only where these relations are valued in the first place, and because the penalty will be incurred over a long period, it similarly will depend on the continuation of relations between the enforcer

agreements, confiscate clients' properties, and engage in activities such as forming "protection rackets." Later I discuss the changes that can lead to confiscation and the measures that people can take to reduce the chance that it will occur.

and the enforced. For instance, a church does not have the power of excommunication over those who have not chosen to gain from belonging to the church community, nor where the community comes to perceive that the church is abusing its power and thus does not participate in the excommunication.

In a similar manner, the enforcer imposing direct costs can be effective only when the parties are in his jurisdiction; he must be able to reach them at the time of dispute. To enforce a loan, the borrower must be within the enforcer's reach at repayment time. In cases of agreements that are consummated at the time of transaction and are taking place among strangers, say at a fair, the buyer may claim that he did not receive the agreed-upon merchandise, or a seller may claim that he did not receive payment. The fair owner, who is the violence-wielding third-party enforcer there, can enforce the trade. The transactors, who may reside elsewhere, with no expectation of meeting again, are tied to each other only by their contract. It is enforceable while they are in the enforcer's territory when they sign it or agree to it.

Reputation is not needed when the costs that the enforcers impose are direct. What the enforcers enforce are "market" transactions, governed by contract. Indeed, as a rule, the enforcer is apprised of the transactions only when disputes erupt. The contracts, then, must fully characterize the underlying agreements. On the other hand, third parties imposing indirect costs can enforce agreements only when they have such powers as the ability to tarnish the reputations of the principals. Such powers are not useful in transactions like the one described at the fair. I elaborate on these notions later.

THE PREVENTION OF CONFISCATION BY THE ENFORCER

In order to maximize the present value of his enforcement activity, an enforcer must ask how his present actions will affect his net gain from subsequent actions. When clients perceive that the enforcer is abusing his power instead of enforcing what he agreed to, they may fear that he might turn on them next. They may, then, take action to protect themselves from such abuse. The effect of such action on the enforcer will depend on whether the cost he imposes on the enforced is direct or indirect.

Under indirect enforcement, extortion can consist of such acts as a threat to tarnish the reputation of a client, making him fear that others will refrain from dealing with him. The chance that the enforcer's engagement in extortion may become public knowledge will increase with additional such acts. When people realize that the enforcer engages in extortion, they will reduce their use of his services. His legitimate earning ability from the provision of third-party services, as well as his power to extort, will then decline. The greater the opportunity that individuals have for securing the enforcement service from a competing third party, the quicker they can reduce their extortion losses by "voting with their feet." The prospect of such losses will constrain the enforcer. Moreover, the indirect enforcer's ability to prevent competitors from offering their services seems to be limited.

The case is rather different for an enforcer using violence. When an enforcer imposes direct costs, the abuse takes the form of confiscation, or of extortion via the threat of inflicting harm. In this case, too, people will begin to realize what the enforcer is up to with successive acts of abuse and will cease using his services. Such an enforcer's confiscation power does not depend on clients' perceptions. One act of confiscation will not greatly increase the enforcer's cost of additional confiscatory acts. The threat to use violence gives the enforcer who imposes direct costs the ability to confiscate the bulk of the gains that have accrued to those using his enforcement services.[11]

In the case of a violent enforcer, parties will not enter into agreements before they take steps to prevent confiscation. As stated, the principals to agreements are not compelled to use any particular third party to enforce them, and they will not secure the services of any third party they perceive as likely to confiscate their gains. The agreement with a third party is enforceable if the present value of his expected loss of future business is larger than his gains would be from confiscation. Alternatively, it can be enforced if he is constrained in some way not to confiscate. A collective-action mechanism can be formed and used for this purpose.[12] The constraint on the third party may serve the additional purpose of helping to guard against confiscation if that should become profitable where it was not profitable before. To preserve his ability to

---

[11] Implicit to the statement in the text is the assumption that all the clients of the enforcer reside in his territory. This, however, does not apply to traders at fairs. The fair owner can sell third-party services only to the foreigners who actually are present at the fairgrounds. These are also the only foreigners from whom he can confiscate, and even then, short of abducting them, only what they bring with them to the fair. He is constrained by potential loss of the prospective income from future users of his fair. Thus, although he uses violence, he cannot confiscate all the property of all his clients.

[12] Collective action is discussed in Chapter 7.

serve as a third party, the enforcer may also constrain himself (Barzel, 2000a).

The enforced may fear, among other things, that the enforcer will extort under the guise of honest adjudication. They can use the collective-action mechanism to require the enforcer to use open adjudication proceedings so that they can detect confiscation more easily and also can force him to apply high standards of evidence. The higher the potential penalty in a given case, the higher the standard of evidence expected. This may explain why, in the United States, criminal conviction requires evidence of guilt "beyond a reasonable doubt" and why, even in civil litigation, the standards in the United States are high compared with those in autocratic states, or those under indirect enforcers.[13]

Once clients perceive, even if incorrectly, that the enforcer is engaging in confiscation, confiscation becomes *more* profitable to him, because the demand for and therefore the value of his future third-party services becomes smaller. To preserve his ability to serve as a third party, then, the enforcer may constrain himself (Barzel, 2000a), or clients may take collective action to constrain him. Later we consider the adjudication procedure, which is another component of the constraining action.

SCALE ECONOMIES TO THE ENFORCER'S POWER

Inflicting punishment is costly. Accumulating power requires effort, and applying it uses up resources. Third-party enforcement accommodates specialization in accumulating enforcement power. The third party accumulates this power, while clients who otherwise would need power to enforce their self-enforced agreements reduce theirs. I demonstrate that, between them, the enforcer and his clients will consume fewer resources in imposing costs and in resisting such imposition than the clients alone would consume under self-enforcement.

Individuals tend to be in equilibrium (i.e., in a balance of power) with respect to each mode of imposing costs and the corresponding means of resisting it. Prior to the emergence of third-party enforcement, for every mode that individuals develop to impose costs, others will develop abilities to resist it. One attribute of this balance is as follows. Consider an asset, say a flock of sheep. One person holds the flock and attempts to

---

[13] This may also explain why, within rule-of-law states, non-state third parties are prohibited from employing capital punishment, or why in the United States the common law prohibits religious groups from suing people who leave them (Posner, 1996, p. 185).

protect it, while another occasionally steals from it. The equilibrium condition here is that, on the margin, a thief's expected cost of stealing one sheep is equal to his valuation of the sheep, and similarly regarding the owner's cost of protection.

Let us now focus on the use of violence for enforcement. Suppose a would-be enforcer proceeds to build up his power. As his power grows, his clients will need less and less power to enforce agreements among themselves. The balance of power that existed initially has now been upset. To avoid such disadvantage, would-be clients will make deals with the enforcer only *after* they agree among themselves to pool their powers to prevent confiscation by the power specialist. The initial balance of power was among independent individuals. After they secure an enforcer for their relationship, the balance becomes one between the enforcer and the group as a whole.[14]

What are the consequences of an increase in the size of the enforcer's clientele? That increase interacts with the problem of the balance of power between the enforcer and his collectively acting clients. Suppose the number of clients increases from two to four. If there was a balance of power before the number of clients increased, clients will now have "too much" power relative to that of the enforcer. To adjust, clients will reduce their own power, and the enforcer will increase his. Compare the situation before adjustment with that after it. I predict that the effect of the changes will be such that (1) the enforcer's ability to take over will be reduced, and (2) the chance of any individual defying him will also be reduced. Enforcement has been improved, and yet the total amount invested in power between the clients and the enforcer has been reduced. As the number of clients increases, then, the total expenditure on power decreases.

Diseconomies to the assembly and application of the collective-action power seem also to exist. As size increases, at some point the magnitude of the effect of the diseconomies will be the same as that of the effect of the economies. In the absence of an external threat, clients will wish to constrain the enforcer's size so as not to exceed this breakeven point, in order to reduce the chance of a takeover. If a takeover occurs in spite of the clients' preventive efforts, then the clients' constraints on the protector, who has now become the dictator, will cease to apply. I predict that after taking over, the protector will increase his power.

---

[14] In Chapter 7, I discuss how members of a group can enforce their own cooperation (i.e., how they form a collective-action mechanism).

OPTIMIZING THE THIRD PARTY'S
CONTRACT-ENFORCEMENT POWER

Individuals look for two major attributes in a third-party enforcer's services:

1. clarity and absence of bias in the delineation of disputed rights
2. success in achieving compliance

The clearer the delineation, the fewer the expected future disputes, and thus the higher the demand for the service. "Bias" reflects a transfer at a resource cost, and its joint value is negative. The more unbiased that people expect the delineation to be, the higher will be the demand for the services. Regarding compliance, its expected rate is also a matter of rights delineation, albeit indirectly. A ruling that is not enforced fails to delineate rights. The lower the rate of compliance, the lower will be the value of the enforcer's services. Individuals will determine whether or not, in spite of the prospect of enforcement, it is worth their while to renege on their agreements or refuse to comply with dispute-adjudication decisions. The more likely they are to renege ex post, the lower the value of the service ex ante.

I have little to say about the clarity of delineation, and I briefly discuss its unbiasedness later. In the rest of this section I focus on the relationship between the enforcer's power and the optimal level of enforcement. In later chapters I analyze the effects of outside threats on the optimum level of power to be held by violence-using enforcers.

In general, enforcement ability involving violence or via any other mode is valued not in terms of its absolute level but relative to others' abilities to resist or to counter it. If, to begin with, there is a balance of power among all individuals, then no one possesses sufficient power to economically enforce others' agreements. I expect, then, that the emergence of the third party will be accompanied by the accumulation of some power on his part, with a reduction in the power of his clients. The greater the amount of power an enforcer has, the fewer the instances in which the parties to agreements he enforces will choose to renege.

Compliance with the enforcer's rulings depends only indirectly on his "true" power relative to that of the enforced. Whether or not the parties choose to comply directly will depend on the information each side possesses about the relative power of each and on the resulting assessment. The nature of that information bears, then, on the question of when power will be used as a threat and when it will actually be deployed.

Given the available information, the enforcer invests in augmenting his power to attain the rate of compliance he desires.

If the sides assess each other's powers accurately, power will not be put to use. Suppose the information is accurate regarding the enforcer's power relative to that of the enforced, as well as the cost to each of using their power. The weaker, whether he is the enforced or the enforcer, knows that he will lose. Therefore, he will concede, not wasting his resources on futile action. The enforced will concede when they realize that they will lose, and then they will simply obey the third-party ruling. The enforcer will concede when he realizes that he will lose; the enforced then will choose to not obey, and will not be penalized. This is a situation where economic (but not necessarily legal) rights are well defined and disputes do not occur. Therefore no resources are spent on capture or dispute resolution.

Obtaining information is costly, and accurate information prohibitively so. Error in the parties' assessments of their relative powers will affect the optimal level of power, will lead to situations in which power will actually be used, and will affect the types of power the sides choose to acquire. These are discussed next.

As previously stated, the actual use of force results from error in measuring relative power between the enforcer and the enforced. The likelihood of such error increases as the difference in power decreases or the accuracy of each party's measurement decreases. The greater the (sum of the) errors in underestimating the other's power relative to the actual difference in power, the higher the chance of power being put to use.[15] When the enforcer's true power is initially greater than that of a subject, and the enforcer increases his power, then the subject is more likely to recognize his inferiority and thus is less likely to resist.[16] Moreover, increasing the *differential* in power between the sides is jointly positively valued.

The power of the modern state is an order of magnitude greater than that of any individual. Still, individuals may choose to resist the state by hiding, by legal gamesmanship, and even by "civil disobedience." In turn, the state does not always choose to prevail. Moreover, in earlier times single individuals did have a substantial amount of power. In medieval England, for example, some barons had large military forces.

[15] Landes (1971) makes this argument with regard to legal disputes.
[16] Although both the concealment of power and its exaggeration are expected, they are not germane to the point here.

The king could not be sure that he could subdue them in case of dispute. As another example, the continuing existence of criminals attests that one should not assume that the state always overpowers individual subjects.

Power is multidimensional, and the ease of assessing it varies. The greater the difficulty in assessing a particular type of power, the greater the assessment error, and therefore the chance that power will actually be deployed increases. Because deploying power is expensive, ceteris paribus, clients prefer enforcers whose power is easy to assess. The successful enforcers, then, are likely to hold power in a transparent form. The same applies to clients. The enforcer is likely to charge clients less for his services if they commit to restrict their power to forms that he can readily assess. When individuals form a collective-action mechanism, they may require the enforcer to maintain power only in forms that are easy to measure. Indeed, they may impose a similar restriction on themselves. Whereas there are many forms of imposing costs, I expect only a narrow subset of these to be in actual use.

Clients of a third party can enter into an array of agreements that may generate disputes and on which they may renege. Ex ante, the higher the level of compliance the enforcer can induce, the higher the clients' valuation of his services. Correspondingly, I would expect him to try to prevent reneging and resistance to unfavorable adjudication decisions. Nevertheless, in at least some cases, the third party may decide not to enforce his decisions. Ex post, clients will compute the benefit and the cost of non-compliance for each outcome. They are idiosyncratic, as are their particular disputes, and they are likely to perceive that they can get away with not complying with some of the decisions against them. Thus, a skeptic will view religious stigma less seriously than will a devout person and will be less likely to comply when the threat of the stigma is the means for enforcement. Similarly, a fleet-footed client will not fear a strong but awkward enforcer as much as will a clumsier client.

The third party can influence the level of compliance by his choice of the amount of power he acquires. What is the value of an extra dose of power to the enforcer, and what is the level of compliance that will maximize the third party's wealth? Consider an enforcer whose enforcement power is insufficient to induce total compliance. Those among the enforced whose true power is less than the enforcer's will yield without resistance if they realize where they stand. They are more likely to recognize their inferiority and yield as the enforcer enhances his power. Initially, however, compliance will be incomplete. With the increase in the enforcer's relative power, the difference in power between him and those who did not comply before will become less. For these, the ambiguity regarding their relative power becomes greater, and the chance of conflict becomes higher.

The net change in the rate of resistance among all clients will depend on the distribution of compliance. It is plausible that as a function of the enforcer's power the distribution of compliance becomes thinner at the tails, as the normal distribution does. It seems highly plausible that, starting at a relatively low enforcement power, the return to the enforcer from increasing his power will first increase, but eventually will fall. The optimal level of power lies beyond the center of the distribution. Beyond the center, the number of those who choose to resist will be smaller with each additional unit increase in the enforcer's power.[17] Inducing full compliance would not be economical; the optimal level of enforcement power will yield less than 100% compliance.

Although increasing his level of power is costly to the enforcer, as the rate of resistance falls with his increases in power, he will spend fewer resources on its deployment. Moreover, as clients recognize more clearly the futility of resistance, they, too, will spend fewer resources on the use of power. Indeed, they will be likely to accumulate less power in the first place. Their expected costs will also be lower, then, and they will be willing to pay the enforcer more for his services. The third party will choose the power and enforcement level that will equate his marginal cost with the marginal gain in expected income from fees due to the increase in the use of his services and the increased compliance.

As the enforcer's power increases, its effect snowballs. When his power relative to that of his clients increases, he will use it less. Thus he will find himself in possession of "standby" power. Such power can be used to enforce agreements among new clients as well, enabling the enforcer to cope with a proportionately larger number of clients.[18] The value of the increased force, then, increases faster than its actual size. A

---

[17] The result holds for the uniform distribution too. For that distribution, the two effects tend to cancel out, except for the truncation at the two ends. Because of the truncation, as the enforcer's power increases, the rate of increase in compliance falls.

[18] The logic here is identical with that behind insuring events that are not perfectly correlated. The same capital (force) can insure (enforce) more than one prospect, and the number of prospects that can be insured (number of subjects) increases faster than the amount of capital needed for a given level of insurance. Indeed, the more certain are the insured that the insurer can pay their claims (overpower them), the less inclined are they to generate "early" claims (to resist).

single large enforcer will do better in this regard than will several small ones. As stated, however, the effect of diseconomies will eventually prevail. In Chapter 8, I elaborate on the scale economies to the formation of enforcement power.

THE DEPLOYMENT OF POWER BY THIRD PARTIES

How far will a third party extend himself to actually enforce agreements that fall under his jurisdiction (i.e., those he has agreed to enforce)? Presumably, he will enforce only those agreements where the gain (including the reputational gain from doing what he has agreed to do) exceeds the enforcement cost, rather than enforce all the agreements he is "able" to. The same logic that concludes that clients will not comply fully yields the conclusion that enforcers will not enforce fully.

Aware that enforcement may be incomplete, individuals who renege on their agreements do not always fear enforcement. The Catholic church, for example, does not excommunicate or exclude from services every individual who has not fully complied with his or her church-mediated agreements, so there will be sinners. Another example concerns individuals under court-imposed obligation for child support in the United States. When such individuals move from one state to another and stop making their support payments, the states to which they have moved do not always choose to flush them out. In other cases, an enforcer may use force to retrieve individuals who have crossed borders to evade their contractual obligations. There is no clear answer to the question, To which state do such refuge territories exclusively belong?[19] It might seem that the difficulty could be finessed by viewing the expectation or the probability that a state would exercise its power as a measure of its degree of control over a territory. That expectation, however, is not (readily) measurable.

The ambiguity about what the state controls is greatly reduced if we turn from levels to changes in them, which we are apt to do when testing theories. For example, I predict that the state's control of the territories in question will increase when the cost of flushing individuals out of their hiding places falls, or when the state's power increases. Measuring

---

[19] We are used to the notion of lines drawn on a map that constitute borders between states. Until recently, however, such lines have seldom existed. Much of the time, no man's land has separated neighboring states, and that territory has tended to change hands frequently.

such changes does not seem daunting. I argued earlier that the state does not possess exclusive power and cannot be defined by it. On the other hand, the definition adopted here can readily be used to test hypotheses. One plausible hypothesis is that as the degree of the exclusivity over the use of physical power increases, the scope of the state also increases.

ALTERING THE PRINCIPALS' INCENTIVES

Third parties possess additional means, more subtle than the direct use of power, to induce individuals to abide by agreements that are not readily self-enforced. These consist of altering the principals' incentives in such a way that their inclination to take dissipating action will be lessened.

Every agreement constrains the parties' behavior, and some impose explicit restrictions on the parties. One example is the restriction whereby college students must meet certain mandatory prerequisites before taking a particular course. Presumably, without the prerequisite, a student might do badly, which could be interpreted as a failing of the school. To protect its reputation, the school imposes the requirement. The school itself, or sometimes the state, enforces the restriction. Returning to the general case, it is too costly for the parties to spell out and enforce all "first-best" stipulations. Consequently, certain otherwise-valued stipulations fail to be made.[20] It is as if the relationship is subject to externalities that the parties find too costly to internalize. Some value is left in the public domain, then, and the parties spend resources on its capture.

A third party, however, may step in and alter the incentives within the relationship in such a way that the (former) principals' gain from capture will be reduced. To illustrate the opportunities for altering the principals' incentives, consider two pre-third-party scenarios. One is a case of a vertical production process where two or more successive independent producers take part in producing the final output. The output is expensive to measure, and in the process of selling it they each attempt to capture the value of some of the not fully measured attributes (or, similarly, the parties spend resources haggling about the price). In the other scenario, two or more fishermen fish the same lake. Each tends to overfish, trying to get the fish before the others do.

[20] The problem is often characterized as one of "incomplete contracts."

In each of those cases, the formation of a partnership in which each partner will receive a share of the venture's output will lower the cost of capture. The reason is that each partner, instead of being a full claimant to his own action, becomes a partial residual claimant. Also partial is the gain from capture, and therefore less of it will take place. Sharing requires an organizing effort and enforcement, as well as having to cope with shirking by the partners themselves. The cost of shirking can be lowered if the partners engage a monitor-enforcer to observe their levels of effort, and, when he finds them wanting, to penalize them.[21] If the projected sum of the organizing costs and the shirking losses exceeds the expected gains from sharing, however, the partnership will not be formed, and individuals (or subsets of them) will operate independently. When the partnership is formed, the monitor-enforcer himself must be induced to perform. Paying a share to him, too, will create such an inducement. Whether the monitor-enforcer is one of the original producers or is an outsider, and regardless of who initiates the change, he is a third-party enforcer.

As to the monitoring, in a vertical production process each individual typically receives the output of another and provides others with his own output. The two operations seemingly can be monitored simultaneously, using the same monitor for both. Thus, to the extent that each of the successive links in the production process is difficult to measure, all these links are expected to be monitored by the same monitor or monitoring team.

In the foregoing cases, the enforcer's threat is to exclude an individual from the group, as well as to withhold his own services. Because he stands to lose from carrying out the threat, it may be difficult to convince the other partners that it will be carried out. The monitoring organization, however, need not also carry out the enforcing, and a specialized power, especially the state, can be tapped to enforce these agreements.

PROTECTION AND THE USE OF VIOLENCE

This section explores the relationship between protection from theft and third-party enforcement. Violence (i.e., interaction among individuals

---

[21] The analysis in the text also applies if the individuals become employees instead of partners. The larger their number, the smaller the self-policing effect of sharing, and the more likely is the employment relationship.

who do not form relationships with one another) is used not only for theft but also for its prevention. Consider two neighbors who may have engaged in theft from each other. A common protector may be able to offer them an attractive deal by reducing their incentive to steal. Parallel to the cases in the preceding section, a single helper may, for example, induce the neighbors to lay bare their border, lowering the return from theft. Indeed, by (horizontally) integrating them, he may altogether remove their incentive to steal. One way of doing that would be to make both of them his employees. In that case they would cease to gain by stealing from each other. By lowering their expenditures on capture, then, the common protector may be able to offer them better terms than what two independent helpers could offer.

Consider a large number of individuals, and suppose that each seeks (1) protection against theft and (2) help in stealing others' assets. I now argue that the separability of the individuals' holdings affects their choice of whether to employ independent protectors or a common one. Suppose neighbors B, C, D, and E seek protection from one another, and M and N are specialized protectors who possess similar amounts of power. B and C employ a protector (M) common to them. C and D employ N, a protector common to them, but different from that employed by B and C. N, when adjudicating a dispute between C and D, sides with D. C may attempt not to comply by securing the assistance of M, his protector in dealing with B. If M agrees to help C, then the protection agreement that N signed with D did not truly secure D's rights. Had D anticipated the difficulty, he would not have signed up with N, and instead might have signed up with M. That would have resolved the particular problem. But if D and E employ a common protector O different from M, a new problem may emerge. Although C then will have only one protector, D will have two: one (M) common to him and C, and another (O) common to him and E. The same problem, then, may recur among C, D, and E. E, too, may then sign up with M. The problem, of course, can affect other individuals connected to these four and to one another. I would expect that the overlap in the protectors' jurisdictions, then, would induce a consolidation of protection under a single protector.

How extensive would the protector's jurisdiction be? The value of a common protector to his clients depends on how easy it is for them to steal, or to capture, each other's property – in other words, how separable their rights are. The more difficult such theft is, the less valuable are the services of a common protector. Territorial attributes are among the factors that affect the ease of theft. Major physical barriers separating two individuals make theft less likely. Such barriers may consist of bodies of water, deserts, or mountain ranges. Sheer distance is a barrier too; individuals positioned far apart are unlikely to steal each other's assets. But if an area is densely and continuously settled, such individuals are connected, albeit indirectly, through chains of those residing between them. Each will seek protection against all his neighbors, and, indirectly, neighbors of neighbors. Thus all will gravitate to the same protector. When an otherwise densely populated area is separated into two by a barrier, the chain may be broken. The more formidable the barrier, the smaller will be the demand for a common protector for the two parts.

Physical power is characterized by its general applicability. Although it comes in many forms, these forms seem to be good substitutes for one another. This is what allows power-using specialists to neutralize one another. Not all enforcers are able to neutralize each other. Suppose that the two pairs of clients (B,C) and (C,D) discussed earlier also secure non-force-using specialists in order to help them capture some other not-well-delineated rights. Here, too, C might attempt to use one specialist to prevent enforcement by the other. These non-force specialists, however, are much less likely than force-users to be able to neutralize each other. The two might be religious organizations. Neither would seem to have the ability to overpower or to neutralize the other.

OTHER TERRITORIAL ASPECTS OF ENFORCEMENT

Enforcement by physical power has at least two territorial dimensions that cause it to differ significantly from other enforcement forms. One is associated with the quite familiar problem of evading enforcement. The other, seemingly previously unrecognized, is in facilitating trade. Both depend on the size of the enforcer's jurisdiction and on the contiguity of the areas he controls. We now consider the first; the second is discussed in Chapter 5.

The jurisdiction of an enforcer seldom, if ever, fully covers the groups under him, nor is its extent ever uniform. A person may renege on his agreement or not comply with its adjudication and evade punishment by getting out of the reach of the enforcer. Where enforcement is by force, leaving the group typically requires moving physically. One may go into hiding, or, more importantly here, seek the protection of another enforcer who uses force (and who, as a rule, controls another territory). As the contiguous territories controlled by the enforcer become larger, most clients will find it more difficult to secure the protection of another enforcer. This is because, on average, in a larger territory clients reside farther from the border, and the ratio of border length to territorial area tends to be smaller, and thus the cost of protecting the border is lower.[22] This, then, is a territorial scale economy to protection. Recall that, in general, although ex post each individual values the opportunity to escape adjudication or enforcement, the lesser is the enforcer's ability to enforce, the less will subjects be inclined to form agreements with him in the first place. I would expect the enforcer, possibly at the behest of his clients, to create a territorial domain such that getting out of it to evade enforcement would be difficult.[23]

ENFORCEMENT BY SOCIAL MORES

In many situations, the cost of using violence for enforcement is low, and it has the additional advantage that it can be applied selectively as the need arises. This is the other side of the coin in regard to the scale economies discussed in the preceding section. The economies lie in the fact that the same power can be used to enforce many agreements. Thus, different agreements may have their own monitors, but they may all be backed by a single enforcement mechanism. When violence is used for enforcement, that means that the state, at least in part, is enforcing the agreements.[24]

The threat of using physical power is not invariably the most efficient mode of enforcement. In the foregoing examples, at least part of each of the arrangements is enforced by non-violent means. Sometimes an appeal to "ideology," "social mores," or "etiquette" is more efficient than the use of violence. For example, the individuals fishing the same lake may belong to a religious organization that takes a tithe from the catch, thereby reducing overfishing. The organization may be able to enforce its rules cheaply. Obeying the rules (i.e., conforming to the ideology) then

[22] The length of the border tends to grow as the square root of the growth of the area. Seen from another angle, when two neighboring states merge with each other, the size of the new state is the sum of the sizes of the two. The length of the new border, however, is less than the sum of the old ones, because the previous common component ceases to be a border in the combined state.

[23] This factor may account for the emphasis on the territorial dimension of the state in the conventional definition.

[24] In Chapter 6, I elaborate on the use of more than one enforcer to enforce an agreement.

will lead to an efficient use of resources. More generally, religious dogmas that impose taxes as shares of output, rather than, say, head taxes, are to be expected where members' output is derived from common resources.

Another example involves protocol on the golf course. Suppose the per-person cost of playing golf depends on how many golfers can comfortably play on a given course in a given time period. The variability in individuals' speed of play is one factor that will affect that number; dawdling golfers will slow all those behind them. Average speed can be improved if the slow golfers either agree to play more briskly or allow faster ones to "play through," to pass them in an orderly fashion. Alternatively, speed can be increased and its variability reduced if golfers use motorized golf carts. The use of carts, however, would preempt walking the course, which many enjoy. Enforcing the use of motorized carts would be straightforward. On the other hand, direct enforcement of appropriate behavior is difficult.

Compare, now, golf courses organized as clubs and used only by members (and guests) and those run for profit, where anybody paying the admission fee can play. We would expect the former to be strong on etiquette, emphasizing the "right" kind of behavior. They will occasionally penalize, and perhaps expel, individuals who do not adhere to the protocol. I would predict that fee-charging courses would be more likely to require the use of motorized carts, especially during high-demand (and high-price) periods, than would membership clubs. The membership clubs will take advantage of their social cohesion to induce speedier play.[25]

Several of the Ten Commandments, as well as other religious rules, can be viewed in a similar vein. The golf example, admittedly much more trivial, however, allows direct comparison between two cases: one where individuals are not bound by social rules, thus requiring restrictions that will lead to behavior that will be relatively easily observable by outsiders, and the other where etiquette is exploited to alter behavior.

CONCLUSIONS

The state, characterized by the use of violence for enforcement, is not the sole third-party enforcer. The state has a comparative advantage

---

[25] Casual evidence supports the prediction.

in imposing immediate large costs, but where other means such as ideology are effective, other third parties have an edge in enforcement.

The enforcer who uses violence poses the threat to his subjects of using his power to confiscate their property. Subjects may get together ahead of time to erect a mechanism to constrain the enforcer, and yet still allow him to have enough power to effectively enforce their agreements. They will require, among other things, that the enforcer use only clear, objective criteria for enforcement. The same criteria are most useful in the exchange of commodities.

The scale economies to the use of power that third parties accumulate may account, in part, for the state's primacy role relative to other third-party enforcers. The state's greatest advantage is in the enforcement of commodity-exchange agreements, as well as other agreements that can benefit from rulings on the disputes (or potential disputes) that are common to many of them.

4

The Choice among Enforcement Forms

Agreements fall into two broad categories: (1) self-enforced and (2) third-party-enforced. As discussed in Chapter 3, the second category can be further broken down into two basic subcategories: (2a) those enforced by non-violent means and (2b) those enforced by violence. Individuals, of course, can also act in isolation (grow vegetables at home).

The definition of the state adopted here assigns to the state's enforcement only the agreements that fall into category (2b). Although the focus of this book is on the state, enforcement by the state shares many features with enforcement by non-violent third parties. The distinctions between self-enforced agreements and agreements enforced by any type of third party, then, may shed light on the nature of the state. In the first part of this chapter I discuss factors that affect individuals' choices between the two main categories; the rest of the chapter is devoted to the choice between the two modes of third-party enforcement.

Before commencing the main discussion, I make several points to enhance clarity. The first is that the agreement categories are not hierarchical. For example, owners of idiosyncratic commodities (authors' private diaries) are expected to protect them by themselves. As these become generic (published diaries), we expect that categories (1) and (2a) will be bypassed and that the state will undertake the protection. It is also important to recognize that agreements are routinely subject to multiple enforcement forms. For instance, parts of agreements may be enforced by violence, and other parts of the same agreements may be self-enforced. Still another point is that the existence of third-party enforcement, as argued in Chapter 2, is conditional on the presence of self-enforced relations. The emergence of specialized third-party enforcement does not alter the basic proposition that *every* relationship must ultimately be *self-enforced*. It allows, however, nesting third-party enforcement *within* self-enforced relationships; in addition, in most cases there is no need to make the caveat when dealing with third-party enforcement. The final point is that action in isolation does not play a central role here, and it is discussed mostly in passing.

LIMITATION TO SELF-ENFORCEMENT AND PROBLEMS WITH THIRD-PARTY ENFORCEMENT

Any number of individuals may take part in a self-enforced agreement. By and large, however, enforcement seems to become increasingly and quite quickly more cumbersome as the number of independent individuals who are parties to an agreement increases beyond two or three.[1] The diseconomies to the number of participants do not seem to be nearly as severe when agreements among them are enforced by third parties. Moreover, as is shown in Chapter 3, once as few as three individuals take part in a self-enforced agreement, each may become a third-party enforcer to the other two. We expect third parties to facilitate the bulk of high-level specializing and of large-scale activities. On the other hand, self-enforcement is expected to facilitate a large range of small-scale agreements, mostly between pairs of individuals, of which marriage is probably the most prominent case. Figuratively speaking, third parties provide the bricks for large, complex structures, whereas self-enforcement provides some of the mortar that keeps the bricks together.

Under stable conditions, at any point in time there must be a balance of power among individuals, each maintaining the level of power he deems optimal. This clearly applies to individuals before they begin to cooperate. Supposing that such a balance exists, would not any individual who increases his power be able to overwhelm the others if the latter did not alter theirs? A modest increase in the stronger person's power seemingly would be insufficient to capture all the assets that the weaker ones have. Indeed, unless the cost or the return from acquiring extra power has changed, given the initial stable equilibrium, the net return from acquiring power must be negative. However, it seems that scale economies to the use of power will become dominant as the stronger one gets still stronger, so that eventually he will totally dominate the weaker ones, and his payoff may become positive.

Consider, in light of the foregoing observation, specialization in protection. In general, at the inception of cooperation, individuals will adjust

---

[1] The self-enforced agreement to form collective action is discussed in Chapter 7.

the skills and capabilities they have already developed. In order to gain the full benefit from specialization in protection, the non-specialists will have to divest themselves of much of their protection ability, or, even better, not acquire protection ability in the first place. Specialization in protection, however, will necessarily upset the balance of power. Given the fact of specialization, the protection specialist's power relative to that of his clients will be sufficient to overwhelm them. When it comes to specializing in protection, then, the clients of the specialist must guard against the latter capturing their wealth. Clients can benefit from accommodating specialization in the use of power only if the protection specialist commits not to confiscate or if the clients develop and maintain collective-action power to control the specialist they allow to emerge.

A protector's commitment not to confiscate will be credible if the present value of his net benefit from not confiscating exceeds his net valuation of the assets that could be confiscated. Under the circumstances considered here, the protector's potential gains would consist of what he could realize from confiscation of the assets that clients have. The net enhancement that protection can provide, and thus his potential net reward, will consist largely of the difference between the cost of protection by him and that by clients themselves. To gauge the relative magnitude of the difference, consider a case where confiscation was not worthwhile: the fairs that were owned and run by the Champagne counts during the Middle Ages. By committing not to confiscate, the count could collect fees that were commensurate with the net value of the trade conducted at the fair. Had he chosen to confiscate, he could have confiscated what foreign traders had brought with them to the fair, but not their entire wealth. Traders, obviously, considered the count's commitment to be credible, in part because they had discretion over what they would bring to the fair. A Champagne count, unlike most of the protectors considered here, had no access to the bulk of his clients' wealth, making his commitment more credible. In more typical cases, the protector cannot credibly commit, and clients have to form a collective-action mechanism to benefit from specialized protection.

THE CHOICE BETWEEN ENFORCEMENT MODES

Neither self-enforcement of agreements nor enforcement by a third party dominates the other over the range of all transactions, or even over all the attributes of given transactions. Four factors seem to affect the choice between self-enforced agreements and agreements enforced by a third party:[2] (1) the time paths of the benefits that an agreement generates for the various parties; (2) the information required to execute and to enforce agreements; (3) the ability to maintain long-term relations; and (4) the cost of punishment. Here we discuss the first three. I address the fourth later on.

The Time Paths of Benefits

Self-enforced agreements differ from third-party-enforced agreements in terms of the pattern of the net-benefit flow that they can support. Self-enforcement can support only agreements that will generate a net value that will remain positive through the entire duration of the agreement for *each* party. Otherwise, at any point during the life of the agreement at which a party perceives that it is no longer beneficial to him, he will withdraw. Under third-party enforcement, it is sufficient that the present value of each party's share in the project be positive at the time of the agreement. However, although the present value need not be continuously positive for each of the parties, it cannot at any time be less than the penalty the third party is expected to inflict.

Provided that the net present value (i.e., the *expected* value) to each participant at the time of the agreement is positive, third-party enforcement can accommodate, among other things, projects with unsynchronized benefit flows, which can arise because of large variability in the outcome or because of definite terminal points. Such projects are not self-enforced. Pure credit transactions, where the flows of benefits and costs for each of the parties necessarily diverge, probably constitute the most significant class of transactions that can be enforced by third parties and are not self-enforced. Under self-enforcement, the borrower would be sure to renege before it was time to repay the loan. The heart of the relationship is in its non-synchronicity, and its value cannot be continuously positive for both parties. The moment the borrower receives the credit, the value of the transaction to him becomes negative, and he is better off not repaying.[3] Cases such as that in which two individuals might engage in a *one-time* non-synchronous exchange also belong in this

---

[2] Ellickson discusses conditions under which two major operations not using the state's enforcement power have functioned: fishing in New England (1989) and ranching in California (1991).

[3] This, as is well known, is why there can be no agreement for sovereign debt.

category. For example, an exchange between a farmer whose apricots ripen in the spring and another whose wheat is harvested in the fall could benefit both. But as long as the interaction is not repeating, the wheat farmer will not deliver, and thus the apricot grower will not provide the apricots to begin with.

For a relationship to be continuously beneficial, it is necessary that the parties interact repeatedly. This requires, in turn, either that both the parties and their projects have a positive chance of living indefinitely or that their operations not be subject to definite terminal dates. For example, two families or two tribes fishing a small lake tend to interact repeatedly.[4] Their continuing contact could result in each unilaterally refraining from taking very young fish because each expects the other to do likewise. Similarly, if the apricot and wheat farmers realize that they (and their descendants) may interact year after year, each may unilaterally deliver some of his seasonal crops to the other.

States can also interact repeatedly. The more stable a regime is, the higher the probability of repeated interactions, and therefore the more willing other states will be to form agreements with it. Rule-of-law regimes seem more stable than dictatorships. A dictator's tenure tends to be insecure, and there is little continuity between a dictator and his successor. For that reason, rule-of-law regimes are more likely to trade and to otherwise cooperate with others than are dictatorships.

Third-party enforcement can accommodate a wide range of agreements in which the condition that the net *expected* value to each participant be positive at the time of the agreement obviously is less stringent than that the value of the relationship remain continuously positive. Therefore, the presence of a third party expands, seemingly greatly, the range of agreements beyond what self-enforced agreements can accommodate.[5]

---

[4] The longer the parties' life expectancy, the easier the formation of the agreement. The life expectancy of a family line is longer than that of its head, as that of a tribe is longer than that of a family. The longevity of a stock corporation does not depend on that of its original owners. It is free, then, from the problem of terminal life.

[5] DeSoto (1989) describes what he calls "informal" operations in housing, street vending, and public transportation in Peru in the early 1980s. He characterizes as informal the transactions that are defined here as self-enforced. He demonstrates the extremely high cost of these informal operations, but points out that legal, third-party-enforced operations in those sectors would be prohibitively costly.

Information Requirements

Two informational issues affect the choice between the agreement forms. One concerns the distinction between implicit and explicit agreements, and the other is the cost a party must incur to learn about his partners' actions. I commence with the value of explicit agreement.

A self-enforced agreement may be tacit, or an "implicit contract" as it is sometimes called. In what sense is a tacit agreement an "agreement"? The parties to self-enforced relationships do not have to come to an agreement; they will act in the same way whether or not they get together and agree on some action. The term "agreement," then, may appear to be superfluous in the context of self-enforced relations. Nevertheless, it seems to contain useful information.

The substance of a self-enforced agreement depends on what each party to it implies he will do. What the parties intend to do will depend crucially on their prior information. In the process of reaching an explicit agreement, the parties exchange information with each other. That information is not available when the agreement is tacit. Turning an implicit agreement into an explicit one makes it clearer, which increases its value.[6] The agreement will be made explicit, however, only when the gain from the information is perceived to exceed the cost of providing it.[7] Moreover, by making agreements explicit, and especially by putting them into writing, the parties make it easier to determine whether or not violations have occurred. This is routinely done in agreements between states, and such was the case with the Magna Carta, the written agreement between king and barons with no third party to enforce it.

A major determinant of the choice between self-enforcement and third-party enforcement concerns the different amounts of information the parties to agreements have about their partners, as a function of the number of partners. The parties to any agreement must be able to determine whether or not the agreed terms have been met. With just two parties, the parties' access to the relevant information is built in. Each knows what he himself has contributed. If each also knows the production function, then except for a random term each also knows what the

---

[6] A person may demonstrate that his time horizon is long by pointing out fruit trees he has just planted. This may be easy to verify, but not easy to notice without the explicit information.

[7] Explicit agreements are not necessarily based on more information than are tacit agreements; the latter may remain tacit *because* the parties already have adequate information.

other has done. Each knows, for instance, if, in the course of their interaction, the other has injured him. Each, then, can obtain at low cost the
needed information. On the other hand, he may be unable to demonstrate the injury to a third party or prove at low cost who caused it. In
such a case, the information needed for third-party adjudication may be
quite costly to obtain.

Three examples will illustrate the difficulty that third parties may
encounter in collecting the information needed to adjudicate disputes
between two principals. In the first example, one person may realize that
he is missing his generic tool, and he notices that his neighbor, with
whom he has been interacting, has newly begun using such a tool. He
may be confident that the neighbor stole the tool from him. However,
his cost of demonstrating that to a third party is likely to be high. The
second example concerns the quality of a theater performance. A patron
may find the performance not up to par, but is apt to find it difficult to
prove that case to others. The final example concerns a victim of domestic violence. The victim cannot easily demonstrate its occurrence. The
resolution of such disputes, then, is more amenable to self-enforcement
than to third-party enforcement. More generally, in a relationship with
just two parties who know their production function, the evidence
needed for a third party to determine who violated the agreement is more
costly to obtain and to transmit than would be the evidence required by
the parties themselves.

The informational advantage that self-enforcement has over third-
party enforcement declines quickly when more than two individuals
interact, even if the interaction is repeated. As the number of parties to
an agreement increases, each finds it more difficult to identify violators.
If, for instance, many individuals had had access to steal a tool left
exposed in a public place, it is then advantageous to use specialists to
collect objective information rather than to use subjective information
in order to pin down blame. Similarly, punishing violators becomes more
difficult as the number of parties to an agreement increases. I predict that
third-party enforcement will prevail when the interaction is among many
individuals.[8]

Numerous individuals are likely to interact in using public roads, in
areas surrounding streams, and in territories occupied by widely ranging

---

[8] A related observation is how the mode of interaction changes from informal to
formal rules in apartment-sharing as the number of roommates increases to more
than two (one, two, many, . . .).

predators and game animals. The sizes of such areas of significant inter-action would seem to substantially exceed the otherwise efficient hold-ings by single individuals. Because many individuals can interact in these situations, third-party enforcement would seem more useful for govern-ing their relationships than would self-enforcement (Lueck, 1989). When numerous individuals interact in "team production" (Alchian and Demsetz, 1972), it is too costly for individual team members to deter-mine who among them may be shirking, so they "employ" a third party, the entrepreneur, to collect the information needed to induce all to perform.

The relationship between the number of parties to an agreement and the enforcement form they choose can be put in different terms. In a two-party interaction, the agreement can internalize the entire relationship. When more than two parties interact and some do not participate in the agreement on how to use their common resources, externalities are likely to crop up. Third-party enforcement may help internalize the externali-ties. Third-party enforcement is predicted to emerge, then, when one deals simultaneously with the entire set of individuals involved, or, in the foregoing illustrations, with the neighbors, and neighbors of neighbors. The third party can increase the value of the property or wealth of all these individuals.

The Longevity of Long-Term Relations

Self-enforcement, as is obvious, requires repeated interactions. When conditions for such interactions become less favorable, I predict that a larger fraction of all agreements will be enforced by third parties. Marital disputes can be used to test that prediction. In the past few decades, marriage has become easier to terminate. The duration of repeated inter-actions within marriage has been shortened, then, making the self-enforcement of the relationship less effective. The recent increase in legal (i.e., the state's) third-party adjudication of marital disputes is consistent with the prediction.

THIRD-PARTY ENFORCEMENT: THE USE OF FORCE
VERSUS THE USE OF OTHER MEANS OF ENFORCEMENT

In Chapter 3, I argued that, by and large, an enforcer using violence has a comparative advantage in imposing large immediate costs on the enforced when he does not rely on lasting relationships between himself and his clients. An enforcer exploiting long-term relations, on the other hand, will require a certain length of time to impose significant costs on others, and at substantial expense to himself. The advantage that a violence-using enforcer has is tempered, however, by clients' perception that such an enforcer can confiscate more easily than can a non-violent enforcer. Clients who control violence-using enforcers will therefore impose constraints on them. Among others things, when their disputes are adjudicated, clients will require a violence-using enforcer to use more careful and more explicit procedures than they would require of other enforcers.

Consider the requirement that an enforcer use careful procedures. Transactors have choices between carrying out their activities more openly or less openly, and between following standards or not following them. Observability is enhanced when the action is open and it conforms to accepted standards. As observation and measurement become easier, I would expect enforcement by violence-using enforcers to become more common.

An enforcer must be able to observe at least some measures of the agreement he enforces, in order to know what to enforce. The information made available to him may be subjective, or it may be objective. I contend that the parties will choose a violence-using third party to enforce their agreement only if he agrees to use, as a basis for enforcement, evidence that can be documented. If a violence-using enforcer were allowed to use subjective evidence, the collective-action authority designed to control him would find it difficult to determine whether or not he had engaged in extortion. Low-quality evidence (i.e., evidence subject to high error rates) also lends itself to manipulation. Because it is unlikely that an enforcer relying on such evidence would be penalized for extortion, he would be likely to extort. Clients, then, will require violence-using enforcers to use objective, verifiable evidence and high-quality information to adjudicate disputes. The more severe restrictions and more stringent requirements imposed on violence-using enforcers, however, raise their costs. Their services, then, will not always be preferred.

Enforcers not using violence also need to observe agreement-stipulated behavior. As discussed in Chapter 3, victims of extortion by such an enforcer can retaliate, to a degree, by withholding their business and persuading others to stop using the enforcer's services. Therefore, such enforcers can expect to have takers for their services even if they use subjective evidence, and even if it is not of the highest quality.

Every enforcer engages, inter alia, in the delineation of rights. This is clearly so for the state (i.e., the force-using third party). Although third parties not using force also delineate rights, it is difficult for outsiders to determine the precise nature of such rights, because the methods used tend to be more subjective. This may explain why the literature that discusses legal delineation implicitly views delineation by the enforcer using violence as the only way of delineating rights.[9]

Another distinction between the two types of enforcers relates to ideology. The presence of an ideology seems to require long-term relations among its adherents. Enforcers not using force maintain long-term relations with their clients, and some of them derive enforcement power from the ideology to which they adhere. Enforcers who rely solely on the use of violence cannot form a common ideological bond with their clients and thus cannot use ideology for enforcement.[10] The former, then, may harness the ideology to reduce the cost of enforcement in ways not open to the violence-using enforcer. Ideology (including such aspects of it as mores and etiquette) can also be created and enhanced; the more potent it is, the more likely it is that agreements will be enforced by long-term relations.

Other factors affecting the choice among enforcement methods include the scale of the operations of the enforcer, and, indirectly, the scope of the institutions formed under him. The choice between enforcement forms depends, then, on the "intrinsic" nature of agreements, on the existing institutions, and on the costs of adapting them to new situations.

It is evident that the differences in ability to enforce are such that neither class of enforcers is preferable to the other for all types of agreements. I now argue that the kinds of information needed for enforcement can have a profound effect on the nature of the agreements the two classes enforce.

---

[9] Third parties not using force, however, may also enforce explicit detailed agreements, especially when their clients are not (fully) under the jurisdiction of a single force-using enforcer. Thus, in past centuries, explicit agreements between Jews residing in different states often were adjudicated and enforced by rabbinical courts with no physical power.

[10] All states seem to rely, to some extent, on ideology (nationality, race, religion). For simplicity, I abstract from this feature of the state. I intend to pursue this issue in future work.

THIRD-PARTY NON-STATE ENFORCERS

A variety of institutions, legitimate and illegitimate, can be used to enforce agreements and resolve disputes. Like the state, criminal organizations use violence for third-party enforcement. Other organizations may employ non-violent methods to enforce agreements. Among those others, such organizations can include tightly knit groups and firms that use long-term relations to enforce their internal operations.

The more expensive it is to make and enforce contracts (i.e., agreements that make use of the state as a third party), the more will people use dispute-resolving mechanisms that are substitutes for the state. The state itself can create such substitute operations. As a rule, however, these are not complementary to protection or to its third-party enforcement. A state that expands its scope of operations necessarily expands its bureaucracy. However, its agents' incentive to operate efficiently is muted, because, as suggested later on, they are rewarded primarily with a fixed wage. The state, then, is at a disadvantage in providing dispute-resolving methods other than the already available third-party enforcement. The more numerous and more valuable the activities in which the substitute mechanisms have a cost advantage, the less the state can exploit the scale economies to protection and to the formation of legal rights. The next few sections discuss some of the substitute organizations.

CLOSE-KNIT GROUPS

In early societies, as individuals began to interact, in some cases they presumably were able to form strong relationships, becoming "close-knit groups."[11] Such groups can form within states as well, with or without the state's consent.[12] The individuals in these groups are close-knit in that they hold common values, interact frequently, and are able to observe one another closely. Members cherish belonging to the group and may

---

[11] Ellickson (1993) defines a close-knit group as "a social entity within which power is broadly dispersed and members have continuing face-to-face interactions with one another" (p. 1320). Such groups also closely correspond to what Taylor (1982) defines as anarchic societies.

[12] Posner (1996) discusses in great detail the interaction between the state and groups within it and the issue of the state's ability to encourage or discourage such groups by its regulatory power and by its tax and subsidy policies, as well as the state's payoff therefrom.

benefit from certain low-cost exchanges that groups accommodate. As long as individuals value membership in their groups, the groups can enforce their rules by the threat of expulsion. The need for enforcement arises because individuals may attempt to take a free ride on the contributions of other members, rather than sharing the burdens that all group members are expected to bear.

Examples of such groups, besides primitive tribes, include ethnic and religious minorities. One prominent close-knit group consists of Hasidic Jews operating in the diamond trade who, with few formalities and at low measurement cost, exchange among themselves diamonds in intermediate stages of production. Another type of group is the social club, where the costs of certain inter-member activities are low, as discussed in Chapter 3 with regard to golf clubs that depend on protocol for enforcement.[13] Sometimes they enhance their enforcement power by charging lump-sum fees up front, fees that are not refundable in case of expulsion.

Religions and religious sects are close-knit groups that also possess an ideology, though they often grow to acquire too many adherents to remain close-knit. Many religious organizations help to form and enforce, at low cost, various agreements, especially within families. A striking example is provided by the Catholic church in medieval Europe. The church had jurisdiction over the "spiritual" life of the Catholic populace. With the consent of sovereign states, it operated its own courts and enforced its rulings partly by spiritual means, including that of excommunication (i.e., "expulsion"), and partly by sheer force. Jurisdictional disputes between the church and various states erupted throughout the Middle Ages, but for a long period they were not so severe as to cause the parties to abandon the prevailing arrangement.

Churches may be organized only partly, and perhaps not from the very beginning, to act as third-party enforcers. A church can impose costs by exploiting any of the relationships it accommodates. To the extent it forms a community, it can impose costs by threat of excommunication. Its ability to impose such a cost is a function, in part, of the fraction of the individuals who can gain by forming various agreements with other members of the group. The larger the number of agreements among members of a given church, the more severe the penalty.[14] We would

---

[13] Ellickson describes the operations of two tight-knit groups: New England fishermen (Ellickson, 1989) and California ranchers (Ellickson, 1991).

[14] This last feature may explain, at least in part, the persecution of non-co-religionists and the intolerance for "heresy" where church members constitute

expect a church, then, to spend resources to try to bring a larger fraction of the population under its wings.

Some churches have adherents in more than one state. Even though most churches have no significant military power, they sometimes are positioned to act as third-party enforcers of agreements between states. The Catholic church in medieval Europe and the oracle at Delphi in classical Greece are two major examples of churches mediating agreements between states.

In the Middle Ages, the popes maintained long-term relations with many Catholic states and were in a position to impose penalties on them, primarily by excommunication. They often arbitrated disputes among states. Because the pope tended to be neutral in regard to relations between these states, his "good faith" was expected. While the papacy was at Rome, the popes actually arbitrated a number of disputes between England and France. Their power to arbitrate between those two states declined, however, when the papacy moved (or was moved) to Avignon, where popes were perceived as more partial to the French.

Classical Greece also provides an example of large-scale arbitration between states. The oracle at Delphi was the prime religious authority at that time and seems to have served as a neutral party in disputes between co-religionist Greek city-states. Even today, the ruins indicate how handsomely Delphi was rewarded for the service.[15]

VERTICALLY INTEGRATED ORGANIZATIONS

One way in which transactors can accommodate non-state-enforced exchange is by taking advantage of vertically integrated organization. Sometimes it is difficult to stipulate the quantity and quality of the products or services that transactors are to transmit to each other. Then delineation of the transaction becomes expensive. If the transactors operate independently of each other, disputes are likely to arise. By integrating vertically, the transactors will become parts of a single organization and will be able to carry out exchanges while largely avoiding disputes

a large fraction of a community. Still, such churches may also have substantial power over non-members, because these non-members are likely to interact extensively with members, and the church may induce its members to not interact with non-members.

[15] Milgrom et al. (1990) demonstrate how agreements among the pairs of individuals within a network of individuals can become self-enforced even when the pairs do not interact repeatedly.

between themselves, or resolving them economically internally when they occur. The reason for this is that when operating within a single organization, the transactors are not full residual claimants to their own actions and are less likely to be in dispute regarding the not-well-defined attributes.[16]

Typically an employer may instruct an employee to perform certain tasks, including engaging in exchange with other employees. In the exchange, an upstream employee typically delivers a product to a downstream employee, and the employer rather than the downstream employee compensates the upstream employee for his effort. As a rule, the precise nature of the tasks employees are to perform will not be stipulated in the employment contract. Performance, therefore, is not made subject to court action, and it must be enforced otherwise. The residual claimant of a firm can enforce the relationship between the firm's employees. The courts are likely to play a significant role in disputes regarding "market" transactions (more specifically, contract transactions), but not those within firms.[17]

An example of this distinction relates to a change in the legal treatment of patents for financial innovations. In 1982, Merrill Lynch was granted one of the first such patents, which subsequently was upheld by the courts.[18] In 1995 the U.S. Patent Office issued new guidelines specifically recognizing such patents. Prior to those developments, one could not have relied directly on state enforcement for protection of the right to financial innovations, since copying without permission was not illegal. One indirect delineation method that was actually used was the employment of the innovator for wage. The firms intending to use such innovations hired the would-be innovators and thus integrated the innovation effort with the other activities of the firm. The use of this method demonstrates a within-firm ability to protect, and thus implicitly to

---

[16] This role of vertical integration was suggested earlier (Barzel, 1982). Vertical integration is discussed in Chapter 5.

[17] By the hypothesis here, the criteria used to delineate rights within firms are looser than (or at least different from) what the courts might require. Judicial and regulatory attempts to superimpose on firms more stringent criteria would defeat the purpose of the firm. If the more stringent criteria could be sustained economically, a reason for the existence of firms would disappear. The regulatory requirement of clearer delineation of the rights of the different resource owners is expected to reduce the scope of firm operations.

[18] The facts in this and the next paragraph, as well as in the following footnote, are from *The Economist*, February 10, 1996, pp. 81–2.

enforce some of the rights to the potential economic benefits of the innovations.

That change in the legal environment made it easier to exchange rights to the use of such innovations in the market, and exchange of innovations in the market was indeed enhanced. Subsequent to the change, financial innovators tended to operate independently of the users of their innovations.[19] This line of reasoning also implies that with the emergence of independent innovators, the financial firms themselves will become less horizontally integrated, as more than one firm can easily use a given innovation. I predict that the greater reliance on contract transactions being accommodated by software patents will increase litigation; previously disputes had to be resolved mostly by self-enforced methods.[20]

As stated, commodities in the intermediate production stage that are costly to delineate by contract can be transacted within firms. This applies not only to transfers within vertical production processes but also to transfers over space. Thus, when contracting is costly, firms may integrate over space to provide a substitute for market transfers. In Chapter 5, I elaborate on the role of integration and on the intertwining of the activities of two or more enforcers.

Similar considerations apply to the delineation of land and to situations where the contribution of productive services to output is difficult to pin down. Regarding land, consider the relationship between two neighbors who seek to reduce their capture losses to each other. They

---

[19] The explanation of vertical integration in the text is consistent with my earlier hypothesis (Barzel, 1982). I argue there that as the cost of measuring the attributes of transacted commodities or services falls, these attributes will be better delineated and will become better suited to court adjudication. As measuring becomes cheaper, then, the need for exchange within firms becomes less, and firms will become less vertically integrated.

The text describes a change in the legal status of the innovations that made legal delineation easier. By my hypothesis, it should have reduced the level of integration. The level of vertical integration did decline subsequent to the court ruling. Note that the argument by Williamson (1975) and by Klein, Crawford, and Alchian (1979) that the purpose of vertical integration is to eliminate opportunities to capture quasi rent is incapable of accounting for the observation in the text. The quasi rent here seems to be a function of legal delineation, a notion that Klein and associates implicitly dismiss in stating that legal stipulations can be easily circumvented.

[20] Under contract exchange, disputes tend to end up in court rather than being resolved by other methods. The United States seems to be at the forefront of using contract exchange. This may explain, at least partly, why the number of lawyers in the United States is relatively higher than in other countries.

might, for example, dispute the use of water from a newly discovered common underground pool. Each could attempt to enhance his interests unilaterally. Alternatively, they could employ a common specialist to assist in their relations. The specialist, usually the state, will internalize, at least in part, what otherwise would have been external effects. One way this is done is by forming borders so as to make capture more difficult.

Considerations akin to those just noted also apply to cases of "team production" (Alchian and Demsetz, 1972), where a monitor can measure the effort of team members, but cannot document it cheaply. How are the associated rights delineated? Because of the difficulty of specifying team members' precise duties, the employment contract does not stipulate these rights, which then are not subject to state jurisdiction. The legal rights in this case consist of the residual claimant's contractual agreement to pay a fixed wage to other team members and his right to fire them without cause, where "cause" means proving in court that there was unsatisfactory performance. The other team members agree to follow reasonable instructions and, as a rule, have the right to quit. The residual claimant's reward depends on the effort he is able to extract from team members by supervising them. He has the economic right to the residual. The team members, too, have an economic right not backed by legal rights – to the amount of shirking they are able to get away with, short of being fired. The courts' role is confined to determining what "reasonable" instructions are and whether or not the agreed-upon wage was paid.

TRADE ORGANIZATIONS

Trade organizations usually centralize some of the operations of merchants or other specialists operating within a well-defined trade. The specialists voluntarily join the organization and agree to abide by its rulings. Services provided by trade organizations include the setting of standards and lobbying for the industry. A few trade organizations provide more direct services to their members. Bernstein (1996) discusses in great detail an organization of the latter kind: the National Grain and Feed Association. Its main function has been to facilitate trade between members. Such trade, as Bernstein persuasively argues, would be difficult to conduct by means of contracts enforced by the state. The main impediment to state enforcement concerns the distinction between the provisions made for the last period and those for ongoing relations.

Individuals maintain long-term relations with each other in order to enforce agreements. Such relationships are not guaranteed to last forever. Parties may wish to provide for the possibility that their relationship will come to an end and that their agreement will therefore unravel. One way of doing that, Bernstein points out, is by including stipulations that will be activated only when the relationship is about to terminate. These stipulations must be enforced by a third party. The state's legal system, however, is not well suited for maintaining such distinctions. A trade association, on the other hand, is able to make arrangements specifically for that purpose. The National Grain and Feed Association provides an extensive arbitration mechanism to resolve disputes between members. Enforcement is achieved by publicizing non-compliance and by expulsion. The effectiveness of their agreements, however, depends on the finality of the organization's adjudication. In recent years, the courts have agreed to review, and on occasion have chosen to override, rulings made by the association. The greater the extent of court intervention, the lower the value of the organization.

CRIMINAL ORGANIZATIONS[21]

Among their other activities, criminal organizations engage in the enforcement of agreements using physical power for enforcement. In this they resemble the state. As discussed in Chapter 6, however, the state and criminal organizations can be viable side by side only if they use different kinds of power. The state's advantage seems to be in the open use of arms and in the use of heavier weapons, such as armored cars. The advantage of criminal organizations is in the covert use of arms. We expect them to use small, easy-to-conceal weapons. States can neither overpower criminal organizations with ease nor effectively compete with them in those organizations' domains. Criminal organizations enforce primarily agreements that the state prohibits, and when they adjudicate their disputes we do not expect them to hold their trials in public, nor to be as fussy as the legitimate state in the quality of evidence they accept. Transactors, then, must be more selective in the agreements they bring to criminal organizations for enforcement.

At equilibrium, there is a balance of power between the state and criminal organizations. The latter find it unprofitable to compete in lines

---

[21] Some aspects of the operations of criminal organizations are discussed in Chapter 13.

where the state has a comparative advantage in enforcement. The borderlines between what the two enforcers enforce, however, are unlikely to be well defined. There is no single ultimate enforcer within that gray area. As an example of not-well-delineated rights, consider a person who made a contractual agreement with another and now perceives that he is about to become a loser under it. Suppose that a criminal organization offers to intimidate his partner. The intimidation may be effective if the partner's other dealings are known to be shady. The person, then, may be successful in wiggling out of his contractual obligation. The rights under the contract turn out to be poorly defined because of the absence of a single ultimate jurisdiction over the particular area. Had the victimized transactor been aware ahead of time of the difficulty of enforcing the contract, he would not have signed it. Rather, he would have chosen not to make any agreement, or else would have made one to be enforced by some other means.

As borderline activities are unlikely ever to be clearly delineated, the jurisdictions of different enforcers are likely to overlap in part, and we expect that disputes will occur. The greater the disputed domain resulting from the presence of more than one power-backed third-party enforcer in a given area, the greater the weakening of individuals' economic rights.

THE EXPECTATION THAT THE STATE WILL TAX WHAT IT DELINEATES

The state provides trade-enhancing delineation services. When clients control their protectors – the case on which we primarily focus – it is plausible that the state will finance its activities so as to maximize its subjects' net wealth. Consider the state charging fees for the transactions it enforces, especially if it provides for the registration of contracts and of (transacted) assets. As reneging and capture activities are likely to increase with the value of the transaction, the state's enforcement cost is likely to increase then too. Therefore, we expect that the fee the state charges will also increase with that value. The state, however, provides service only for the contractually delineated attributes of transactions. Assuming that a property tax is imposed for that purpose, I predict that it will be based on the value the property is expected to fetch when put up for sale. This is also its lien value to a bank, what the government could get if it sold the asset, and indeed what a thief would receive if he sold it on the open market.

The model here leads to the additional prediction that a state that imposes transaction taxes will tax commodities at a rate higher than the rate it imposes on services. The reason for this is that contractual specifications are used extensively in the sale of commodities, whereas non-contractual delineation, by reputation, for example, is more prominent in the sale of services. It is observed that at least some of the time, the state actually taxes commodities at a higher rate than that for services.[22] The same rationale may explain why income taxes are imposed on market income (i.e., contractually earned income) but not on home production, which is earned without the use of state enforcement. The factors that facilitate delineation may also facilitate tax collection. Ease of collection, then, may also, or alternatively, explain why property taxes are assessed only on market values, why sales taxes are often imposed on commodities but not on services, and why home production is not subject to income tax.

CONCLUSIONS

Agreements can be self-enforced or enforced by a third party. For enforcement, the latter can use either long-term relations or force. Self-enforcement's edge is in two-party agreements that others have difficulty in observing; its weakness is that the present value of the agreement must be positive to both throughout the life of the agreement, thus excluding, among others, any lending agreements. Third-party enforcement using long-term relations is effective in agreements that traverse national borders and in cases in which the cost of measuring the attributes of the transaction at transaction time is high. The use of force seems to be a low-cost form of enforcement, but the power the enforcer amasses poses the threat of confiscation to his clients. Clients will not let a specialized violence-using enforcer emerge before they make arrangements to control him; otherwise they could not prevent a takeover. When clients can control their protector, they will impose high standards on his adjudication procedures to prevent abuse of power. Other third-party enforcers will require less control, because they are self-policed to a greater degree.

Besides the state, third-party enforcers include organizations like close-knit groups (these, as a rule, are small), churches, trade organizations,

---

[22] Note, however, that the sale prices of various commodities and services cover components not enforced by the state, such as the quality of theatrical performance.

firms, and criminal organizations. Each has its unique comparative advantage, and thus we expect each to provide a subset of enforcement services. For example, I predict that vertically integrated firms will be found where the cost of measuring the downstream moving products is high. As that cost declines, such as when standards emerge, I predict that the role of contracts and the role of the state will expand and that firms will become less vertically integrated. Finally, as long as subjects control the state, I predict that the state will act so as to maximize subjects' wealth. In terms of taxation, this implies that transactors and property owners will be taxed in proportion to the protection and enforcement services the state supplies.

5

Anonymous Exchange, Mixed Enforcement, and Vertical Integration

INTRODUCTION

In the discussion that follows, I use the terms "agreement" and "contract" in very specific ways that require definition.

> **Definitions. Agreement:** *A relationship that encompasses the entire agreed-upon interactions of a transaction.*
>
> **Contract:** *An agreement, or part of an agreement, that the state takes on itself to enforce and adjudicate.*

By these definitions, then, the scope of the state will increase with an increase in the extent of contracting.

In this chapter, I claim that, as a rule, the state enforces only the contractual components of individual transactions; transactions, as a rule, have additional attributes, and these are enforced by other means. As is obvious, I predict that a decrease in the cost of contracting will induce transactors to cover more of the commodity attributes in their contracts. I also predict that a decrease in that cost will generate a number of more "macro" effects:

1. Legal delineation and anonymous exchange will become more common.
2. The level of vertical integration (defined later) will decline.
3. The extent of the market and the role of the state will increase.

By the model here, then, the cost of contracting and the precise contents of agreements can significantly affect the scope of the state.

Discussing first anonymous exchange, I argue that when information is costly, only caveat-emptor transactions meet the conditions for anonymity, and only these are enforced fully by the state. The state *never* enforces entire non-caveat-emptor agreements; other enforcers enforce part or all of such agreements. The nature and the consequences of mixed enforcement, tightly wound with vertical-integration issues, occupy the rest of this chapter.

Obviously, enforcers using exclusively long-term relations for enforcement cannot enforce anonymous exchange. Neither can anonymous exchange be self-enforced, because that would require strictly synchronous exchange, which is unattainable. I proceed to discuss, then, third-party enforcement of anonymous exchange.

COSTLESS PRODUCT INFORMATION, ANONYMITY, AND THE EXTENT OF THE MARKET

The fundamental assumption that accommodates anonymity in the Walrasian model is that commodity information is costless.[1] Under costless information, buyers can assess their purchases without incurring any expense. Thus, among other things, they cannot be cheated, and warranties to assure product quality are superfluous. Even lending and borrowing are easy to arrange then. Loans need not be secured, as lenders are certain of the probability of repayment and will grant only "good" loans. Credit transactions are equally easy to enforce then, and exchange need not be instantaneous.[2] An additional assumption implicit to the Walrasian system (though ultimately embedded in the first one) is that property rights are well defined. This assumption clearly implies no theft. When people do not fear theft, and when they can assess costlessly what others offer, enforcement, too, is costless. There is no need to spend resources in learning about whom one deals with or in maintaining long-term relations. Although, seemingly, anonymity characterizes the Walrasian model, because it is costless to determine the identity of trading partners, the notion of anonymity is not really meaningful there.

The extent of the market is one of the main concerns of this chapter. The "market" of the Walrasian system is a point in space where all buyers and sellers of a commodity are located. Goods have to be transported when buyers and sellers are dispersed, and the cost of shipping has to be accounted for then. Monopoly issues aside, given scale

---

[1] Hayek, in "The Meaning of Competition" (1948), first delivered as a lecture in 1946, incisively discusses problems that the zero-information cost assumption generates.

[2] A related consequence of costless information is that all commodities are perfectly liquid, and therefore there is no need for cash.

economies to specialized production, transportation costs fully determine the extent of the market.

The farther away a commodity is shipped, especially when several modes of transport are used, the more times it changes hands, and the larger the number of transportation specialists providing the service. No matter how many links the chain of exchanges contains, when information is costless the transactors incur no extra cost of exchange. For instance, there is no reason that a producer of a commodity would transport it to the market himself.[3]

Relaxation of the costless-information assumption drastically affects the shipping problem. When information is costly, buyers spend resources to evaluate the offered merchandise before they agree to buy it. The evaluation costs are distinct from those of transportation and will be incurred every time the merchandise changes hands. Indeed, transportation services have to be evaluated too. Exchange costs can be reduced if the producer (or an intermediate trader in the chain) bypasses some of the transport and exchange intermediaries. This action, however, lowers the level of specialization and the gain from specializing. The extent of the market, as well as the gains from it, then, will depend not only on the costs of shipping but also on the costs of evaluating commodities and services.

TRADE BY REPUTATION VERSUS TRADE BY CONTRACT

How does the evaluation of commodities exchanged by contract compare with their evaluation when the exchange is backed by reputation? Consider three individuals, B, C, and D. B is a seller of a commodity, and C and D are its buyers. B can delineate the commodity in a contract or back it with his reputation. One concern that buyers may have is the ease of transferring the commodity to a third party. Suppose first that B's commodity is delineated by a well-specified contract. B can then readily transfer it to C. In his turn, C can also transfer it to D almost as easily by reassigning the contract he has with B. B might be a manufacturer, C an itinerant salesman, and D a final consumer. The consumer may have no reason to trust the salesman's assertion of the quality of

---

[3] Under costless information, the improbability of double coincidence – of each of the transactors offering precisely what the other desires – is of no consequence. Individuals can repeatedly reexchange their products (stored at the least-cost location) at no extra cost until they encounter suppliers offering the products they actually desire.

the commodity, but he may agree to deal with the salesman because he can rely on the specification of the commodity in the contract.

Suppose that B sells wheat. If he is a reputable seller, and because delineating the wheat in a contract would be costly, he may certify its value by his reputation. Relying on his reputation, he may find it easy to transfer it to C as well as to D. The reputation, however, is not attached to the commodity. Once the commodity is transferred, the effect of B's reputation ceases, and C cannot transfer it to D with equal ease. The contractual rights that the protector delineates and enforces, then, accommodate exchange by specifications, which may be anonymous.[4] On the other hand, when reputation backs the exchange, it is crucial to know the identities of the exchange parties.[5]

The distinction is illustrated by the move from larger to smaller batches of a commodity. As long as it is clear that specimens within batches are similar to each other, then the larger the batch, the smaller the per-unit measurement cost, and with it, the cost of contract delineation. For instance, the large-scale producer of a commodity, say tomatoes or flowers, is likely to use contracts in trading with wholesalers. The retail seller of the commodity, however, is more likely to use his reputation to guarantee its quality to his many buyers.

Brand names are often attached to commodities, which makes them easy to transfer. It may seem that the producer's reputation itself is transferable by branding the commodity. The ease of transfer, however, is not the property of the commodity, but rather of the reputation of the brand owner.[6] Transfer is easy only when the recipient is aware that the issuer is reputable. When B uses his brand name to sell a commodity to C, C can easily transfer it to D only if D trusts the brand (i.e., if the producer has created long-term relations with D as well as with C).

This discussion generates the following implications: (1) I predict that extra effort will be devoted to contractual delineation of commodities that typically change hands more than once. The other side of the coin is that commodities that have been delineated contractually can be pre-

---

[4] The market, in this sense, is non-discriminatory. It matters not what is the race, sex, religion, age, or any other characteristic of an exchange party.

[5] When the buyer uses cash, only the identity of the seller has to be known. But the state then implicitly guarantees that disputes regarding the cash the buyer has delivered to the seller will be subject to its third-party enforcement.

[6] Note that the cooperation of the state is required to enforce the brand name itself and to prevent imitations, whereas the seller's reputation is of no use for preventing imitation.

dicted to change hands more times than commodities that are delineated by reputation or brand name. Moreover, producers may use fewer intermediaries ("cut the middlemen out") to sell the latter type of commodities to consumers, reducing the number of hands the commodities go through. (2) As discussed later in this chapter, as the cost of the contractual delineation of a commodity falls, the prediction is that it will be sold over a larger territory.

CAVEAT-EMPTOR VERSUS FUTURE-OBLIGATION TRANSACTIONS

Individuals will not trade unless they are properly informed about what they are getting. The simplest way to acquire the information is by inspecting the merchandise on the spot before buying it. This is what people do under the rule of caveat emptor. Caveat-emptor exchange probably has taken place since time immemorial, especially where towns have existed, and now is commonly employed in produce markets and flea markets.[7] Presumably the parties actually transact only after they have decided that what they have chosen is satisfactory. They inspect garage-sale furniture, taste fruit-stand cherries, and test-drive used cars before buying any of these. Such trade, however, encompasses only a small fraction of all exchange.

Caveat-emptor transactions are costly in that the best time for inspection is not necessarily the time of exchange, especially because the things that pairs of transactors wish to get seldom are available simultaneously.[8] In addition, some commodities and most services are consumed by the act of inspection. If such commodities are inspected before the agreement is made, then under caveat emptor the buyer has no incentive to pay. If payment precedes inspection, then the seller has no incentive to provide good quality. Long-term relations can be established to overcome these problems. Thus, even in produce markets not all transactions are caveat-emptor transactions, as sellers often occupy the same stalls for long

---

[7] The term "caveat emptor," or "buyer beware," does not properly characterize these transactions; rather, both parties must beware. The transactions are symmetric, as each obtains something from the other. The seller usually receives cash, but like any other commodity, its value may be less than what it seems. Contemporary sellers inspect bills for watermarks, and in earlier times sellers bit into coins to determine if they were truly gold.

[8] Note that inspecting a commodity at transaction time often constitutes a duplication of effort, since commodities are "inspected" by the act of consumption.

periods, and some buyers become steady customers. This reduces the haggling and the need for inspection. As elaborated later, establishing long-term relations amounts to the suppliers agreeing in the present to provide something in the future.

Caveat-emptor transactions are instantaneous, and their enforcement is relatively simple. It requires only that the enforcer see to it that each delivers what he agreed to.[9] Transactors often agree to make delivery in the future. The enforcement of such agreements, whether by long-term relations or by the use of violence, is less simple. The difference between these two enforcement forms is crucial to our problem, and I discuss it through much of this chapter.

In general, the stipulations in any agreement must be sufficient to apprise the enforcer of what he is supposed to enforce. The information that is sufficient for enforcement under violence-using enforcers, however, is very different from the information that has to be provided to enforcers using other means of enforcement. As argued in Chapter 3, we expect clients to impose more stringent requirements on the evidence used by contract enforcers than on the evidence used by enforcers of other agreements. Whereas the information used by non-violent enforcers may be implicit, that used by the violence-using enforcer must allow adjudication based on explicit stipulations (supplemented by the laws governing the transaction).

Besides stipulations regarding commodities and services, contracts may also contain stipulations regarding the attributes of the transactors. A contract that stipulates only the former and is silent regarding the latter meets the condition of anonymity. Its enforcer does not use information about the exchange parties, only about the exchange entities.

The two types of enforcers incur different information costs in the enforcement of exchange agreements, and each has a comparative advantage in a subset of enforcement issues. The next section addresses the within-transactions exchange and enforcement of the different attributes of commodities.

An exchange agreement, especially by contract, has to make clear what is exchanged. If grain is exchanged, a unit to measure it by, a "bushel," say, must be selected, and its attributes described. Standards for a commodity must be established, and these may be general or specific. As an illustration of the progression of standards toward greater

---

[9] It is not clear to me how the enforcer knows what the parties agreed to. The resolution of this problem, however, does not seem germane here.

specificity, "wheat" is a more specific standard than is "grain," "soft wheat" is more specific than "wheat," and "No. 2 St. Louis wheat" is more specific than "soft wheat." Where standards are available, contractors are likely to use them. When more specific standards are adopted and contractors use them, delineation becomes more comprehensive, though the specifications are unlikely ever to be exhaustive. As discussed later, we expect the weight of the contract content in agreements to increase, then, and reassignment to become easier.

Transactors have leeway as to how accurately to measure each attribute of the exchanged commodities, as well as the level of enforcement of the exchange. They face a trade-off between the accuracy of measurement and the means of enforcement. As a rule, enforcement by violence is cheaper than enforcement that uses long-term relations, but the measurements that the former requires are more costly than those required by the latter.

MIXED ENFORCEMENT

Commodities, even "simple" ones, have many valued attributes. The agreement governing a transaction is likely to stipulate the standards for only some of its attributes; others are too expensive to stipulate or to enforce.[10] The transactors, however, will nevertheless exploit those not covered by the agreement.

Two very different agreements can illustrate the use of multiple enforcers for different attributes of a transaction. One is the exchange between a theater company and its patrons, and the other between marriage partners. In the former, the state enforces attributes such as "when," "where," "identity of principal actors," and "price." They are stipulated contractually by public notices, as well as implicitly by the ticket. Not covered by the contract is the quality of the performance, which is enforced by reputation.[11] It is conceivable that the transaction would not be profitable under either form of enforcement if carried by itself. It may become profitable, however, by employing the two simultaneously within single transactions, each enforcing a different subset of

---

[10] The contract-theory literature, which invariably assumes that the state is the sole third-party enforcer, designates the phenomenon of not stipulating and enforcing all attributes "incomplete contracts." By the terminology used here, it should be called "incomplete agreements."

[11] Left in the public domain is the differential in value between the high-value seats and the uniform selling price for all seats in a price class.

attributes.[12] The state, as discussed in Chapter 10, has an advantage in enforcing standardized contracts. I predict, then, that it will enforce a larger fraction of the attributes of a long-running Broadway play than of a one-shot production, because the payoff to standardizing in the former is higher.

The individual marriage agreements are also enforced by more than one enforcement method. The attributes the state enforces are encompassed in the marriage contract and the laws governing it. One of these is the property division in case of divorce. The ease of measuring property relative to other marital attributes is in conformity with the earlier assertion that the state will undertake to enforce the easier-to-delineate stipulations. Other aspects of the marriage agreement are self-enforced. These include, for example, the daily effort each spouse is to contribute to the household. In addition, religious institutions enforce still other provisions, such as those regarding children's education in some marriages. As mentioned in Chapter 4, the state's share of enforcement is predicted to increase with a shorter duration of the marriage. Personal attributes, obviously, are at the heart of the marriage agreement. Not surprisingly, the agreement cannot be reassigned. Discussed later are predictions of what characterizes the attributes that will be stipulated in the two forms of third-party agreements, as well as those that will be left to self-enforcement.

ANONYMOUS EXCHANGE

As stated, under costless information there is no difficulty in knowing the person one deals with, nor what the characteristics of the person are. Anonymity is not an issue there, then. It becomes relevant *because* acquiring the information is costly. The question then is, Under what conditions can one conduct trade anonymously, dispensing with knowing the identity and characteristics of the trading partner?

Anonymous exchange can take two forms. One is caveat emptor. The other, more diverse form includes explicit future-delivery transactions

---

[12] The timing of payment poses a problem within a problem. The seller is likely to find it expensive to enforce the collection of the admission fee after the show, even if contractually stipulated, and consequently may require that patrons pay in advance. The state enforces this requirement; the police help to restrict admission to only ticket holders (i.e., those who have already paid). Buyers agree to pay in advance, presumably because they believe that they can tarnish a performer's reputation in case he delivers less than what he promised.

and the exchange for cash of guaranteed and brand-name commodities. As discussed later in this section, the second form is anonymous only in a restricted sense. While restricted, it is instrumental for extending the market.

Caveat-emptor transactions are attractive because they dispense with the parties' need to maintain personal relationships. As discussed earlier, they are expensive in that inspection may be cheaper later than at the time of the agreement, and some forms of inspection are difficult to arrange. The need for synchronicity can be dispensed with by allowing the transaction to span a period of time. Maintaining anonymity in future-delivery transactions, however, is problematic.

Unlike future-delivery disputes, caveat-emptor disputes can occur only at transaction time. In caveat-emptor transactions the third-party enforcer simply ascertains that each side delivers what was agreed to, thus preventing the stronger or the quicker from getting away with plain theft. In future-delivery agreements the transactors stipulate in the present the price and the specifications that the merchandise is expected to meet at some future time. Dispute at the time of the agreement is highly improbable, because the merchandise is not inspected then. However, as delivery trails the time of the agreement, and as conditions often deviate from the predicted path, it is highly likely that one of the parties will turn out a loser and will be eager to renege.[13] Disputes can also arise if the recipient perceives that the quality of the merchandise does not meet the specifications.

Analysis of the exchange of brand-name commodities for cash (assumed, for simplicity, to be costless to transact) brings out issues both of future delivery and of anonymity. The seller does not care, and therefore does not seek to know, with whom he is transacting (i.e., he is not concerned with the buyer's identity).[14] On their part, customers do not need to inspect the merchandise if they believe that they can punish the seller by not buying from him in the future. Customers' relations with a seller whom they can punish are long-term rather than anonymous. Had the seller been a stranger hawking his wares at a street corner, buyers would have been less confident about what they were getting. A similar argument applies to the exchange of a guaranteed commodity for cash.

---

[13] The parties can specify the price prevailing in the market at delivery time, but then there must be some (hidden) reason why the transaction itself is not carried out at that time.

[14] A caveat to the text is due, because different buyers are prone to affect the seller's brand name differently.

To enforce a future-delivery trade, the transactors must be within the enforcer's jurisdiction at delivery time. Even if they are, enforcement may still fail if the would-be loser does not possess adequate resources to make good on his promise. Anonymous exchange provides no information on transactors' wealth. Anonymity, then, reduces the value, and the probability, of such exchange. If anonymity is to be maintained, the parties may simply revert to caveat-emptor transactions that are completed at the time of the agreement.

By transacting indirectly through intermediaries, however, the principals to a transaction can overcome the difficulty of dealing with each other while remaining anonymous to one another. The intermediaries agree to receive merchandise from sellers at pre-specified terms, and they agree to deliver to the ultimate buyers merchandise that is, as a rule, subject to the same specifications. The ultimate parties need to know only the specifications of the merchandise. By dealing with the intermediaries, the buyers can be anonymous to the sellers. As elaborated later in a discussion of futures contracts, the intermediaries themselves, however, must be "nonymous." They must have a brand name and the ability to guarantee their actions. They cannot maintain anonymous relationships with their customers, then, though their customers may be anonymous to them.

The existence of intermediaries and the specifications they use are valued for more than merely facilitating trade between strangers. The intermediaries are specialists, dealing with multiple customers. They may create standards, and where standards already exist, they tend to enforce specifications that meet the standards. Standards are cheaper to stipulate and enforce than are tailor-made specifications. In addition, the presence of standards tends to imply the existence of economical methods to ascertain whether or not the standards are met. Producers can produce to the standards, buyers can purchase by them, and, to use current jargon, the goods becomes "commoditized." Any number of people can join the network, all tied together through the intermediaries, while not having to know each other.

THE REASSIGNMENT OF AGREEMENTS

The higher the degree of specialization and the greater the shipping distance, the greater the number of times commodities are likely to change hands before reaching the final users. The number of links in the chain of shipping is not constant, nor is the number of sales intermediaries that connect the original producer of a commodity and its final user. The ability to reassign an agreement makes the parties' rights and obligations more liquid.[15] The greater is a specialist's ability to reassign an agreement, the higher is the value of the transaction.

As stated, transactors may (but do not have to) include stipulations regarding their own personal characteristics in their contracts. On the other hand, the personal attributes of the transactors are essential to agreements, or parts of agreements, enforced by long-term relations. This highlights a fundamental difference between the two kinds of agreements. Contracts will not be used unless their stipulations are sufficient for carrying out the transaction; for that reason, then, they are relatively easy to reassign.[16] As elaborated later, the ultimate transactors to futures contracts can readily reassign their contractual obligations. Reassigning agreements enforced by long-term relations is seldom automatic and often requires the consent of the other party.

As stated, contracts encompass only parts of agreements. How do their non-contractual terms affect their reassignability? For completeness, consider first caveat-emptor transactions. These transactions are fully governed by their contracts. The state, which is the enforcer of contracts, has simply to determine that the parties deliver what they agreed to. If the agreement is merchandise for cash, the state has to ascertain that the merchandise has been delivered and the cash is not counterfeit. All else is up to the transactors, who presumably assured themselves beforehand that they wanted to make the deal. In that case, the identity of the transactors is of no consequence. These transactions are concluded instantaneously, however, and the reassignment issue is moot.

Agreements to exchange brand-name commodities for cash are governed only in part by contract. Such relationships are asymmetric; they are anonymous to sellers as they view buyers, but sellers cannot be anonymous to buyers. At least a part of the exchange is enforced by the brand name (or by guarantee). Correspondingly, the parties on one side are usually permitted to reassign their role to others, but those on the other side are not. In the sale of new appliances, for example, the buyer's

---

[15] Telser and Higinbotham (1977) elaborate on the enhanced liquidity that reassignment ability generates.

[16] Although contracts must be sufficiently informative to allow the state to enforce them without recourse to provisions not included in them, the parties do not have to explicitly stipulate "everything." The enforcer is expected to be aware of, and to act on, stipulations that are embedded in custom or in the law (especially the common law).

right to reassign the manufacturer's guarantee when reselling the appliance is usually provided for contractually. The manufacturer, on the other hand, cannot reassign its obligation to another. In a later section dealing with vertical integration, I discuss one method of partial reassignment.

In some cases, agreements may be enforced without state assistance. Of those in which the state does take part (caveat-emptor transactions excepted), the agreements invariably also contain components that are enforced by long-term relations.[17] In some, one of the parties may be anonymous, and in others neither is. In the former, the contractual rights in the dealings with the anonymous party can quite readily be reassigned, but those in the relationship with the brand-name party cannot.

FUTURES VERSUS FORWARD CONTRACTS

A comparison between "forward contracts" and "futures contracts" will further illuminate what agreements govern and the problem of their reassignability. Typically the ultimate parties to futures contracts are strangers. Parties to forward contracts, on the other hand, operate under long-term relations. Futures contracts delineate in great detail the commodity transacted, and the commodity delivered must meet the specifications in the contract. "What you see (in the contract) is what you get." Forward contracts are not as detailed as are futures contracts. Unlike futures contracts, the contractual terms of forward contracts do not encompass the entire agreement; long-term relations govern the remainder. Implicit in the agreement encompassing the forward contract is the provision that the seller will deliver a commodity with an optimal (or near-optimal) set of attributes. The long-term relations serve to enforce this provision.

Disputes are resolved differently under the two forms of agreement. One source of delivery disputes is that the non-performing party's wealth may be insufficient to compensate the other. The parties to forward contracts use their long-term relations to enforce their agreements. Their positions are symmetric here. When the market price at delivery time is higher than that agreed upon, the seller may encounter a performance problem. A lower market price poses a similar problem for the buyer.

---

[17] Indeed, the sale of a used appliance still under warranty is usually under caveat emptor, except for the guaranteed aspect.

Each commits long-term relations to the relationship, and the potential loss for one is similar to that for the other.

The enforcement of delivery in the case of futures is quite different. The futures organization possesses a brand name, while its customers are anonymous. This is similar to the previously considered sale of guaranteed commodities for cash where the seller possesses a brand name while buyers are anonymous. In the case of selling guaranteed commodities, however, buyers fulfill their commitment at transaction time, and thus no problem arises in enforcing the terms to which they agreed. In futures, the enforcement problem remains, and to resolve it the ultimate transactors are required to make cash deposits. These deposits largely dispense with the problem of the adequacy of transactors' wealth and with the need for state enforcement.[18]

Deposits are needed because determining customers' capacity for bearing losses is expensive. Because it is difficult to know who will be able to back up his obligation, "inefficient" default might have been common in futures trades with no deposits. Although deposits impose a burden on the depositors, they largely eliminate the problem of default (or the need to know transactors' personal characteristics). Because the deposits are contractually stipulated, they facilitate the reassignment of these contracts. The ultimate parties in futures contracts routinely reassign their contracts (i.e., their rights and obligations). On the other hand, reassignment of forward contracts usually requires permission, because the offer of the assignee may be inferior to that of the original transactor.

Disputes regarding quality are also handled differently by the two kinds of agreement. Forward contracts require a lower effort in specification and in measurement than do futures contracts. Although measurement is necessary in any transaction, in the forward-contract transaction it can take place when the commodity is actually used. A user who finds the commodity he has received deficient can resort to their long-term relations to punish the seller. The forward contract's advantage over a futures contract derives from the lower cost of measuring any attribute under the former and from the problem that some attributes are too costly to stipulate in a futures contract. As futures are governed by explicit specifications only, suppliers who control the levels of the unspecified attributes will provide low levels of the positively valued ones and high levels of the negatively valued ones. The "low" and "high"

---

[18] The holder guarantees the safety of the deposits by his brand name.

are in comparison with the levels that would have been stipulated in a more elaborate contract.[19] In forward contracts, the levels of these attributes are expected to be near optimal.

Futures contracts spell out all the promised quality attributes of the transaction. A futures dispute can only be a contract dispute, and thus it is adjudicated by the state. Strangely enough, intermediaries are essentially neutral parties in disputes with their clients regarding quality. The rulings in such disputes may indeed go against the intermediaries. What they lose on one side, however, they tend to gain on the other. Suppose that after taking delivery, a futures buyer claims that the commodity has failed to meet the contract specifications. He bought it from an intermediary, and he takes the intermediary to court. If the intermediary wins the case, the story is over. Suppose, however, that he loses. The intermediary himself operated under the same contract when he received the commodity from the seller. The ruling made by the court implies, then, that the seller is liable for the same damage the intermediary was required to pay the buyer. What the intermediary loses as a defendant, then, he gains back as a plaintiff, or by the threat of becoming one. The litigation, therefore, is in essence between the ultimate buyer and the seller who originated the contract.[20]

In the case of forward contracts, the levels of many of the valued attributes are part of the encompassing agreement but are not stipulated in the contract. The state, then, has no jurisdiction over these attributes. Disputes regarding them must be resolved by appeal to the long-term relations backing the agreements. Reliance on the long-term relations, however, makes reassignment of the agreement difficult. The reliance on the courts in disputes regarding futures makes their reassignment (relatively) easy. The higher the likelihood (as perceived by transactors) that they will gain from reassigning a contract, the greater the advantage of using the futures contract.

A dispute over non-contractual aspects of an agreement tends to weaken the long-term relations among the transactors. A severe dispute

---

[19] Carl L. Alsberg (1926) provides evidence that supports this assertion. Note that only a small fraction of commodities futures are carried to maturity; actual deliveries are mostly by forward or spot contracts.

[20] The ultimate seller of futures is the warehouse. The warehouse buys commodities from individuals who may be unable to guarantee them, in case they are found toxic, for example. Therefore, the warehouse performs the function of inspecting the commodities to determine that they meet the required specifications. The warehouse then guarantees to the buyers of futures the commodities it delivers.

may even result in termination of those relations, removing a link from the chain of exchanges between producer and consumer. The exchange might proceed via formation of an alternative long-term relation, but that obviously would be costly. The greater the reliance of an agreement on non-contractual components, the wider the scope for non-contractual disputes, and the greater the difficulty of executing the exchange.

THE JURISDICTION OVER AGREEMENT ENFORCEMENT

The trade of commodities requires their physical transfer. Only immediate neighbors whose landholdings abut can trade commodities directly. To trade with non-neighbors, producers can travel with their merchandise, but they will need permission from the landowners whose land they traverse. Moreover, that method fails to fully exploit specialization opportunities. Alternatively, people can trade by forming chains of trades across the successively connecting holdings of various neighbors. The simplest way to effect such trade is by caveat emptor at each transfer juncture. That, however, requires inspection of the merchandise every time it changes hands, and the total cost of such repeated inspections increases with the number of transactors in the chain.

Two very different organizational methods can be employed to transmit a commodity through a chain of transactors while avoiding some of the inspection costs. One is to use a single contract that is applicable to the entire chain. A problem here is that both ultimate and intermediate parties must reside under the same enforcer (i.e., within the same state). Alternatively, the agreements can be governed, at least in part, by direct long-term relations between successive pairs of transactors. In that case, then, each link requires a separate long-term relation. The larger the number of links, the greater the chance that trade will be disrupted. Long-term relations, however, can be used both within and across states, whereas contract enforcement requires a single enforcer.

Individuals residing in separate states that do not honor one another's contracts cannot use the state to enforce their exchange. Such transactors either can form direct long-term relations or can operate within firms. The latter is advantageous when the exchange between independent transactors is prone to disputes. Consider, for example, shipping a highly variable and highly perishable commodity. If the exchange is between independent transactors, disputes and other forms of capture are likely. If, instead, the shipping is organized within a firm, here a multinational one, the chance for dispute is lowered. The firm, of course, must

93

possess enforcement power over its employees. To enhance that power, it may, for example, employ members of a close-knit community such as a religious or ethnic group (Greif, 1994). However, unlike trade within firms, trade among independent transactors is not subject to the shirking that can occur in the former. I elaborate on commodity movement within firms in the section after next.

TERRITORIAL SCALE ECONOMIES

The ability to contract, even if for only some of the attributes of a transaction, seems to be of great value, especially when the merchandise changes hands many times. As stated, territorial continuity is required for the exchange of commodities.[21] Violence-using third parties also require territorial continuity; they have to be able to move their forces across the territories they control. Moreover, the trade of commodities by contract is subject to scale economies with respect to the continuity of territory; as a state expands, the opportunities to use contracts also expand. The ability to exchange commodities by contract is lost when the potential exchange parties reside in different states that do not honor each other's contracts.

When commodities are not altered in transit, and when the individuals participating in chains of trades are the subjects of the same enforcer, contracts can greatly facilitate the transfer of the commodities. The reason is that in spite of the sequence of ownership transfers, the use of contracts makes it possible to confine disputes regarding the attributes governed by the contracts to the ultimate trading parties. The intermediate parties, like those in the case of futures, "catalyze" the transfer of the commodities, but need not be involved in the dispute.[22] The individuals in the chain are all bound by a single contract – a contract that is reassigned each time the merchandise crosses a property boundary. In order to enforce the chain of trades, the enforcer has to have control of

[21] Territorial continuity is less important for services, especially for intellectual rights.
[22] A close analogy to the decreased need for intermediate parties' inspection that contracts provide is with the transferability of bills of trade that functioned in Scotland more or less as money. These were endorsed by a succession of individuals. The latest recipient was concerned only with the solvency of the original issuer, not the solvency of any of the intermediaries in the chain. The original issuer presumably was one with a highly regarded brand name.

an unbroken land (or sea) route connecting the trading parties.[23] A third party using physical force for enforcement has a comparative advantage in maintaining such control. Third parties not using violence, such as firms or religious organizations, seem not to have a comparative advantage in maintaining jurisdiction over a continuous territory.[24] Thus, for example, whereas the Catholic church has as many adherents as China has subjects, the former cannot secure the movement of commodities among its dispersed members without traversing others' jurisdictions. But any two individuals in China may trade with each other, in that their merchandise will traverse a territory that presumably is controlled by a single third-party enforcer.

The control of contiguous territories by a single third party provides the related advantage of economies of scale to trade by specification. The economies here result from the ability to use standard contracts rather than custom-made ones. One example of the use of such contracts is in futures markets, where the exchange organization fixes a standard, and all the exchanges it effects conform to that standard. The larger the third party's territory, the greater the economies to the use of such contracts. Because the power-backed third-party enforcer is operating in a continuous territory, he has a comparative advantage in enforcing contract exchange. Contract exchange, in turn, relies heavily on the use of standards endorsed by the state.

The more easily that different specimens of commodities and services can be brought under a common denominator, or "commoditized," the easier is their contract delineation, and thus their reassignability. The more specific that commodity standards become, the greater the specialization to be expected in shipping the commodity. Shipment is facilitated by the fact that the commodity is more adequately described when given to the shipper. As long as the recipient believes that the commodity has not been altered, or, when altered, that responsibility can readily be assigned, the original specifications will suffice. We see later that a similar, though more circumscribed, arrangement may apply

---

[23] The use of public roads largely finesses the problem of using a whole chain of trades, but the requirement for a continuous territory remains. I elaborate on the economics of public roads in Chapter 10.

[24] The German Hansa is a counterexample. It connected the participating states by a treaty and maintained the integrity of their sea routes. However, it did not possess physical power with which to enforce the treaty. This implies that the distinction between the types of third parties is largely quantitative rather than qualitative.

to the vertical transmission of commodities through the production process.

As discussed in Chapter 10 in conjunction with legal institutions, the state has a comparative advantage in improving and enforcing standards. On the other hand, where commodities or services are idiosyncratic, or even where they are generic but do not require territorial continuity, enforcing agreements without the use of force is likely to be cheaper. As the cost of providing generic commodities or services decreases (increases) relative to that for idiosyncratic ones, power-backed third-party enforcement (i.e., that by the state) will expand (shrink). In Chapter 12, I discuss further these territorial economies and the reduced need for vertical integration that they accommodate. I also argue there that where people newly stand to gain from exchange within an area that formerly was subject to the jurisdiction of another enforcer, the state is likely to extend its jurisdiction to that area. Such expansion can take the form of merger; it can also be achieved by creating an empire.

VERTICAL INTEGRATION: THE RELATIONSHIP BETWEEN MERGER AND CONTRACTING

Long-term relations can serve independent parties trading with each other as well as parties that move commodities within organizations. The firm is the main form of organization engaged in within-organization exchange. One advantage the firm has is its relatively low rate of disputes regarding such exchanges (Barzel, 1982). The firm owner or the entrepreneur will instruct employees to move commodities from one to another. This can take place at a juncture in a shipping operation, or as part of a production process in which one employee, after operating on the commodity, hands it to another. The upstream employee, who is paid a wage rather than being rewarded for his output, can gain little from deliberately providing low-quality commodities; neither can the downstream employee gain much from spending resources to get high-quality specimens. Therefore, they are unlikely to have disputes regarding what they give and receive. Where independent transactors effect the exchange, disputes among them are more likely to arise. Because the relationships among employees are not governed by a contract, the state cannot adjudicate them. Rather, the employer is the third party with power to enforce relationships and resolve disputes between his employees.

I proceed by exploring the enforcement role of vertical integration.

Definition. *Vertical integration:* A state wherein a residual claimant of a firm, or of some other organization, assumes responsibility for two or more vertical operations.

The assumption of responsibility is a key ingredient here. As defined, the level of vertical integration within an existing firm can increase or decline. Indeed, not all the within-firm transfers between two merged firms contribute to the level of vertical integration, and in at least some of its components a merger may *lower* the level of integration. I argue that the level of integration in a firm is a matter of degree. It depends on the extent to which the firm uses its own power to enforce its operations. Within-firm operations that the state enforces do not fall under the firm's jurisdiction, and thus, by the definition here, should not be counted as part of its vertically integrated operations.

Consider how a firm operates on the attributes of a commodity it produces. The price it can expect to receive for the commodity will depend on buyers' evaluations of its attributes. Abstracting from interactions between attributes, the amount the firm will spend on each attribute will depend on the extent buyers are able to evaluate it. The firm obviously will not spend resources to enhance (or preserve) the value of an attribute that buyers have failed to measure. Commodity attributes can be divided into three categories:

1. Those the firm can increase (or maintain), and buyers can profitably measure.
2. Those the firm can increase (or maintain), but buyers cannot profitably measure.
3. Those that can be expected to remain unaltered (or can be prevented from being altered), and that buyers can profitably measure.

Note, first, that although the physical commodity seems to fall within the jurisdiction of the firm, the firm need not own the economic rights to all attributes of the commodity. I hypothesize that the firm is likely to assume ownership of the first two categories of attributes, but that the third is likely to be exchanged by contract and thus will not be owned by the (integrated) firm. In terms of the level of vertical integration, the point is that the cost of measuring an attribute may change as it moves downstream in the production process, and it is advantageous to exchange it in the market at a point where measuring it is relatively less costly.

Suppose that a manufacturer B sells to an intermediate producer C a component to be incorporated into the latter's own product. The quality of the component can be easily measured, both when it enters C's operations and when it leaves, and C commits not to alter it. Under these conditions we expect the manufacturer to guarantee the component to the final consumer E, who is the client of the intermediate producer. The manufacturer's guarantee of his product to the final consumer makes the execution of the intermediate transactions easier. The intermediate producer C need not be concerned with the guaranteed component of his exchange. He has no reason to inspect the merchandise the manufacturer sends to him because he will not be penalized if the component has defects. Even though the original producer B sells the commodity to C, he retains the legal and economic ownership of the guaranteed attributes.

As an example, suppose that an apparel manufacturer guarantees certain attributes of his products to the ultimate consumers. The manufacturer uses a retailer to distribute the product. When a guaranteed attribute of the apparel turns out to be flawed, then customers' complaints might seem directed against the retailer. In the final analysis, however, the complaints are against the original guarantor. The manufacturer is the residual claimant to the guaranteed aspects of his operation.

To grasp more fully the nature of within-firm transfers, consider extending the foregoing case. We begin with an innocuous extension and then move on to a more significant one. Suppose that we add firm D to the vertical array B, C, and E. B produces the component that C incorporates into its product that it then sells to D. Here, too, B guarantees its product directly to E. Firm D now acquires firm C, and the merged firm is called C + D. D's merger with C need not alter the guarantee provision; B continues to guarantee the product to E. The product that C formerly sold to D is now transferred internally within C + D. The component that B produces, however, is not part of the vertically integrated operation, because the residual claimant of the firm C + D does not assume responsibility over the guaranteed component and therefore is not such a claimant over it. Rather, B continues to be the residual claimant to the variability in the products it guarantees.

I now show how merger can actually *reduce* one component of vertical integration. The vertical array still consists of firms B–E. Suppose that while processing a commodity, C's cost can be reduced if it allows one of its valued attributes to deteriorate. D's cost of measuring that attribute as C transmits it would be prohibitive. C, then, has no incentive to preserve the attribute if it sells the commodity to D. As long as C and D operate independently, C can be expected to let the attribute deteriorate. B, therefore, will not guarantee the attribute to E. Suppose, however, that the attribute can be measured at low cost both when B transmits the commodity to C and when D transmits it to E. Once C and D merge, then, the guarantee becomes attractive. This, indeed, may be why the two may choose to merge. As stated, C + D must commit to B that it will not degrade the guaranteed attribute. The merger of C and D has increased vertical integration. The C + D commitment to maintain the level of the attribute allows B to guarantee it to E. B's guarantee to E seems the more fundamental operation here, and in this respect, C's merger with D results in a *lower* level of vertical integration.[25]

B, for instance, may purchase fresh vegetables from farmers. C and D provide two successive links in transporting the vegetables to E, a supermarket. Freshness, a highly valued attribute, is easy to inspect when B prepares the vegetables for shipment, as well as when they are unloaded at the supermarket. Under the most economical packaging method, however, it is expensive to inspect the vegetables while in transit. Shippers' costs are lower when they skimp on maintaining freshness. If shipper C operates independently of D, and the low-cost packaging method is used, each could blame the loss of freshness on the other, and thus freshness would not be adequately maintained. As long as the two continue to operate independently, freshness can be properly preserved only if they employ a more expensive packaging method that accommodates low-cost inspection in transit.

To the extent that various links in the chain are independent, the agreements between them could be enforced by caveat emptor, but they are more likely to be enforced by long-term relation. Either way, as long as C and D operate independently, each, in his turn, has to assume the responsibility for freshness, and so B will not guarantee freshness to E. Merged, however, B can transact with E if C + D agrees to assume responsibility for freshness. C + D then will be the residual claimant to that attribute and will have no incentive to skimp on its maintenance. C + D presumably will simply instruct its employees to take the necessary steps to maintain freshness. The merger between C and D allows B

---

[25] The view in the text conforms to Grossman and Hart's notion (1980) that the firm consists only of the aspects that are not contracted out.

to leapfrog both and contractually guarantee freshness to E, thus *lowering* integration in preserving freshness.[26]

The more attributes that one transactor guarantees to another across intermediate producers, the less the scope of the intermediate producers (firms), and the greater the scope of contractual relations. Moreover, the number of links that the guarantee may leapfrog is not constant. The pesticide producer supplying the farmer who sells to B may guarantee product safety to the final consumers, and the farmer's seed supplier may guarantee to the retailer that the produce will withstand frost.[27]

The foregoing discussion demonstrates that merger and vertical integration are distinct concepts and that merger can reduce the level of vertical integration. These conclusions, then, are not merely matters of definition, though the definition that I offer seems appropriate to the issue at hand. A question such as "Are a franchiser and his franchisees vertically integrated?" cannot be satisfactorily answered if we simply try to determine whether they "belong" to the same firm or are separate firms. By the definition here, on the other hand, the question can be readily answered. Moreover, the *level* of integration is not constant here, but depends on the fraction of the exchanges between the franchiser and the franchisees that are enforced within the operation.

Consider, for example, the effect of a lower cost of legal delineation, due, say, to a decrease in the cost of measuring commodity attributes, or to the formation of new standards. By the model here, we expect the degree of vertical integration within firms to decrease, and we also expect firms to increase the rate at which they spin off some of their operations. This is a sharper prediction than the models of Williamson and Klein and associates offer. To them, vertical integration is binary; it is either present or absent, and it will occur when quasi rents are significant. The existence of situations in which the ease of legally enforcing different

---

[26] Similarly, the doctrine of privity (successive relationships to the same rights of property) applies to legal liability across a vertical chain of transactors.

[27] One scenario for testing the general hypothesis here is as follows. The introduction of refrigerated cars (and of preservatives) has reduced the spoilage of perishable commodities such as meat and vegetables. The introduction of containerized shipping has reduced merchandise damage and theft in general and especially at transfer points. Because of such innovations, damage discovered at destination can more easily be attributed to the original producer when he indeed was responsible. It is expected that the share of contracts in the agreements regarding the affected commodities has increased subsequent to the introduction of the new technologies.

stipulations varies allows us to test our model. The ease of enforcement presumably depends on what there is to enforce. The greater the comparative advantage the state has in enforcement, the more likely it is that a stipulation will be agreed upon contractually, the lower will be the level of vertical integration (both within firms and through the dissolution of firms), and the larger will be the scope of the state. This illustrates the edge that the view of vertical integration proposed here has over the models of Williamson and Klein and associates, as those models do not offer such a clear prediction.[28]

CONCLUSIONS

Exchange agreements must be enforced. The enforcement of instantaneous, caveat-emptor exchange is relatively simple, in that the enforcer has only to ensure that the parties have actually delivered what they agreed to. Enforcement of all other forms of exchange is multidimensional. An enforcer who has a comparative advantage in enforcing one component of a transaction does not necessarily have such advantage in its other components. In particular, the state's advantage is in enforcing the easy-to-measure attributes of a transaction, whereas enforcement based on long-term relations is advantageous for difficult-to-measure attributes. The firm is one institution using long-term relations for enforcement. It employs individuals who would have spent significant amounts of resources on capture from each other if they had been independent transactors. Because employees' remuneration is not directly tied to performance, their incentive for capture is lowered, and so is the potential for dispute.

Transactions that are enforced by reputation-based long-term relations cannot be anonymous. On the other hand, caveat-emptor transactions, as well as those based on standards or commodity specifications that are enforced by the state, can be anonymous to at least one of the parties. Agreements in which a party can be anonymous are easy to reassign. They are especially attractive in long-distance trade and in multistage production. Enforcement by the state requires territorial continuity, and the transactions the state enforces are subject to territorial scale economies. As the costs of measurement and other contracting costs

---

[28] My earlier discussion of financial innovations in Chapter 4 elaborates on the distinction between these models.

decrease, and as standards become more common, we can expect (1) the importance of vertically integrated firms to decline, (2) contracts such as futures to become more common, and (3) the state to expand, sometimes by acquiring an empire.

6

Jurisdictional Issues

THE VIABILITY OF MULTIPLE THIRD PARTIES

In early society, at the inception of the evolution of interactions, anyone could become a third-party enforcer. No organized power yet existed to stop third parties from emerging. Because enforcement was diverse, numerous third-party enforcers could exist simultaneously, and more than one may have attempted to enforce the same agreements.

Third parties are able to charge a fee for the services they provide because their clients value these services. They set the fee so as to maximize their wealth. A third-party enforcer will not form agreements with individuals who are indifferent to whether or not to belong to his organization. Such individuals' cost of "defecting" is low, and thus the enforcer's power of enforcement over them is very limited. Given their predilection not to comply, an enforcer who allowed them to belong to his organization would only cast doubt on his enforcement ability. Indeed, if enforcement is to be effective, then to the marginal person in the enforcer's clientele the prospect of switching must be seen as resulting in a quantum loss of wealth. The size of that potential loss must be sufficient to prevent the individual from quitting under most of the anticipated cases of enforcement. The amount of the potential loss from quitting is what defines the community from which one might be expelled or excommunicated.

One result of the quantum-loss condition is as follows. Consider the enforcement services offered by two third-party enforcers. Their potential clients attach a value to the service of each of the two enforcers, taking into account the possibility of switching to the other. Correspondingly, each enforcer ranks the individuals according to their valuations of his service. The two enforcers are viable side by side only if one's rankings significantly differ from the other's. Otherwise, clients' cost of switching would be low, and then neither enforcer would have much enforcement power. Indeed, no two identical third-party enforcers are simultaneously viable. Enforcement, then, is not a service that can be supplied by "perfectly competitive" suppliers; it cannot be a competitive industry. If two such third parties attempt to compete, one or both will not survive. To survive, each enforcer must use his own method to enhance his power, and the two enforcers must differ in the character of their enforcement power.

JURISDICTIONAL OVERLAP

One ingredient in the definition of the state is that it is the exclusive user of violence for enforcement. By the definition, then, a state cannot accommodate competing third parties that also would use such power for enforcement. But what is the state's domain, that is, the domain with respect to which it has exclusive power? Given that the state uses physical power, which is employed in physical space, that domain has to be territorial, and essentially continuous. I have just argued that if two or more identical enforcers should attempt to operate in a particular area, at most only one of them would be viable. Two or more non-identical enforcers, however, could coexist. The question arises whether or not the state necessarily controls a unique geographic area. Or is it possible that several violence-using third-party enforcers can coexist within a geographic area such that parts of that area lie in more than one state?

I maintain that essentially there can be no jurisdictional overlap among states within a geographic area. In some cases that may seem to occur, but then neither state has true jurisdiction over the territory, and such territory tends to be in the public domain. On the other hand, the domains of criminal organizations, discussed primarily in Chapter 13, tend to overlap those of legitimate states. These organizations, however, seem to rank clients differently than the state does, allowing the two to exist side by side.

We now turn to trade opportunities between states. A state has the power to enforce contracts between its citizens when they reside in it. Consider two individuals residing in two different states. Can they form enforceable exchange contracts? The two states, relying on long-term relations between them, may agree to honor such contracts. However, in the absence of agreement between the states, I expect that such contracts will not be enforced.

Contracts that straddle state borders fall into three classes. In the first two, each enforcer controls an exclusive territory. In the first of these, the two contractors reside in different states under different enforcers, and in the second they are the subjects of two distinct enforcers, but reside in the same state. In the third, the contractors reside in a territory that the two enforcers claim simultaneously. I consider each in turn.

The first case applies to individuals who reside in and are subjects of different states, each with its own exclusive territory. It seems that such individuals cannot form enforceable contracts. When the contractors reside in different states, the enforcer in one cannot force a contractor in the other to perform. Therefore, a contractor who stands to lose from performing his contractual obligation will not perform. A losing contractor may choose to perform in order to retain his reputation, but then it is the reputation rather than the state that enforces the agreement. Contracts that could not be enforced would not be signed in the first place. Instead, as long as the parties reside in different states, they either will altogether refrain from making any agreement with each other or will make agreements that are self-enforced or are enforced by third parties not using violence.

The second case concerns contracting between two individuals who reside in the same state but are the subjects of two geographically exclusive states. One of the two (or both) must be a "foreigner." The foreigner's own state, however, is in no position to enforce his contract. On the other hand, his state of residence has such power. As long as the state agrees to enforce the contract, the two contractors are only nominally subjects of different states; in practice they fall under the jurisdiction of the state where they both reside.

In the third case, two states claim jurisdiction over some of the same territory. The territory, then, is in dispute between the two. Each may claim the right to enforce contracts there. If both enforcers attempt to back their claims by force, but the supremacy of one or the other is not established, contracts there are not enforceable by either, and revert to the public domain.

CONSTRAINTS ON OWNERSHIP BY FOREIGNERS

Foreigners, like locals, are subject to the local force-using enforcer, but the two groups are distinct. How does the behavior of subjects of a state differ from that of foreigners residing in it, and what accounts for the difference in their treatment by the state? Virtually all states admit some foreigners into their territories.[1] Foreigners interact among themselves and with the subjects of the host country. Some of the interactions are placed under the enforcement of the power-backed third party, and some are otherwise enforced. As transients, foreigners are not likely to belong to groups formed by local residents nor to form long-term relations with such groups. They are more likely, then, to interact with local residents by contract than are the latter among themselves.[2] This applies most forcefully to short-term tourists (and, in some respects, to illegal immigrants), less so to longer-term visitors such as foreign college students and trade representatives of foreign firms, and least to "permanent residents."

The third-party enforcement that a state offers to foreigners tends to differ from that offered to its citizens. What can explain these differences and the changes in them? For reasons explained in Chapter 8, the state seldom charges on the margin for the use of its third-party enforcement services. The cost of these services usually is borne by the general taxpayers, and these, as a rule, are citizens, not aliens. States sometimes impose restrictions on non-citizens, such as restrictions regarding the ownership of land or other assets. The restricted ownership tends to lower the opportunity for conflict that would require state adjudication. I hypothesize that such restrictions serve to prevent an excess burden on those bearing these costs. One implication is that the more prone to litigation a class of assets is, the greater the likelihood that restrictions on the ownership of such assets by foreigners will be imposed.[3]

THE REACH OF COLLECTIVE-ACTION MECHANISMS

In Chapter 3, I argued that collective-action mechanisms are needed to control enforcers, especially those using violence, and in Chapter 4, I dis-

---

[1] Not addressed here is the interesting question of the factors that affect the state's choices of to whom to grant citizenship. Elsewhere (Barzel, 2000a) I have discussed the related issue of what distinguishes those individuals whom the state chooses to enfranchise and those whom it does not.

[2] The portion of the total relationships that transients will conduct by contract seems indeterminate on a priori grounds. It depends, among other things, on transients' access to the host states' courts (likely determined endogenously) and on how tight their connections with each other are.

[3] The state provides other services that are financed by general taxes and provided at zero marginal charge. Here, too, I predict that foreigners will be restricted if they can be cheaply identified when using such services.

cussed some of the features of such action. Collective action can be initiated specifically for prevention of abuses of power, as well as for other purposes. Whatever its origin, the question arises whether or not an existing collective-action mechanism will be used to control more than one enforcer.

I have just argued that of two or more identical enforcers competing for the same set of clients, at most one is viable. Therefore, a collective-action mechanism that attempts to control more than one enforcer has to be able to cope with diverse forms of power. Consider now the prior questions about the nature of the clients' power that the enforcer must be able to overcome and the nature of the collective-action authority in charge of controlling the enforcer.

The powers of different enforcers using physical power seem to be similar. Offensive and defensive weapons are, to a substantial degree, similar. Clients, especially under the balance of power that existed prior to the enforcer's emergence, tend to use the same kinds of weapons used by the enforcers, partly in attempting to resist the latter. The collective-action mechanisms that clients organize and operate may use similar weapons as well. Although the sides are unlikely to use identical weapons, the ability to inflict physical harm seems to be the dominant form of power here.

The weapons used by other types of enforcers are more diverse. Consider the church. The church's power lies in the ideology that it exploits to penalize members' non-compliance. What is the nature of the power that the enforced might use to resist the church's enforcement? It is not even clear what the notion of the prior balance of power means in this case. Individuals who attempt to avoid compliance cannot respond in kind short of organizing their own religion. Consider the confiscation of members' wealth by church officers and ways to prevent it. Suppose the head of the church attempts to extort wealth from members by, for example, discovering minor infractions and threatening to expose them and to exaggerate their significance. There is little each individual can do to protect himself. However, as suggested in Chapter 3, the agreement between enforcer and clients is self-policed in part because the increase in the scale of extortion generates a force that counters it. The existence of such self-correcting forces may prevent large-scale abuse. Still, some abuse may take place. Can the collective-action mechanism erected to contain the violence-using enforcer prevent such abuse? The general answer is negative. The state may find it difficult to collect the information required to determine harm. Had it been able to collect the information cheaply, most likely it would have been asked, to begin with, to become the enforcer of the agreements the church took on itself.

Moreover, there is no reason to expect the head of the church to reside within the jurisdiction of the violence-using enforcer. Many religions are not confined to a single state, and hence no particular state is necessarily in control of the head of such a church. The state can impose costs on the church, but is less effective in penalizing its head. A head of a church who resides in a state that attempts to control him may be able simply to shift his headquarters to another, perhaps more tolerant state.[4]

Clients' means of control over any organization to which they belong must be appropriate for the idiosyncrasies of each situation. The clients who control an organization may simply be the ones who created the organization by getting together ahead of time for that purpose. They may keep control of its officers the way rule-of-law states keep control of their armies' chiefs of staff. Such is the case with various international organizations that have been established and are controlled by member states. Other organizations that operate in more than one state often are organized by individual entrepreneurs who solicit clients' participation. This is the case with the ruling bodies of various sports, such as the International Tennis Federation. Clients can avoid extortion by leaving the organization, hopefully to join a competing one.[5] In any case, control here is by non-state enforcers.

States may attempt to control such organizations, but their power tends to be confined to their geographic borders. States can easily control organizations erected to facilitate trade between pairs of states, because the organizations will be viable only if both states allow the trade. Each state may be able to prevent its own subjects from belonging to organizations operating in more than one state, but it will have little additional control.[6] Some third parties operate entirely within a single state. This is so where they operate within states that prohibit their subjects from

---

[4] Similarly, incorporated American firms that do business in many states may shop around for the best state in which to establish their (legal) headquarters.

[5] The method by which condominium owners prevent condominium organizers from abusing their power is instructive here. Condominiums are originated and initially controlled by entrepreneurial organizers. However, the entrepreneurs commit to eventually turning control over to the voting members of the condominiums. Presumably, the entrepreneurs perceive that they can increase their profits by the pre-arranged transfer of control.

[6] The International Olympic Committee has penalized some individual athletes by barring them from competing. These individuals have had singularly little success in attempting to get state courts to rescind those penalties.

belonging to international organizations, as well as where they could have no significant economies from operating beyond a state's borders. The state may choose to use its enforcement power to regulate such organizations. On their part, such organizations often may take advantage of, and benefit from, the state's enforcement power.

Another aspect of this problem relates to the enforcement methods used by organizations that operate in more than one state. Multinational corporations and joint ventures between corporations registered in different states are among the organizations whose operations span the jurisdictions of two or more states. The activities conducted within these organizations are less amenable to power-backed third-party enforcement than are those conducted in organizations confined to single states, since the jurisdiction over many of the former type of activities is less clear than that over the latter type. Therefore, the multistate organizations are expected to rely more heavily on other enforcement mechanisms. They might, for example, commit a large amount of resources, whose value would decline (though they would not easily be vulnerable to capture by others) if others within the organization should perceive non-performance.

LOCAL AUTONOMY

What is the rationale for, and the extent of, local autonomy?[7] Consider states that grant local autonomy to local authorities over local issues. The local authorities then may assume more of the residual from local activities, which allows a better match of costs and benefits than when the state controls local affairs from the center. Certain activities that fall within the domain of the state may affect a well-defined subset of individuals. Creating an authority to carry out such activities and to assume responsibility or take credit for the outcome tends to enhance efficiency. Local autonomy may be more local or less local. A whole hierarchy of local autonomies, such as of cities within counties, counties within provinces (states, in the United States), and provinces within the federal system may be created.[8]

---

[7] Tullock (1994) discusses extensively the optimal level of local government with its different layers.

[8] Confusingly, the term "state," besides its core use here, has another meaning, not consistent with the main one. The federal system of the United States conforms to what I define as a state, whereas the 50 states are local units within the system. Naming these federal units "states," however, has a historical basis, as originally the states were intended to be more independent than they are now.

Any third party can have a locally autonomous third-party subordinate to it. It seems sensible to view a community as having autonomy if it has a court and a police force to enforce its rulings and if a subset of its own highest-level rulings is not subject to appeal. On the other hand, it does not seem useful to consider an organization to be autonomous if a higher, "ultimate" authority with enforcement power can overrule at least some of its rulings.

> **Definition.** *Local autonomy is a situation in which a third-party enforcer is subordinate to a higher authority within the domain governed by the latter.*

I focus on local autonomy under the state, but most of the discussion applies to other third parties as well. Local autonomy, obviously, is a matter of degree.

> **Definition.** *The degree of local autonomy is the fraction of contracts within a local area whose ultimate adjudication occurs at the local level relative to the total of (legitimate) third-party-enforced contracts in that area.*

To illustrate, consider transactions between retail buyers and sellers within one of the states of the United States. To the extent that contract disputes regarding such transactions can reach that state's supreme court (with the Supreme Court of the United States having no jurisdiction), those transactions will be included as part of the numerator in the measure of the state's autonomy.

The delineation of rights between any two jurisdictions can be problematic, and this includes delineation between the local and the more encompassing authorities; disputes can arise there too. As the earlier discussion implies, local autonomy will be granted where separability of rights is relatively easy to delineate. The more frequently that different individuals, assisted by their legal advisers, interpret differently what falls under local jurisdiction and what falls under state jurisdiction, the less well satisfied is the separability condition. The more poorly satisfied is the condition, the less well defined are legal rights. When the two authorities delineate the same rights in inconsistent ways, resources are likely to be spent trying to capture some of the poorly defined rights. I expect that as these difficulties become more severe, the jurisdiction of the higher authority will be expanded. I elaborate on these notions in Chapter 12.

An increase in local autonomy resembles the previously discussed lowering of the degree of vertical integration of firms, and for similar reasons. Consider conditions where it becomes easier to break down cleanly into well-delineated components what initially fell under the higher jurisdiction. The granting of local autonomy, then, will generate fewer ambiguities in what each level controls, and the enforcers will become more clearly accountable for their actions. Conversely, when the separation of functions between the local and central authorities becomes more difficult, more authority will be moved from the former to the latter. This change is akin to an increase in vertical integration, where conflicting interests are turned into more harmonious ones, at the expense, however, of greater bureaucracy.

LOCAL AUTONOMY IN PROTECTION

Separability also applies to each individual's need for protection from theft. Consider an individual who seeks protection both against plain theft and against a full-fledged conquest by another state. The skills needed for the two types of protection seem sufficiently distinct that if the tasks are undertaken by two protectors, no serious jurisdictional disputes between them should be expected. The clients, then, can secure a local protector (the "police") for protection against plain theft, and a statewide protector (the "armed forces") against a takeover by another state. It seems that within small communities seeking protection from various kinds of theft, separability of enforcement between protectors is difficult. A single protector seems able to provide protection more effectively than can several independent ones.

Similar but somewhat more complex considerations with regard to local autonomy apply to the relationship between colonizer and colonized. The colonizer has the power to determine the extent of local autonomy and the extent of the ultimate enforcement of adjudication decisions in imperial systems. In Chapter 11, I argue that a basic objective of some imperialistic efforts has been to form a unified legal authority over the entire territory controlled by the imperial power. Whatever their purpose, colonies, by the definition here, constitute an integral part of the empire and are subject to the state's power-backed third-party enforcement. Colonies can differ greatly in the extent of the autonomy they are granted. During the heyday of the British Empire, dominions such as Australia and Canada had much greater autonomy than "plain" colonies such as Kenya, and the latter differed in that regard from crown colonies (Hong Kong), mandates (Palestine), and so forth. Without attempting to detail such differences, whatever the degree of autonomy of the individual units, England was the ultimate third-party enforcer of the entire empire.[9]

CONCLUSIONS

Enforcement cannot be subject to "perfect competition." The enforcer must have power over the enforced, and thus switching enforcers must be made costly. Given that the state is defined by its exclusive control of violence, two states cannot control the same territory, nor can contracts between individuals residing in different non-cooperating states be enforced. Different enforcers, however, can coexist. That can include, besides states, both criminal organizations and other non-violent enforcers, whether "local" or traversing state borders.

Local autonomy is attractive when local issues are easy to separate from national issues, and we expect local authorities then to be granted their own courts and police forces. However, to the extent that the separation is not perfect, we expect resource-consuming disputes over jurisdiction to arise. Similar separation can take place between local police forces and a national armed force.

[9] The forms of the different subordinate units presumably reflected the character of the different colonies and the ease of separating the local jurisdiction from the central one.

7

Collective Action and Collective Decisions

This chapter commences by arguing that individuals must form collective-action mechanisms to protect themselves from their own protectors.[1] We next consider the erection of a collective-action mechanism and the ability of that mechanism to punish defectors. The discussion then turns to the peculiar nature of the balance between the power of this mechanism and that of the protector and the measures needed to prevent the protector from taking over. We continue with a discussion of the decision-making mechanism, vote allocation, and the need for a voting supermajority. The prevention of capture and the notion of rent-seeking follow. Then comes a discussion of controlling the protectors without collective action, followed by considerations of expanding the state and the accompanying collective-action mechanism. We close with conclusions.

THE NEED FOR COLLECTIVE ACTION IN CONSTRAINING PROTECTION SPECIALISTS

Rule-of-law regimes, that is, regimes where clients control the protection organizations, are characterized by the relative ease with which they can be turned into dictatorships and by the difficulty of restoring the rule of law once it has been lost. Both difficulties stem from the problems of collective action. Unless individuals cooperate to prevent dictatorship from emerging and to overturn it once it seizes power, the strongest individual among any unorganized group can subdue the rest, one at a time, and thus become and remain a dictator. Not only can a dictator be

---

[1] I believe that Olson (1965) was the first to connect the difficulties in effecting collective action with the theory of the state.

expected to enrich himself at his subjects' expense, but also he can be expected to adopt oppressive measures to lower the opportunity for revolt. Individuals, then, have reason to fear that a dictator will harm them.

Assuming that the group under consideration is neither tiny nor very diverse, no single individual has a significant stake in preventing a dictator from emerging or in opposing him once in power. Absent cooperation, then, no one will take action to prevent the emergence of a dictator or to overthrow an existing one.[2] As is well understood, the reason is that the gain to each will be higher if others bear the cost of such action. Individuals must act collectively to protect themselves and their rule of law from dictatorship.

Definition. *Collective action consists in simultaneous actions by a number of individuals.*

Such action presumably is triggered in response to a given signal. Simultaneity of actions is a necessary condition for success of the collective action. In the case here, the collective action must be self-enforced. The self-enforced action of the operation of the "Law Merchant" modeled by Milgrom, North, and Weingast (1990), or the reactions of many individuals to, say, a reduction in the price of a commodity, do not constitute collective action. Milgrom and associates do not claim the action they model to be collective; however, it may superficially appear to be so, as it connects merchants into a single network. The functioning of the network, however, does not require *simultaneous* actions by the merchants. Each individual in those illustrations gains independently of others' actions. They take similar actions at the same time simply because they all respond to the same signal. In the case of collective action, on the other hand, each can gain only if many act simultaneously.

The usefulness of collective-action mechanisms for the provision of public goods is well recognized; a primary collective good of concern here is the delineation of legal rights by legislation. Apparently not well recognized is the notion that preventing the emergence of dictatorship is also a collective good, nor that a good whose production requires simultaneous actions by many individuals, where the gain to each from acting

---

[2] This is not to imply that dictators are secure. They are often toppled. Groups tend to be diverse, and sometimes individuals from a dictator's inner circle (siblings, bodyguards, generals), rather than the oppressed, are the ones who overthrow the dictator and gain significantly from it. Ousting a dictator seldom brings an end to the dictatorship; we expect the dictator's successor to become a dictator too.

individually is negative, is a collective good. Moreover, it is not too difficult to discover private means for the production of most public goods. Such production may not be "efficient," but it still may take place, as evidenced by the private production of television broadcasts and of innovations. On the other hand, it seems inconceivable that subjects could prevent a dictator from emerging in the absence of collective action.

In order to protect themselves from confiscation by their specialized protectors, clients must organize their collective-action mechanism *prior* to initiating relationships with those protectors. Letting an individual become such a specialist first would be tantamount to inviting him to become a dictator.[3] Moreover, clients must continue to maintain that mechanism after contracting with the protector, because the threat posed by his protection organization is continuous.

The literature on effecting collective action is concerned primarily with specifying conditions for such a mechanism to function, and it offers empirical examples, mostly anthropological, describing their actual modes of operation. The literature seems to provide an incomplete analysis of the mechanism, however. Moreover, as far as I can ascertain, an analysis of how collective-action mechanisms may *originally* have been formed is entirely absent. I start by offering some of the necessary ingredients for the initial formation of such a mechanism and then move on to other collective-action issues. It is important to recognize that the initial formation occurs when social institutions are, at best, embryonic, since, to belabor the obvious, their existence cannot have been based on collective action.

The per-person cost of reaching agreement to form a collective-action mechanism seems to rise with the number of persons involved. It seems plausible that collective-action mechanisms would have emerged at the onset of socialization and of specialization, when the groups involved were small and reaching agreement was relatively easy (Chai and Hechter, 1998). The continuing existence of a collective-action mechanism requires that at no point in time will the power of any individual (or any organized subset of individuals) within it increase to exceed that of the rest of the organization. This must hold throughout the life of the organization. The number of members in the group cannot be too small,

---

[3] Wittfogel (1957), in my opinion, is one of the most astute students of the state, both empirically and theoretically. He does not recognize, however, the need for the prior existence of a collective-action mechanism to prevent dictators from emerging.

however. When that number is small, an exogenous change that resulted in an increase in power for a very few individuals could then too easily upset the balance needed for maintaining the collective-action mechanism.[4] I expect the number of individuals who organize to take collective action to be small, but still to exceed some minimal size.

THE FORMATION OF COLLECTIVE-ACTION MECHANISMS

As a preliminary simplifying step in the analysis, suppose that individuals are identical in all relevant respects and are well informed, and voting and the formation of voting decisions are costless. It is relatively easy to determine, then, when the collective-action mechanism will be successful, in that arrangements are easy to evaluate; any arrangement that is acceptable to one will be acceptable to all. Moreover, when individuals are identical, it would seem that no subset of them could form a stable coalition to exploit others. Therefore, we expect that the mechanism generating the highest net gain to each person, and hence in total, will be adopted. The ability to punish is a necessary component for the inception of such a mechanism. The participants *agree* to be *coerced*. They will consent to collectively punish those among them who are not contributing their share of the agreed-upon tax or effort, thus to induce them to contribute to maintenance of the collective action. Under the stated conditions, however, the coercion mechanism will never be activated. Because they are identical, either no individual will deserve punishment or all will, but then there will be nobody to mete out the penalty.

The absence of actual punishment in the model just described may conceal the need for repeated interactions among the members of the organization to enforce their agreement. Unless individuals believe that they will be punished when not contributing to the organization, they will not contribute. In the case of "conventional" public goods, effecting punishment is relatively easy. When the collective-action mechanism is used to provide such goods, exclusion from the group is sufficient to induce compliance. Exclusion simply deprives the person of the good. For example, one collective service is third-party enforcement of agreements. Individuals excluded from that service must forgo forming such agreements with other group members; they are restricted, then, to

---

[4] The numbers of individuals in families are small, and tyranny seems a common occurrence within them.

self-enforced ones. I point out in a later section on the prevention of takeover by a dictator that punishment is more problematic when such prevention is the public good.

In what follows, I relax the simplifying assumption that individuals are identical with each other.[5] Individuals do differ in many ways, such as in strength, intelligence, wealth, age, sex, and location. Because individuals are diverse, their gains from the actions that the collective undertakes may differ, the costs they impose are not necessarily the same as those imposed by others, and the costs of excluding them may differ too. As collective-action mechanisms are organized, it is not clear ahead of time which individuals belong in a particular collective-action set. Stated differently, among the individuals who are not members of the organization, which are the "true outsiders," and which are "defectors" from it?[6] The diversities of people come into play in forming and activating a collective-action mechanism. They make exclusion easier than it is often asserted to be, because the criteria for exclusion to prevent free-riding can be "custom-made."

ENFORCEMENT POWER OF COLLECTIVE-ACTION GROUPS

How can groups that form collective-action mechanisms compel their members to comply with their decisions? No individual will contribute to the effort if the contribution is not made mandatory. The effectiveness of the collective action, then, crucially depends on compliance by all or most of the members of the group, and the group must find ways to enforce its decisions. At this early stage, however, groups are still without third-party enforcement power; rather, all the agreements must be self-enforced. Here, as in the general case, self-enforcement requires repeated interactions.[7] I argue later that when a

---

[5] Chai and Hechter (1998), in modeling the collective-action mechanism, assume that all individuals are identical. In reality, however, diversity seems to be the norm. As suggested in the text, diversity is important in the present context.

[6] Later in this chapter I claim that the group is likely to require a unanimous vote or a near-unanimous vote for collective decisions. It is expected that individuals not perceived as beneficiaries of the collective action, who thus would be expected to cast negative votes, would be excluded from the group in the first place.

[7] The literature on collusive behavior to raise prices discusses the problem of cooperation among individuals extensively. One of the conclusions it reaches is that the more successful the price collusion, the higher the gain from defection. Here the gain from defection does not seem to increase with greater success in cooperation.

collective-action mechanism is used to prevent the seizure of dictatorial power by a protection specialist, the possibility that the repeated-interaction mechanism will collapse has to be addressed. I first consider the enforcement problems arising from the possibility of such collapse.

Non-compliance must be dealt with collectively. The group must first determine whether or not an individual has complied with the group's decision. If it determines he has not, it must organize the collective-action mechanism to impose a penalty. Suppose the penalty is ostracism – prohibiting group members from speaking or trading with the offender. For some individuals in the group, meting out the penalty might be expensive; perhaps they could gain significantly by communicating or trading with the outcast. The attempt to impose penalties will be ineffective unless all or most group members abide by the decision. Individuals, then, must perceive in the first place that their gains from non-compliance with the penalty would be less than their resulting losses of future benefits. When some individuals are expected not to contribute to the production of the public good, since penalizing offenders is also a public good, the remaining individuals must perceive that their gains from not doing their share in the penalizing would result in greater losses of their future benefits.

Because individuals differ, the problem is not necessarily one of infinite regress. Each action generates a distribution of outcomes to the diverse members of the group. Consider, again, imposing the penalty of not interacting with the offender. At least some of the time, most group members will perceive the cost to themselves of imposing the penalty to be very low, and we expect these individuals to comply. More generally, if, to begin with, the perceived penalty for not complying with the group's production decision is high to most individuals, and if the cost of imposing penalties in cases of non-compliance is low, the collective action can be carried out.

Several mechanisms, not mutually exclusive, can be used to induce or coerce individuals to comply, to make "defection" costly, and to prevent free-riding (e.g., by evading taxes). These mechanisms can also prevent individuals from collaborating with the protector when the latter attempts a takeover. Some of the available methods are the previously mentioned ability to exclude, intermarriage among participating families, the holding of hostages (Klein and Leffler, 1981; Williamson, 1983), and imposing costs on defectors by creating or exploiting common values (ideology) that tie individuals to each other.[8] Although the "social" arrangements used to enforce decisions by collective-action mechanisms seem to be of utmost importance, there is little that I, as an economist, can say about most of them. I simply assume that such arrangements exist and are put into use.[9]

THE BALANCE OF POWER BETWEEN THE COLLECTIVE-ACTION MECHANISM AND THE PROTECTOR

The collective-action mechanism is a center of power, and when its organizers allow a protection specialist to emerge, another power center is created beside it. By its very purpose, the collective-action mechanism must have the power to contain the specialized protector. Are not the clients then in a position to confiscate the wealth their protector may accumulate while doing his job? It would be prohibitively costly to perfectly contain the protector, and so he is given some leeway in using his power. Does not the leeway given to the protector enable him also to gain some confiscatory power? Indeed, the protector has some leeway to act "arbitrarily" with no fear of penalty. Being able to do something, however, does not mean it is worth doing. As long as conditions are unchanged, the relationship between clients and protector is under a self-enforced balance. They are in (presumably stable) equilibrium. *Neither* party would find it worthwhile to try to amass all the power in

---

[8] Taylor (1982) defines as "anarchic" those societies with no concentration of power. He discusses methods they can use for attaining order. Among these are intermarriages and the withholding of private goods from transgressors (i.e., exclusion). He cites studies of primitive societies using these methods. It seems that anarchic societies employ the punishing power of collective action to achieve internal order. Therefore, some of the same methods Taylor discusses can be used to enforce collective-action decisions.

    Note that a society that chooses not to allow concentration of power must forgo the gain from specializing in the use of power. As elaborated later, such a society becomes vulnerable to others that have chosen to specialize in violence. Indeed, we may have here an explanation for the initial emergence of states, an explanation that eluded Taylor and others. When an outside threat is expected, the society may *choose* to turn itself into a "state" in order to acquire the ability to repel the threat.

[9] A subsidiary mechanism for enforcing collective action is that in which the protector takes part in enforcing the collective decisions. Indeed, as discussed elsewhere (Barzel, 2000a), a sitting dictator who wishes to secure the cooperation of his subjects may *initiate* the formation of a collective-action mechanism and commit to participate in enforcing its decisions.

its own hand; it would be too costly for either to attempt to dominate the other.

Consider now the trade-off that the collective-action organization faces between the amount of power it maintains and the probability that the protection specialist will take over.[10] The trade-off must take account of random fluctuations in the powers of the two sides, as well as their errors in estimating these powers. To start with, the collective-action organization must have more power than the protector has. The greater the excess, the less likely that a dispute regarding who is stronger will arise. In addition, given the potential for a random surge in the protector's power, or a decrease in that of the collective-action organization, the chance that the protector will attempt a takeover within any given span of time is less when the initial discrepancy is greater. Because maintaining more power is costly, power will be maintained to cover normal contingencies, but not extraordinary ones. Given this scenario, as long as conditions do not change drastically, the balance of power will be maintained, and the protection specialist will not attempt to take over.

Although there is a balance of power between the collective-action mechanism and the protector, the situation is clearly asymmetric. The protector is likely to become better off if he takes over. On the other hand, the collective-action organization needs the specialized skills the protector has. It has to protect itself from takeover by the protector, but it would defeat its own purpose by taking over the protector. I expect, then, that the collective-action mechanism will have more power than the protector has. The events that resulted in the Magna Carta, described later in this chapter, illustrate the case where the collective-action organization (the council of the nobility) had more power than the ruler, but used it only when facing an attempted takeover by him.

The balance of power here is of an unusual type. The organizers of the collective-action mechanism must make arrangements to determine when its power should be activated and must see to it that they are able to activate it then. The process of activating that power, however, seems to be cumbersome. Its individual contributors are not specialists in the use of power. Consequently, substantial effort may be required to assem-

---

[10] The rationale of the argument that follows is the same as that in Chapter 3 regarding the amount of power the protection specialist has to hold to induce compliance.

ble that power, and its weapons may be blunt.[11] Making good on the threat of using that power is expensive, and we expect that individuals will be reluctant to activate their power. Under normal circumstances, however, the *threat* of activating that power will be sufficient to hold the protector back. Such a force will be convened only if the payoff appears large enough to more than cover the cost. Put in other terms, the protector has a *comparative advantage* in the use of violence. In the aggregate, his clients have more power than he does. Because the clients' comparative advantage is in activities other than the use of violence, it is expensive for them to mobilize their power. If they are willing to incur the cost, however, they can have an *absolute advantage* in power.[12]

PREVENTING DICTATORIAL TAKEOVER

The agreement between clients and protector presumably will be crafted to hold under a wide range of circumstances, though such agreements are not fail-safe. The mere existence of a collective-action mechanism does not preclude the possibility that a person, from within or from the outside, might attempt to take over. In addition, the would-be dictator is expected to take advantage of the fact that the *prospect* of a takeover might emasculate the collective-action mechanism.

Obviously, the agreement underlying a collective-action mechanism itself must be self-enforced. One condition necessary for its functioning, as well as for punishing defectors, is that of repeated interactions among the participants. Participants in the collective action expect to gain from such actions in future periods. Similarly, penalties for non-performance in the present are imposed in future periods. The mechanism will collapse in the absence of repeated interaction. Can such repeated interaction be maintained after a dictator takes over? Should an individual who defects to the side of the would-be dictator fear a penalty in the future? In case the dictator succeeds in becoming *absolute*, the answers to both questions are clearly negative. If such an aspiring dictator is expected to succeed, his supporters will not fear reprisal, for, when installed, the absolute dictator will ban and uproot the previously existing collective-action mechanism. The game ceases to repeat itself then.

---

[11] It is often asserted that democratic states confronting dictators are subject to the same problems when attempting to mobilize their forces.

[12] John Wallis must be credited for the suggestion to exploit the distinction between comparative advantage and absolute advantage as a way to look at this proposition.

I argue that although protection specialists often may be successful in enhancing their power, seldom will they gain enough power to dismantle the collective-action mechanisms. The reason is that in the absence of a severe shock, such as that due to war, a protection specialist with dictatorial aspirations will have a hard time convincing people that he can actually succeed. Obviously, the supporters of a failed aspiring dictator can be punished.

In rule-of-law states, that is, in states where subjects effectively control their protector, there seems to be a continuing tug-of-war between the protector and his controllers. As circumstances change, the relative powers of the sides ebb and flow. The agreement between the collective-action organization and the protector, however, is designed to survive in spite of such constantly shifting conditions. A shift favoring the protector need not destroy the agreement, although it will make the protector better off. He may then gain the support of defectors from the collective-action mechanism. His power will be *enhanced*, but, as a rule, not sufficiently to allow him to take over. A shift in the balance of power toward the protector will weaken, but not destroy, the collective-action mechanism, and the game will continue. Consequently, those identified as defectors who assisted the protector in gaining more power may still be penalized in future periods by those who did not defect and did not choose to support the aspiring dictator. A full-fledged dictatorship with the attendant destruction of the collective-action mechanism is likely to arise *only* as a result of a very severe shock, usually from actions by other states. I elaborate on these considerations in Chapter 15.

By my interpretation, the events that led to the Magna Carta keenly illustrate a change in conditions that led to an attempt at large-scale confiscation. That attempt, undertaken by a king widely viewed as autocratic, eventually triggered the activation of a collective-action mechanism and culminated with the king's capitulation.

The story is as follows.[13] In the early years of the thirteenth century, King John, who had vast holdings in France, was twice severely defeated in battle there. Those wars can be characterized as "king's wars" rather than "national wars," in that they directly affected the king's wealth and his power and had relatively little effect on his English subjects. Subsequent to those defeats, King John took two kinds of confiscatory actions. The purpose of those actions probably was to reconstitute his power vis-à-vis the English nobility. One was to increase the rate and

[13] Holt (1965), a major authority on that episode, is my main factual source here.

frequency of some of the "customary" taxes imposed on the nobility. Such taxes traditionally were meant for military preparedness, but it was not immediately clear whether or not the extra funds were actually needed at that time; it took some time for the barons to recognize that those taxes were excessive. The other action consisted of a series of court cases against individual noblemen accused of treason. Although by then the courts had some reputation for independence, the king still had a great deal of control over them. Those cases resulted in conviction of the accused individuals and in the confiscation of their property. Isolated from each other, it seems that each act of confiscation could have been interpreted as a high-value random draw from the sets of possible determinations of innocence or guilt and the associated penalties in case of guilt.[14] Only as those one-sided decisions against individual noblemen accumulated were the nobility able to infer their confiscatory nature and realize that the rest of them were in danger of also falling prey to the king.

The king's initial success must have enhanced his power. It may also have encouraged the view that he was likely to pursue dictatorial power by proceeding with his confiscatory policy. Although for a while the king's gamble seemed well taken, ultimately it did not pan out. The decision to activate their collective-action mechanism took the nobility some time. When they finally acted, they were able to assemble formidable power, in spite of some defections. The king was forced to retreat and accept a new agreement – the Magna Carta – with his subjects. The Magna Carta curtailed the king's power. It required that there be consent for the imposition of the war tax, and it delineated more clearly the rights of the nobility, thus making easier the detection of confiscation such as that effected by John.[15]

As a final point here, consider the relationship between the longevity of a regime and the chance that the protector will engage in confiscation. I hypothesize that the chance of confiscation decreases as stability is enhanced. Stability facilitates the long-term relations necessary for self-enforcement. As stable conditions continue to prevail, the safeguards against confiscation will remain in place longer, reducing the chance of

---

[14] Because barons had contacts with foreign rulers, it was difficult to rule out the notion of treason.

[15] Venice provides another clear illustration of the use of the collective-action mechanism. In the early days of that city-state, on several occasions, the reigning doge, the elected head of state, was suspected of plotting to become dictator and was deposed by the elected council.

confiscation by the protector. A reason for this is that as time passes, clients gain experience in controlling the protector's power.

Individuals are expected continually to strengthen their collective-action mechanism and to tighten their control over the protector in order to reduce the ability of the protector or any other individual to gain exclusive control of power. I predict that in rule-of-law states, as time passes, the protectors who pose the most severe threat, whether king or chief military commander, will become less the residual claimants to the protection effort and more the recipients of fixed pay. The history of the republic of Venice provides a dramatic example of such an evolution. Over centuries of the rule of law, subjects imposed progressively tighter constraints on the doge, the head of state, reducing him from a position of substantial power in the early periods to a largely ceremonial figure later on. The power of the doge, who was elected for life, was reduced, and power was put into the hands of less-threatening committees whose members were elected for short periods.

COLLECTIVE-ACTION DECISION-MAKING: VOTE ALLOCATION AND SUPERMAJORITY RULES

How are collective-action decisions made? In any sizable group not dominated by a dictator, individuals should have a voice in decision-making. Each decision-making format gives each individual a certain weight (including zero weight) in the decision. The volume of sound participants were able to produce constituted one system of weights.[16] Here I concentrate on decision by counting votes. Who gets to vote, and what weight is allotted to each? The decisions made by the collective-action mechanism are agreements among the participants. Under the conditions here, such decisions, including those by voting, must be self-enforced. How are voting decisions made under self-enforcement?

Decisions, whether or not by voting, are valuable only if they can be implemented. I predict that, at least early in the life of a collective-action mechanism, voting decisions will not be made by simple majority, nor will each person be given one vote. Voting decisions made by the majority of the members of a group are not, in general, enforceable. No third party exists here to effect enforcement. Rather, those in favor of a particular action must be in a position to enforce it themselves. For voting

---

[16] Decision by volume of sound was in actual use in the English Parliament in the Middle Ages, though only for "minor" matters.

to be meaningful, the winners and the losers of a decision made by voting must perceive that the former are sufficiently more powerful than the latter that they can enforce the decision. We cannot expect 51% of any set of individuals always to have the power of enforcement – the power to overcome the resistance of the other 49%.

Consider allocating votes in proportion to individuals' power, rather than one vote per person. When votes are so allocated, and assuming that power is additive, the majority of voters will also have the preponderance of power.[17] Therefore the majority will be in a position to enforce its decisions.[18] Under this vote allocation, actual voting will reveal where the power lies, and any measure receiving a favorable vote can be enforced. Moreover, the losers will not resist because they will *know* that the majority can force them to yield.

In reality, vote allocation is unlikely to be strictly proportionate to voters' power, and for that reason, decisions will not be made by a simple majority. Because the measurement of power cannot be highly accurate, neither the actual power behind a vote nor its perception by the two sides will be exactly equal to the "true" power or to the perceived power. Moreover, the degrees of power exercised by individuals are constantly changing, and it would be too costly to continuously keep track of the changes and adjust voting power accordingly. Therefore, at any point in time, a minority consisting of only 49% of the votes may believe that it has become stronger than the 51% majority. To overcome this problem, the organizers of the collective-action mechanism may choose to implement only decisions made by a supermajority large enough so that most of the time the two sides will recognize the superiority of the majority power.

A rather different reason for adopting a supermajority or even a unanimity voting rule relates to the desire to preclude wealth-transfer opportunities.[19] Some individuals will seek opportunities to exploit the decision-making mechanism even if their gains are at others' expense. The existence of such opportunities will reduce the joint value of the

---

[17] If powers are not additive, a simple majority may still be inadequate to enforce the voting decisions.

[18] Timothy Dittmer originated the idea that a collective decision must be backed by a preponderance of power. Given this condition, where decision is by voting, and where there is no third party to enforce the decision, vote allocation is expected to be in proportion to voters' power. See Dittmer (1997).

[19] Buchanan and Tullock (1962) were the first to analyze the properties of the unanimity voting rule. The rationale for the use of that rule here follows theirs.

organization; the fewer such opportunities, the higher the organization's value. We expect, then, the emergence of provisions that will make transfers less likely (Barzel and Sass, 1990).

Consider individuals' attempts to make transfers to themselves by exploiting their voting arrangements and the prior problems of formulating decision rules to reduce the chance of transfers. An individual who wishes to generate transfers to himself via voting will need others to collaborate with him. Those collaborators would have to form a "subsidiary" collective-action mechanism and be able to coerce the rest to submit to the transfers. It seems, however, that any attempt to form such a group would be self-defeating. Even those who could perceive themselves as beneficiaries of a particular transfer might be reluctant to agree to a voting rule that would accommodate transfers.

In general, an individual will support a decision, including one on a voting rule, only if he perceives that it will increase his present value. The present value here consists of the sum of the particular decision on the agenda and the decisions it will bring in its wake. In the case here, individuals initially in the majority may recognize that eventually they could be relegated to a new minority. Once the property of the initial minority was confiscated, and perhaps individuals in the minority were disposed of, a new majority might form to exploit some of the members of the former majority. Indeed, most individuals would fear that eventually they would come to be in the minority. To prevent that from happening, individuals would require a self-enforced arrangement in which they would feel secure that they would not be expropriated in the future. It does not seem likely that credible commitments to that effect could be made. On the other hand, decision-making by unanimity is likely to assure such an outcome.[20] Because strict unanimity has its own problems and might result in no action of any kind, decisions may instead require only near unanimity. In the discussion that follows, the term "unanimity" is extended to also mean "near unanimity."[21]

---

[20] It is not clear to me that such a decision itself is self-enforced.

[21] Unanimity was the decision rule in the Italian city-states in the Middle Ages, where rule of law prevailed. Waley (1988) states that in the nascent communes of medieval Italy, "decisions required the approval by acclamation of this [conciliar] body" (p. 36). Moreover, "councils could only reach decisions if a quorum was present; this often was two-thirds of the members" (p. 37). He also states (p. 38) that for important resolutions, supermajorities of those present were needed, consisting of 3/4 or 4/5 and sometimes even of 10/11 or 16/17. It seems plausible, though Waley does not state so explicitly, that in the last two cases the councils had, respectively, eleven and seventeen members. If such was the case, then the rule

Even though individuals are not identical, the unanimity requirement is not as stringent as it might appear. A necessary condition for unanimity is that every voter perceive himself a net gainer (or every one a net loser) from the proposed action of the collective-action organization. Consider a project whose aim is to produce a public good valued positively by all. One way to ensure that every individual will become a *net* gainer from the project is to cover its cost by assessing all individuals the same *proportion* of their valuations of the output of the public good. Where that public good is defense, the benefit takes the form, at least in part, of lowering the probability that marauders will capture individuals' holdings. It is not unreasonable to expect all participants in the collective action to lose in case the marauders are successful. When all physical property is equally at risk, then under risk neutrality a property tax at a uniform rate sufficient to cover the entire defense cost would meet the necessary condition for unanimity. If any individual perceives the value of the gain in extra protection to exceed the tax cost, then all will, and thus the affirmative vote will be unanimous. Similarly, if one views the tax as exceeding the project's benefits, so will all the rest. Whereas under unanimity only those projects with total benefits greater than total costs will be approved, where less than unanimity is required, voters may approve projects with total costs in excess of total benefits.[22]

When individuals' interests regarding the production of the public good are perfectly aligned, such that when one gains all gain, votes will be unanimous no matter what the design for vote allocation is. In reality, the alignment of individuals' interests is unlikely to be perfect, making the vote allocation relevant. In practice, votes often have been allocated on the basis of individuals' property values. Earlier in this chapter, however, I argued that in state institutions individuals' votes will be proportionate to their power.[23] If the correlation between power and

---

was simply one of "near unanimity"; it prevented any single person from having veto power.

[22] Certain protection projects will benefit a subset of individuals. When these projects and their beneficiaries are distinct, the collective-action mechanism is expected to tax the beneficiaries specifically for such projects. An example is the protection of export routes. The protection benefits the particular exporting industry, and a tax on the exported commodities is to be expected. The tax on the export of wool in medieval England, its primary export then, was such a case.

[23] I have encountered just one instance of allocating votes in proportion to voters' power. That took place during the republican era in ancient Rome (Crawford, 1978, p. 194).

property value were perfect, it would not matter which one was used. Although not perfect, the correlation does in fact seems to be high, and there are two reasons to prefer the use of property value. First, measuring property value seems to be considerably easier than measuring power. Second, attempting to build more power to gain votes has a distorting effect, but as long as wealth is measured accurately, accumulating more wealth is not distortive. Individuals could gain voting power by exaggerating their wealth, but because wealth is taxed, such exaggeration is unlikely. I expect, then, that collective-action mechanisms will be based on vote allocations and assessments proportionate to the values of individuals' holdings.[24] Finally, I expect that given the difficulties with unanimity voting, as already stated, voting decisions will require only near unanimity.

The unanimity condition or even the near-unanimity condition will prevent the undertaking of projects that would benefit a large but less-than-overwhelming fraction of the voters. The minority may consent to such projects if properly compensated, but arranging for such compensation seems sometimes to be very expensive. Unless all decisions are unanimous (which becomes less practical as groups expand and become more diverse in their voting interests), certain decisions will lower the wealth of some individuals. As an organization is formed, I expect it to impose constraints on itself to reduce the scope of abuse – of making decisions amounting to wealth transfers from some to others. As time passes and the safeguards against voting abuse become more effective, the organization may allow decisions to be made by less than unanimous votes or near-unanimous votes.

The more successful that individuals are in preventing transfers, the wealthier they will become in the aggregate. Still, it does not pay to try

---

[24] That was roughly how votes were allocated in the medieval English Parliament; moreover, "major" decisions required unanimity (Barzel, 1997b).

When vote allocation is by property, individuals with no measurable property will have no vote, and "one person, one vote" will not be observed. Slaves have no property, and the model here predicts that they will not be allowed to vote. In classical Athens, slaves did not get to vote. Moreover, by the model here, the allocation applies only to the group members who have power. There is no a priori reason to expect votes to be allocated to newcomers with no military power. It is not surprising, for example, that in Athens, *metics* (the foreign residents in the city who did not participate in military activities) did not get to vote. Athens is often condemned for not being a true democracy as it did not grant the franchise to *metics* or to slaves. Whatever the term "democracy" may mean, which is by no means clear, maximizing, by the model here, is likely to lead to decision by voting, but not necessarily to "one person, one vote."

to perfect the safeguards against appropriation of minority wealth by the majority. This line of reasoning implies that in their collective action, individual maximizers will find it too expensive to eliminate all transfers. Transfers, often attributed to "rent-seeking," are not inconsistent with maximizing. Their occurrence should not necessarily be viewed as dissipating. I next argue that at best the concept of rent-seeking is useless.

RENT-SEEKING

The concept of "rent-seeking," thought to result from state policies and to lead to the dissipation of wealth, has become deeply rooted in the literature by now. In this section I argue that it should be uprooted. I contend that the line of reasoning underlying the concept of rent-seeking is faulty and that its use tends to preempt the quest for understanding of the phenomenon to which it refers. The term itself is most unfortunate.[25]

As construed, rent-seeking supposedly is wasteful. Waste has the connotation of avoidable costs (or of available, but unrealized gains). The existence of waste, however, is inconsistent with maximizing behavior. Individuals are expected to make a systematic and deliberate effort to eliminate waste, or dissipation. Indeed, they are expected to do so whether the waste is *private* or *public*. On the other hand, they will not attempt to eliminate what appears to be waste when the cost of elimination would exceed the gain. The term "rent-seeking" itself is unsatisfactory. The maximization assumption implies that every individual will exploit *every* profit opportunity. Consequently, *all* action constitutes rent-seeking. The term, therefore, is superfluous.

To illustrate the problematic nature of the concept of rent-seeking, consider the use of valued resources at rush hour. These are often rationed by congestion, rather than by price. Rationing by congestion or by queue may appear to be dissipating. Congestion occurs on the state-controlled highways, and seemingly the state could (and some say should) eliminate it by the appropriate pricing. Congestion, however, is also a common occurrence in privately owned supermarkets. As is obvious, the supermarkets' owners *choose* not to price the queue out of existence. Presumably, owners deem the cost of eliminating the rush-hour

---

[25] Cheung (1974) forcefully argues that dissipation is inconsistent with maximization. Becker (1985) shows that public policies tend to be efficient.

queue to exceed the gain. Owners, of course, may be mistaken. Our working assumption, however, is that they maximize given the information they have. It seems to me that we must apply the same logic to government operations. I contend that if we take proper account of *all* the costs incurred by governmental action, the costs of pricing the highway in order to eliminate rush-hour congestion would exceed the gains that the more refined pricing would generate. If that is the case, actual implementation of the policy some have recommended to eliminate (what may appear as) public-sector dissipation would incur higher costs than the gains it would generate.

The notion that what people actually do is always optimal is, of course, a tautology; people do what they choose to do. My contention that we can predict changes in the level of the apparent dissipation is not tautological. Suppose, for example, that individuals' cost of time increases. My prediction is that the owners of supermarket, as well as those of highways, would then adopt more elaborate pricing methods or impose restrictions so as to reduce queuing. The notion of rent-seeking does not produce such predictions; indeed, it seems to produce no predictions, and thus it is a "notion" rather than a "theory."

Social scientists often have offered prescriptions to reduce the loss to rent-seeking. These prescriptions imply that these social scientists possess definitive knowledge of the situation at hand that permits such prescriptions. This confidence in what they "know" tends to discourage skepticism, to obscure the recognition that perhaps we need to understand better what is going on. It tends to deter the pursuit of any explanation other than rent-seeking for what we observe.

Olson (1982) is one of the most prominent scholars dealing with rent-seeking transfers. He considers them to be the main obstacles to economic growth. He ignores the possibility that individuals, in their maximizing attempts, can use their collective-action mechanisms to impose restrictions on actions in the public sphere, as well as the fact that certain "constitutional" restrictions are designed to prevent such transfers (Barzel and Sass, 1990). He also ignores the fact that individuals stand to gain from eliminating existing costly transfers in both the private and public sectors.

Related to rent-seeking is the asserted inefficiency of dictatorial states. It is often claimed, occasionally accompanied by telling illustrations, that dictatorial regimes operate very wastefully. Some of the illustrations make it clear how easy it would be to raise per-capita income in such states. Overlooked, however, is the fact that his subjects' welfare is unlikely to weigh heavily in the dictator's deliberations – his priorities lie elsewhere. Whereas the changes suggested might raise his subjects' income, they might also lower the dictator's personal safety. The dictator well might choose not to adopt policies that would yield higher income to his subjects, and instead look to his safety. In this case, too, what looks like waste may be the result of optimizing, here by the dictator, rather than of rent-seeking.

AN EVENTUAL SUBSTITUTE FOR COLLECTIVE ACTION

Contemporary rule-of-law states do not seem to possess collective-action mechanisms. How does this observation square with the earlier claim that individuals must erect and maintain such mechanisms to avoid dictatorial takeover?

I first discuss how the creation of several coexisting military forces that are largely independent of each other, a "divide-and-rule" measure, provides at least a partial barrier against dictatorial takeover.[26] This measure, along with others discussed in the next chapter, can allow a state with a well-established rule of law to dispense with the rather costly collective-action mechanism.

The notion of the "separation of powers" is in the same spirit as the main idea here. Montesquieu was the first to promulgate the idea. The Federalist papers (originally published 1787–8) greatly elaborated on this notion, as, more recently, has Ostrom (1971). In my view, the prior existence of rule-of-law institutions is a necessary condition for the introduction of separation of powers. The authors mentioned earlier seem not to have recognized the vital importance of this condition. The fact that the original thirteen states of the United States were governed by rule of law allowed such separation under the conditions that prompted the writing of the Federalist papers. That, however, is not the general case, as Riker (1976) points out.

Certain actions can be taken by rule-of-law states to reduce the burden of maintaining a collective-action capability. The simplest way to reduce the burden is by altogether dispensing with the collective-action mechanism. Indeed, no collective-action mechanism seems to be in evidence in most contemporary rule-of-law states. Now, I have been asserting

---

[26] The divide-and-rule argument is usually applied to a state governed by a foreigner, whereas here it is applied by a state governed by its own collective-action mechanism.

throughout that individuals who are in a position to become dictators are likely to seize the opportunity if it arises. Absent proper constraints, then, the chief of staff or some other militarily powerful individual might well take over. One possible explanation for why states with no apparent collective-action capabilities have not been taken over is their tendency to maintain several military forces that are largely independent of each other, which tends to deter such takeovers. It must first be recognized, however, that a necessary condition for success in avoiding dictatorship is the right timing in the creation of such forces. I argued earlier that the collective-action mechanism must be erected before anyone is allowed to specialize as a protector. A similar argument applies to the timing of the creation of these independent military forces. It would be too late to attempt such a balancing move after a single commander had already taken control of the entire military force of a state.

Consider a state possessed of a collective-action mechanism wishing to divide its military power into several independent units. To begin with, it will be easier for the collective-action mechanism to control a number of relatively independent and not-so-powerful military units than a single monolithic one. Rule-of-law states, then, can be expected to subdivide their military forces into units that are independent of each other, coordinated, when necessary, by the collective-action mechanism. I now argue that, in addition, and perhaps more importantly, the existence of such independent units may *by itself* be an effective barrier to the rise of a dictator.

An additional powerful force seems to be present here. A person aspiring to become a dictator must secure others' cooperation. A potential supporter would evaluate the costs and returns from providing such support. The assessment of others' actions is an essential ingredient in the payoff computation. Resisting the would-be dictator would become very costly if the latter otherwise had adequate support for the takeover. But cooperating with anyone aspiring to be dictator likely would prove equally costly if he should fail. The success of an aspirant will depend crucially on his ability to commit credibly to reward his supporters. It is not clear to me on a priori grounds what form such commitments could take. Experience strongly suggests, however, that securing the support of one's subordinates tends to be easier than securing the support of others. A necessary condition for securing subordinates' support is having sufficient time to interact with them.[27] Now, when all the armed forces are

---

[27] Appointment duration is discussed in Chapter 6.

unified under one command, its commander, if well established, may be able to secure the support of his subordinates. As there is no organized force to oppose him, he is in position for a takeover.

The aspirant's ability to secure the support of military units not under his command seems much more difficult. The commanders of these other units are likely to be doing well for themselves under the existing conditions. The aspirant will need their help if some of their individual forces are as strong as the force that he commands and can rely on. He may also need their help if only their combined forces clearly are stronger than his own. To secure their help, he must convince them that he will make them better off. A contractual commitment is of no use here because there is no third party to enforce it. Neither is a self-enforced agreement workable under these conditions. The reason for this is that the parties here may view the probability of continuing interactions as low, because dictators themselves are often overthrown. In addition, a full-fledged dictator will have the power to eliminate whomever he chooses. Because the commanders of any substantial forces might be seen as threats to himself, he might wish to get rid of them. Such commanders would have good reason to be wary of the promises the would-be dictator might make. They would be unlikely to offer their support to the aspiring dictator, then. Without such support, the dictatorial aspirations are likely to remain dormant.

The same considerations seem to apply to an existing dictatorship. The dictator will be likely to divide the military into independent forces to reduce the chance that any of them will topple him. Dictatorships and rule-of-law regimes differ here in one major respect. Suppose a dictator is killed. There is a significant chance that whoever kills the dictator will become the next dictator. There is also a chance that there will be a struggle among contenders to determine the next ruler. On the other hand, in a rule-of-law state, we expect that anyone who kills the head of state will be punished and that the succession will be constitutional, as was the case after President Kennedy's assassination.

The use of independent military forces appears to be a factor, perhaps *the* factor, preventing a military takeover in the United States. In the formative stages of the United States, each of the thirteen colonies had, and kept control of, its own militia. Those militias continued to play their independent roles between 1776 and 1789, the year of the constitutional convention, and beyond. According to Riker (1987, ch. 8), as the nineteenth century progressed, the states devoted fewer and fewer resources to their militias. A possible reason for that decline was that among the provisions of the constitutional convention was the formation of the marines. That was a land force attached to the navy and independent of the army. By the view here, that made the role of the militias in preventing a coup less vital. It is of some interest to note that currently the army, navy, and air force are substantially independent of each other.[28] Even the protection for air-force bases, obviously a land-force specialty, is by air-force personnel, not army personnel. The air force is not the only military branch with airpower; indeed, each of the other three main forces has some airpower – the army has combat helicopters, the navy has both carrier-based and land-based aircraft, and the marines have their own air support. Neither are these the only independent military powers. The U.S. National Guard, a remnant of the state militias, is another independent force, controlled by governors rather than by federal authorities. Several additional independent forces, military and semi-military, exist today in the United States, including the Central Intelligence Agency and the Federal Bureau of Investigation. Finally, as elaborated in the next chapter, the police forces in rule-of-law states are independent of the military.[29]

The existence of independent power centers seems to constitute a barrier to a full-fledged dictatorship even in states where the rule of law is not so firmly established. Military juntas have orchestrated many overthrows of existing governments. Such juntas most often consist of a *coalition* of military commanders. These coalitions, it appears, take deliberate measures not to allow any individual to become a full-fledged dictator.[30] Rather, they rule collectively, by committee. As a rule, such juntas seem to be less repressive than are individual dictators. The reason might be the desire of individual members of a junta to create safeguards against single-person control, for fear of finding themselves at such a person's mercy.[31] The move to (or back to) a rule-of-law mode seems much more likely for such regimes than for regimes under single dictators.

[28] Today the navy has its own airpower. It, rather than the air force, controls the jet fighters and bombers operating from its aircraft carriers.

[29] It is evident that the relationship between the executive and legislative branches of the United States government is self-enforced. One role the judiciary performs is arbitration of disputes between the other two branches.

[30] The assassination of Julius Caesar illustrates the effort by group members to prevent one of them from becoming dictator. Caesar's allies killed him, apparently because they feared that he planned a dictatorial takeover.

[31] Olson (2000, p. 34) makes this argument in a similar context.

MERGERS AND TREATIES AMONG STATES

To this point the discussion has focused on single groups of individuals and the within-group collective-action mechanism. Mergers of such groups can have some advantages, as well as costs (Chai and Hechter, 1998). As a small group's collective-action mechanism becomes entrenched, its individuals may feel sufficiently secure from the danger of internal takeover that they will choose to merge with a similar group so as to take advantage of the scale economies to protection (and other economies in state-level operations). Small groups that contemplate merging their protection organizations are expected to do so on condition that their within-group collective-action mechanisms merge as well. As small units merge to become larger ones, however, problems of wealth transfer are likely to become more acute, especially if the groups are relatively homogeneous internally, but differ significantly from each other.[32] I expect the desire to limit transfers to be a factor that affects the structure and the size of the state.

Large states pose a threat to their small neighbors. Small states may attempt to cooperate with each other to avert being conquered by a large one. Agreements among states must be self-enforced, and the temptation to defect is bound to be strong at times. One method of reducing the chance of defection is by merger, where the individual states submit to the combined power of the new one.

Rule-of-law states may find it easier to merge than will dictatorships. Most likely they will have existed for a long time and will have accumulated records of performance that will be satisfactory to each other. A major concern for each of the merging states will be the issue of the confiscation that might take place within the merged state. They can avert confiscation by merging their collective-action mechanisms and, like individuals forming a collective-action mechanism, by formulating procedures such as supermajority voting that can significantly reduce the prospect of confiscation.

The evolution of Switzerland to what it is today conforms closely to the foregoing expectation of how states will merge. In the second half of

---

[32] If variability is measured by the statistical variance, then the variability of the merged group is necessarily greater than the average variability of the constituent groups. This is true even if members of each of the groups are randomly drawn from the same population.

the thirteenth century, three freemen states, or cantons, formed a federation to defend themselves against their German and Austrian (Habsburg) neighbors. The number of cantons in the federation continued to grow until 1815, when it reached its current size. When the cantons merged, they instituted rules that minimized the chance of transfers among themselves. Three major features have distinguished Switzerland throughout its history: (1) the firm rule of law that governs it, (2) the substantial local autonomy of the cantons, and (3) a well-armed population. Of all contemporary rule-of-law states, Switzerland, arguably, is the only one that evolved, essentially uninterruptedly, from a voluntary beginning.[33] In Chapter 13, I discuss in greater detail local autonomy and conditions for merger, such as by forming a federation.[34]

CONCLUSIONS

The foregoing discussion may have conveyed the impression that we should expect the rule of law to be the historically prevailing form of rule. It is essential to recognize first that absolute control over protectors would be prohibitively costly, and therefore a protector will, on occasion, take over and become a dictator. Second, when the takeover is successful, the newly emerged dictator, in order to establish and maintain his dictatorial powers, will attempt to get rid of the collective-action mechanism if it is still in operation. Rule-of-law states are able to avert dictatorial takeover quite effectively. There, only seldom is a protector expected to prevail and become a dictator. The fact that dictatorship has been the most common form of rule in the past is not, in my view, inconsistent with the argument presented here. As stated earlier, a rule-of-law state can be turned overnight into a dictatorship. On the other hand, and this is an important ingredient here, unless the dictator allows it, erecting a collective-action mechanism under a dictatorship is very difficult.[35] A dictatorship can evolve into a rule-of-law state, but the process seems exceedingly slow.[36] Therefore, in one

---

[33] One might claim a similar status for the United States, in spite of its emergence from the colonies of England.

[34] In Chapter 12, I compare treaties among dictatorships with those among rule-of-law states.

[35] Olson (1982) discusses in great detail the difficulties of erecting collective-action mechanisms not sanctioned by the state.

[36] Elsewhere (Barzel, 2000a) I have considered forces that might induce a dictator to turn his regime into one governed by rule of law.

sense, a rule-of-law state may have the upper hand in a confrontation with a dictatorship, but once the rule of law is upset, restoring it can take a very long time, which may account for the commonness of dictatorships.[37]

---

[37] In later chapters I briefly discuss some of the distinguishing features of dictatorships.

8

Tying the Protector's Hands: The Agreement between Subjects and Protector

Protection specialists presumably have a comparative advantage in providing protection services. Protectors are needed for deterrence of violence. In turn, specialists in protection require skill in the use of violence to perform their task. Some forms of protection are subject to scale economies. The scale economies to enforcement by force have been discussed extensively in Chapter 3. Protection subject to scale economies is provided efficiently when the same protector or set of cooperating protectors protects many individuals. Protection, therefore, can entail a large-scale assembly of power. The assembled power and its head can be controlled by the protector's clients or by the protector himself. A protector who is able to gain such control may use it to become a dictator.

Creating a collective-action mechanism is a necessary condition for preventing protectors from taking over. The costs of activating the mechanism, however, seem substantial. To reduce the probability of takeover, individuals are expected to undertake measures to restrain the protectors, thereby reducing the burden of activating the collective-action mechanism.

Individuals, besides directly activating their collective-action mechanism, can prevent themselves from becoming easy prey to their protector by the way they form their agreement with the specialized protector and by the restrictions they impose on him. The agreement that individuals make with their protector is expected to be incentive-compatible. Reducing the protector's inclination to take over, however, requires incentives very different from those that promote efficiency in more conventional circumstances.

In the discussion that follows, I argue that as long as the protector does not possess dictatorial power, the clients, rather than the protector, hold the purse strings to the protection budget. Clients determine what taxes to impose and at what rates and how to spend the tax revenue. I argue that they, and not the protector, retain any budgetary surplus and have to make up any deficit. Obviously, this holds only for rule-of-law states. In a dictatorship, the dictator controls the government finances.

THE ABSOLUTE DICTATOR: THE SOLE
RESIDUAL CLAIMANT

Why should subjects be so wary of dictators? Do we need to exclude benevolent dictatorship? After all, it is not impossible that a dictator could be just and compassionate. Most dictators claim to be such. A dictator's benevolence, however, cannot be taken for granted. Worse, benevolence seems to be an attribute conducive neither to becoming a dictator nor to staying in power. Subjects have reason to be suspicious of the claim of benevolence and to view benevolent dictatorship as a low-probability outcome.

To better understand the cause for subjects' concern, consider the actions a dictator must take to ensure that he stays in power. We begin with a limiting case to make the issue more transparent and then introduce more realistic considerations. An individual or a group that deposes a dictator is likely to be rewarded by inheriting his position.[1] A dictator can be secure in his power if his subjects have neither the initial ability to overthrow him nor any opportunities to acquire such ability in the future. The overthrow of a dictator requires human and non-human resources, especially time and weapons.[2] To ensure his stay in power, a dictator must prevent his subjects from acquiring the resources needed for an overthrow. Therefore, after gaining power he must first confiscate his subjects' wealth, including the product of human capital. He must then constrain them to the minimal-consumption level required to produce the output he extracts from them, as that level leaves nothing for uses other than sheer survival.[3] Except for subjects' minimal-consumption level, then, the dictator is expected to keep the entire output they produce.

---

[1] The situation in rule-of-law states is quite different. The assassin of the head of such a state, if caught, is likely to spend his life in prison, or even lose it.

[2] It may also require the ability to organize collective action. I briefly discuss this issue later.

[3] Olson (2000, pp. 111–34) argues persuasively that by using a regressive tax structure, along with various constraints, Stalin was able to extract most of the wealth of the Soviet Union.

A dictator will try to avoid using even a payment scheme that on average awards subjects their minimal-consumption level but is subject to variability, because that could still be a threat to him. He will be even more keen to avoid a scheme requiring subjects to cede to him a fixed amount equal to their average level of production, rather than their actual production. Under such schemes, those lucky individuals who might have experienced a positive random shock would be allowed to retain the difference between their actual pay or income and their actual needs. They might be able, then, to amass the resources needed to finance a rebellion. To prevent that from happening, the dictator will prefer to make payments commensurate with actual needs, taking on himself the effect of whatever income variability there is. The more successful he is, the closer he is to becoming the sole bearer of the residual income of the state and thus its true owner.[4] If he were totally successful, he could veritably announce *L'état, c'est moi*. I consider as "absolute" the dictator who can costlessly achieve such an outcome.[5]

In reality, because it is costly to monitor and police subjects, the dictator must let them retain some wealth and have some leeway in their action. Still, individuals who currently are relatively free and well-to-do will be extremely wary of the prospect that a dictator might emerge, because they would have to fear that he might deprive them of much of their wealth, turn them into slaves, or even take their lives. Individuals, then, will attempt to fashion the agreement between themselves and the protector they employ so as to reduce the chance that the protector might be able to become a dictator. Thus, for instance, the city-states of medieval Italy adopted extreme measures clearly designed to prevent any individual from taking over. Finer's discussion (1997) of Florence illustrates the case. He emphasizes the cumbersome nature of the Florentine governance institutions and states that the same pattern held for all other Italian city-states (aside from Venice). He concludes that the reason for that was the desire to prevent dictatorship, as "nothing was more feared than the dominance of a single family" (book III, p. 984).

---

[4] As I have argued (Barzel, 1977), estimating the minimal consumption of every individual would be prohibitively costly, and when an underestimate is actually used, the person cannot survive. We do not know, however, if the large numbers of deaths of peasants and of others who died from starvation under Stalin's regime were due to this factor.

[5] The dictator may also restrict his subjects' freedom of action, though this seems superfluous under the specified conditions.

THE PROTECTOR: THE SUBJECTS' EMPLOYEE

Consider a protector retained by a group of clients. Suppose, momentarily, that they make him the sole, or at least the primary, residual claimant to the protection effort. Being such a claimant, especially in terms of protection vis-à-vis other states, there is a high probability that he will amass sufficient resources and independent power to enable him to become a dictator. This is because the outcome of the protection effort is subject to large swings. Winning would greatly reduce the potential damage that could have been wreaked by the enemy, and possibly would yield handsome loot. The total value of winning, then, would be enormous. Conversely, a loss in war would be devastating. Therefore, the residual claimants to such an enterprise will be subject to large swings in wealth. If an individual or a small subset of individuals is the primary residual claimant to that wealth, a successful war might yield them sufficient resources to take over the state. Making a producer the residual claimant to his action, including the action's side effects, would be efficient. In the case of protection, the unaccounted-for side effects would seem too large to maintain that arrangement. I discuss the terms of the agreement between clients and protector in the rest of this section, and turn to the restrictions they can impose in the next.

The form the protector's reward takes will delineate his share in the residual income of the protection effort. Before addressing the general case, I compare two polar arrangements for remunerating the protector: (1) fixed price and (2) cost plus. Under arrangement 1, subjects will pay the protector a fixed periodic amount, akin to an insurance premium. That amount must be large enough to cover the entire expected cost of protection. On his part, the protector must make all protection arrangements. Most significantly, he will be allowed to *fully benefit* from the outcome and will be required to shoulder the *entire burden* of the outcome of the protection effort. Under arrangement 2, the subjects will make the protector their employee. Besides his actual defense expenditures, they will pay him only a salary.

The fundamental difference between the two arrangements is in who bears the consequences of the protection effort. Under the first arrangement, assuming, momentarily, that the protector meets its terms, the clients' wealth will be unaffected by how the protection effort is conducted; they will make only fixed periodic payments. If the protector's protection effort turns out to be successful, he will emerge as its sole beneficiary. He also must shoulder the entire burden of any protection loss; he must fully restore any damages the enemy inflicts on his clients. The protector, then, is the sole residual claimant to his own action. Under the second arrangement, the protector's net reward is fixed, and the clients are the ones who must bear the consequences of the variability in the outcome of the protection effort.

Abstracting from the clients' own contribution to the protection endeavor and its effect on the outcome, the first arrangement would seem to be incentive-compatible and thus the more efficient of the two. Under it, the protector would have no incentive to shirk, whereas under the wage contract he would have such an incentive. The efficiency claim is valid, however, only if the protector delivers – a big "if" in this case.

The protector is not likely to deliver under the given conditions, for two distinct reasons – one due to a wealth constraint and the other due to enforcement problems. I consider the wealth constraint first. Clients who use the fixed-price method to reward the protector receive, in effect, a performance guarantee. Given the clients' lack of expertise in protection, they would like to acquire the protection services subject to a guarantee, since a guarantee here would ensure a performance of the appropriate "product quality." This guarantee is comparable to the one a fire-prevention expert provides to less well informed clients seeking fire protection by agreeing to repair any fire damage (i.e., by tying his preventive service to fire insurance).[6] A guarantee, however, is problematic here, because the protector's wealth constitutes a ceiling on guarantee payments and for that reason limits the effectiveness of the guarantee. A loss in war likely would result in losses not only to numerous clients but also to the protector himself. Such losses would be large. If, as is likely, the protector's wealth were inadequate to make good on the full amount of the guarantee payments, we would expect his protection effort, too, to be inadequate. Indeed, the protector is induced to gamble by undertaking, among other things, projects with negative joint value, because he will fully gain if the gamble succeeds, but if the gamble fails, he will default, and others will have to bear much of the loss.[7]

[6] Risk aversion is barely, if at all, a relevant factor for corporate and other commercial fire insurance. The guarantee of the quality of fire-prevention services is, in my view, the primary reason for insurance in that case. See Barzel (1997a [orig. ed., 1989, pp. 56-7]). Mayers and Smith (1990) also offer an informational explanation and provide evidence for it.

[7] In any case, had the would-be protector been so wealthy as to be able to meet in full such guarantee payments, would he have bothered to produce and sell to others a service that would endanger his life?

The second reason the protector is unlikely to deliver – that concerning enforcement – is especially pertinent in the context here. Because no third party exists as yet, performance on the guarantee agreement cannot be enforced by a third party. Neither is self-enforcement an option here; under the circumstances considered, the agreement ceases to be self-enforced. As just argued, an agreement giving the protector a free hand to assemble a force adequate for protection would also enable him to become a dictator and confiscate his clients' property. The protector would be better off becoming a dictator than honoring the guarantee payment.[8] He will then choose to "defect." For these two reasons, clients will not make the protector the full or primary residual claimant to the protection effort.

In the second form of remuneration, clients employ the protector for a wage and also cover his actual military expenditures. At the same time, they bear all the other consequences of the protection effort and become the residual claimants to its outcome. The protector is not the residual claimant then; his skills earn him a salary, but nothing else. Therefore, by becoming a protector he is not moving into a position that would enable him to finance a takeover. By making his subordinates employees as well, rather than independent contractors, neither are those employees in a position to finance a takeover.[9] Fixed wages, of course, induce shirking. The later section on incentives discusses the remuneration of the protector as a partial residual claimant.

RESTRICTIONS SUBJECTS IMPOSE ON THEIR PROTECTORS

To further reduce the chance that the protector will take over, and yet still achieve the desired protection results, his employers will supervise him and instruct him to perform certain tasks. They will also impose

---

[8] A caveat is due here. The more initiative that is required of participants in fighting (and other collaborative efforts), the smaller the gain to the protector from confiscating the wealth of individuals with whom he would have liked to have collaborated.

[9] Remunerating the protector and his subordinates by wages happens to perform another major function. In the adjudication of disputes, a subject of later chapters, the adjudicator may rule in favor of those who pay him the most. Such payments, or bribes, constitute expenditures of resources to capture wealth that otherwise would be owned. When the adjudicators are paid a wage, spotting and preventing bribes would seem to be easier than when they become residual claimants to disputes, because only in the former case is their wealth largely restricted to their accumulated wages.

restrictions, such as on the size and makeup of the forces he commands, and his tenure. These restrictions, to some degree, are substitutes for each other, and, as a rule, we do not expect all of them to be imposed at the same time. I now discuss some of the restrictions.

Restricting Force Size

We expect the clients to restrict directly the size and power of the force the protector controls. They will attempt to ensure that as long as they maintain their collective power, no protector (or likely coalition of protectors) can amass as much power as they can assemble collectively. For that reason, the size of the regular armed force in a rule-of-law state in time of peace is predicted to be less than that in a dictatorship of similar size. When the need to assemble a larger force arises, subjects themselves may provide the necessary force and keep it under their control. The need to restrict size may explain why English kings in the early Middle Ages were not allowed to maintain a significant standing army or to hire foreign mercenaries. Moreover, subjects may impose or retain such restrictions as the force is increased.[10]

Until about 46 B.C., Rome was a republic, subject to the rule of law. While it had been expanding its territory, it had not been very restrictive about the armies it let its generals command. The rule of law came to an end because the republic lost control over its large armies in faraway lands, and its generals turned it from a republic into an "empire." Those commanders were largely independent of their home base in Rome, living on the loot from their conquests. At some point the restraint that those independent forces exerted on one another ceased to be effective. Eventually Julius Caesar prevailed in his rivalry with the other generals and then overpowered the constitutional government.

Complementarity among forces and the difficulty of separating their contributions to protection are reasons to place such forces within a single command. The degree of complementarity in the performance of protection is likely to vary between different forces. Such forces are also likely to differ in terms of the threat they pose to their clients. The lesser the complementarity and the greater the threat, the smaller the gain from placing these forces within a single command. Indeed, as argued earlier,

---

[10] In the United States, the armed forces have some leeway regarding the size of each force. Congress (rather than the executive), however, maintains control over the number of commissioned officers – the core of the force – and it also must approve promotions to the higher ranks.

when the forces are organized and controlled separately, they are likely to counterbalance one another. This, for example, seems to be one reason why police forces and army forces are separately organized.

Each type of force is most efficient on a particular scale (or range of scales). Not all forces, however, will be allowed to operate at their optimal scale. I expect some forces to be held below their optimal scale so that clients can contain them, but clients will not restrict the size of forces that do not pose a serious threat. Forces such as those assigned to dig trenches do not pose a threat to confiscate. The optimal scale for this kind of force may be less than the intended scale for the armed forces, the main protection organization, allowing the scale for other forces to be larger. To the extent that the optimal scale for a non-threatening force is smaller than that for a potentially threatening one, it will be allowed to operate at its optimal scale. Naval forces tend to fall into the latter category, since their ability to threaten land possessions is limited.[11] Another major such force is the one needed to protect against local, high-transport-cost theft. Moreover, we expect such a force, if not complementary to a threatening one, to be organized independently in order to increase efficiency. Indeed, some of these forces are allowed to operate privately, as is the case with certain security and cash-transfer services.

Restricting Tenure

The shorter the tenure that the clients grant to their protector, the greater the protector's difficulty in consolidating his control of power. A protector needs time to form alliances and negotiate enforceable agreements that will secure the support of subordinates and other potential collaborators. A restriction on his tenure will reduce the chance that the protector can form such alliances.[12] We expect, then, that clients will restrict

---

[11] This apparent feature of naval forces may account for the fact that a relatively large number of constitutional states, including classical Athens, Venice, Holland, and England, held vast but dispersed overseas empires.

[12] In Chapter 15, in comparing the rule of law with dictatorship, I argue that subjects in rule-of-law states are likely to retain the right to select the protector's successor. This implies that they will not allow hereditary monarchies to emerge. If the argument is correct, such monarchies must have evolved from an initially dictatorial rule. The current Belgian monarch, however, is descended from one installed by a new constitutional regime and given a non-trivial amount of power by it. Note that hereditary monarchies need fewer resources to determine succession, and contested successions are very expensive.

the protector's duration of service. Examples of such restrictions imposed by rule-of-law states are not hard to find. In classical Athens and in pre-imperial Rome, military commanders appointed in time of emergency were given a great deal of power. However, in addition to the fact that often they were not even professional soldiers, they were allowed to serve for only brief periods, six months in Rome. It is not surprising that none of those commanders was able to use his position to become a real dictator.[13] Many of the city-states of medieval Italy appointed successions of city managers, called "podestas," to lead them. Waley (1988, p. 42) states that "the podesta in the early fourteenth century served for a period of six months (a one year period of office became rare after the mid-thirteenth century)." Both in the United States and in Israel the term of the military chief of staff, while not constitutionally set, is quite short.[14] Moreover, in rule-of-law states, war heroes tend to be "retired" early. On the other hand, as is obvious, subjects cannot restrict dictators' durations of reign.

Other Restrictions

Clients can impose additional restrictions on their protectors. The nature of such restrictions will depend, in part, on the potential for confiscation of the resources under the protector's control. I hypothesize that clients will identify the threatened protection resources and make arrangements to contain the threat prior to forming an agreement with a protector. For instance, both the infantry and the more mobile quick-strike units pose such a threat, and precautions must be taken regarding each of them. Clients can be expected to monitor the movements of such units, especially when they are assembled in large numbers or in close proximity to the clients.

Other, more specific restrictions on the size and equipment of forces can be expected in situations that render their control difficult.[15] I predict that these forces will be divided into relatively small units and will not

[13] "Dictator" was the title the Romans gave to their short-term commanders. That was the origin of the term.

[14] "General John Shalikashvili, chairman of the Joint Chiefs of Staff . . . has served two two-year terms. . . . His decision to step down would be in keeping with the tradition for JCS chairmen, none of whom has served more than two terms." *Seattle Times*, January 29, 1997.

[15] In rule-of-law states, the protector is given little discretion over defense appropriations and over the nature of the forces under him. This facilitates control where direct supervision is difficult.

be given control over the means of transporting themselves to the center. This last restriction most likely applied, for example, to the English forces located in the far corners of the British Empire. Such precautions, presumably, were insufficiently applied in republican Rome.

Some protectors have been required to disperse their properties among those of their clients. Protectors then could not defend their own properties without, at the same time, defending the neighboring properties of their subjects. Moreover, when the properties are mingled, subjects can more easily detect when a protector is assembling a force that might threaten them. That may have been the reason why the royal (and some noble) properties in medieval England were scattered throughout the kingdom.

Subjects occasionally require the protector to be an outsider. Outsiders incur greater costs in interacting with insiders than do insiders when interacting among themselves. Outsiders, then, are less able than insiders to collude with insiders and take over. The individual selected as city manager (the podesta) in a medieval Italian city-state had to be an outsider.[16] Until well into the twentieth century, a European royal line left without an heir would often be replaced by an outsider.[17]

INCENTIVE PROBLEMS ASSOCIATED WITH PROTECTION

Earlier in this chapter it was stated that an efficient method for organizing protection is to use a large-scale protection force servicing the whole state. In addition, protection that requires team production (Alchian and Demsetz, 1972) calls for a large organization. Such an organization, however, can pose a threat to clients. I expect that clients will employ such protectors largely as fixed-wage employees so as partially to alleviate the threat. Fixed-wage employees cannot accumulate sufficient wealth to finance a seizure of power. However, wageworkers, including those employed in protection, can gain by shirking, and their effort must be supervised. The cost of supervision and the cost of the remaining shirking, "bureaucratic cost" in the context here, tend to

---

[16] The podesta was restricted further in many ways. For example, he needed the council's permission to leave the city during his time in office (Waley, 1988, p. 42). Greif (1994) discusses in detail the role of and the restrictions on the podesta in the twelfth and thirteenth centuries in Genoa.

[17] In addition, the protectors, as a rule, are not permitted to impose arbitrary sentences on nor extract arbitrary fines from subjects judged to have committed infractions.

dampen the effect of the scale economies to protection. I expect that a balance between the scale economy and the inefficiency of wage labor will be struck.

Here, as elsewhere, decentralization tends to enhance efficiency because of the fact that the lower the level of a unit, the more of a residual claimant it is to its own operations. As measuring individual contributions becomes easier, the protection organizations can be expected to become less centralized, giving individuals more discretion over their own operations. Similar considerations apply to whole military units. As contributions become easier to measure, then, the size of the centralized military force is predicted to shrink, and different forces are more likely to be organized independently of one another. Put differently, little overlap is expected in the output of independent units. Thus, if military strategy dictates the use of cavalry separately from the use of foot soldiers, I expect the two forces to be organized independently. Indeed, when separation becomes easier, I expect that more of the activities will be provided by for-profit organizations.

Where separation is difficult, the prediction is that individuals, or whole units, will be employed on a fixed-wage basis, rather than operating as independent contractors. Otherwise, when different protectors were in charge of protecting different individuals, conflicts among them could easily arise. This issue, brought up in Chapter 3, will now be considered further.

Suppose two neighbors seek help in protecting themselves. Should they employ two independent protectors or a single protector common to them? Conflicts among neighbors tend to arise when their properties are not clearly demarcated. Protectors have to delineate clearly what they agree to protect. If the neighbors employ different protectors, the protectors may delineate differently their supposed common border. Each protector is a residual claimant to his own effort. The potential for dispute, then, is transferred from the neighbors to the protectors. On the other hand, when a single protector is employed for both, presumably he will delineate a unique border. Moreover, the protector can reduce his cost of performing the service by delineating the border in such a way that the potential for dispute will be reduced. Protection under such a single enforcer is horizontally integrated.

Compare, in this light, the protection provided by the police with that provided by the armed forces. As a rule, the delineation of borders between individuals and between small communities is far from perfect. Protection is needed, then, and protecting one person or one community against theft tends to protect the neighbors too. Such services, however, seem fairly easy to separate across communities. We expect such protection, then, to be provided by the police on a local basis. On the other hand, the protection that the armed forces provide to individuals and to communities does not seem well demarcated even across large communities. If so, its scale economy covers a larger territory than that of the police. This may account for the local independence of the police, and the absence of local independence within the military.

The restrictions that clients impose on protectors raise the cost of protection. Here, too, then, clients face a trade-off between a higher threat that their wealth will be confiscated and a lower cost of protection. Seeking the most efficient protection effort under the restrictions, we expect the clients to promote greater coherence between their own and the protector's interests. The clients are likely to provide their protector with incentives that resemble the inducements offered to corporate chief executives, such as shares, bonuses, and performance-adjusted salaries. Under such incentive schemes, the protector bears some of the income variability of the protection effort and thus becomes a partial residual claimant. By the same token, subjects do not then bear the entire burden of variability, but they bear some – the remaining portion. The higher the share a protector bears, the better his performance, but, as just argued, at the cost of a higher chance that he might take over.

Clients are also expected to allow their protector some organizational discretion, such as more vertical or horizontal integration when that will increase the value of the protection organization. By allowing that, clients can secure their protection more cheaply. As we will see later, the legal machinery and other resources that accommodate trade are complementary to police protection. Clients, then, may place the legal machinery (and the other resources) under the jurisdiction of the protector who provides police services.

Because protectors are only partial residual claimants to their own activities, the coherence between their own and their clients' interests is not complete. They will not be inclined to pursue all the projects that could yield a joint positive present value. Consider the pursuit of war. A successful war would bring loot and greater security to the citizenry. But the protector may be disinclined to undertake a winnable war because his personal cost would be likely to exceed his gain. We expect his subjects, then, to implement procedures to evaluate possible military projects and to instruct the protector to undertake the ones they view as desirable. This seems to have been one of the main functions of organizations like the medieval and modern parliaments, and perhaps also the medieval councils.[18]

The discussion to this point indicates that rule-of-law states differ from dictatorships in terms of the restrictions imposed and the allocations of power. Clients impose restrictions on the scale of the protective power allowed under the protector's control, so as to lower his ability to confiscate their property. These restrictions are major determinants of the scale of a state governed by rule of law. A protector who takes over a state and becomes a dictator is unlikely to preserve the scale that the clients prescribed to him when he was their employee. Freed from his subjects' restrictions, he alone will decide on the scale of operations and is likely to try to expand the size of the state he has seized.[19] Moreover, being a dictator, he is more of a residual claimant to the wealth of the state. He (i.e., the state) is likely to undertake all projects with positive present value. The greater bureaucracy that state projects entail will temper this effect, however.

Regarding the control of power, as long as dictatorship is averted, no protector is expected to have exclusive control of the state's power. The power that the protectors are given is likely to be dispersed among them, and their employers may maintain a power center too. These powers tend to be in balance, neutralizing each other. A dictator, of course, will control the bulk of the power in his state.

THE FIRM: A MODEL OF THE STATE?

Like firms, states can be organized in various ways. The state, as seen here, shares certain basic features with the firm. In some other major

---

[18] As mentioned earlier, the tenure of the podesta, the city manager of an Italian city-states, was six months. Consequently, his lifetime income crucially depended on his reputation, on how his performance in office would be perceived by future employers. Waley (1988, p. 43) states that "some of these men [podestas] came to specialize in the office and move on regularly from city to city." It is expected that the need to instruct a podesta to undertake projects beneficial to his employers would have been much less than, say, for the Venetian employers of the doge, who served for life, or for the councils of hereditary monarchs.

[19] The incentive for a dictator to keep a permanent army and expand his state is likely to have effects on his neighbors. Consider two neighboring states that initially were operating under the rule of law, but one of which was then taken over by a dictator. The size and other features of a dictator's force are not constrained by his subjects, and he is expected to increase the military strength of his state. To counter the newly threatening dictatorial neighbor, the constitutional state, too, may amass a larger army. It may relax the restrictions on its own protector, and thus it faces a greater threat from within. To a degree, then, dictatorship is "contagious."

respects, however, the two differ. Comparing them is interesting for its own sake; it is also instructive in providing a better understanding of the constraints on the protector.

States can operate under at least two major forms of organization that will govern the relationship between protector and clients, or subjects. One, the main focus in this book, has its origin in a set of individuals who make an agreement to employ a protection specialist who will then become their employee. The protector undertakes to build up defense organizations that he manages under the clients' supervision. In the other form, where a dictatorship emerged right from the beginning or where it replaced the original state, the dictator assumes the initiative for the protection organization. Elsewhere (Barzel, 2000a) I have discussed a dictatorial ruler (protector) who, to enhance his wealth, initiates various agreements with his subjects. He may, among other possibilities, set up an institution like the English Parliament, an institution that will make decisions by vote. That institution will participate in protection decisions and will be granted the right to impose taxes or, indeed, to refuse to impose taxes.

Condominiums and common-stock corporations show parallels with the state that emerges from the ruler's initiative. In those enterprises, an entrepreneur sets up the organization and gives it a constitution. He manages the enterprise and secures investors-voters to cooperate in financing it. In the case of a common-stock corporation, the entrepreneur often will sell stock in the corporation he has created and will remain its manager, while personally retaining much of the stock. Such an entrepreneur resembles the ruler who establishes a parliament and then relinquishes some of his control over it. Common to the state and these commercial enterprises, the role of the initial manager tends to decrease with time.

Partnerships and cooperatives show parallels with the state that emerges from an initiative by the governed. Such firms are established by the partners or by the members of the cooperative. Those principals employ specialized managers to run their organizations. The partners or the cooperative members tend to maintain tight control over the managers and constrain their actions. Such control methods are not unlike those employed by clients to control and constrain specialized protectors.

Both the state and these business enterprises are characterized by the restrictions the participants place on themselves at the outset of their operation. Opportunities for wealth transfer within organizations are always present. For example, where decisions are made by majority vote, majorities may attempt to capture some of the minorities' wealth. The attempts to effect and to prevent such transfers consume resources. I hypothesize that the previously mentioned restrictions serve, in part, to reduce the opportunities for wealth transfer within organizations. The fewer such opportunities, the higher the net value of the organization, and the higher the return it will bring to its originators (Grossman and Hart, 1980; Barzel and Sass, 1990). Some of these restrictions will be incorporated in the franchise or the constitution of the organization, where the organizers will limit the areas into which the organization will be allowed to go.

By their very design, such organizations are prepared to handle problems that cannot be handled as cheaply in the market. Market or contract transactions are basically those between independent entities: between individuals, between individuals and organizations, or between organizations. In Chapter 6, I suggested that many transactions are "mixed." They consist of many components, some of which will be conducted by contract in the market and will be enforced by the state, whereas others will be enforced by other means. I hypothesize that individuals tend to organize their interactions so that when disputes arise, they will be adjudicated by the mechanism best suited for their idiosyncrasies. Thus, disputes that involve market transactions, or the components of transactions that are in the market, will be adjudicated by power-backed third parties. On the other hand, organizations such as firms, by appropriately altering the incentives for the individuals involved, are able to handle internally many problems that would be more costly to have adjudicated by a power-backed third party.

The distinction between agreements that are enforced by a power-backed third party and those that are otherwise enforced, however, is also what differentiates states from firms. The organizers of firms and their partners embody their agreements in contracts that are enforceable by the states in which they operate. These contracts often are sanctioned by the state and sometimes are explicitly placed under its auspices (chartered corporations and cities in medieval England, stock corporations and condominiums registered with the states in the United States today). On the other hand, an agreement between protector and clients must be self-enforced. Even in the case of an explicit agreement, as with the

Magna Carta, surely the most celebrated such agreement, there exists no third party to enforce it.[20]

Managers of common-stock corporations may attempt to transfer wealth from shareholders to themselves. Such transfers are particularly difficult to prevent when ownership is dispersed. As just asserted, organizers make provisions to reduce wealth transfers within their organizations. Firms can take advantage of the power-backed third-party enforcement of the state, as well as other forms of agreement, to prevent transfers. The prevention of transfers seems at least as difficult in the case of the state. The state, too, must develop mechanisms to reduce transfers by the protection specialists who may use their force to confiscate clients' wealth, as well as mechanisms to prevent the majority of voters from confiscating the wealth of the minority. The agreements that underlie the state, however, do not have access to the power-backed third-party enforcement that is available to firms. Given this difference between states and firms, I predict, for example, that the restrictions that rule-of-law states impose on how commanders can use the armed forces under them will be more severe than those that shareholders impose on their chief executives in running their firms, the reason being that only the latter can be constrained by a power-backed third party.[21]

One more feature, and a more fundamental one, differentiates states and firms: the assignment of the residual. Economic action is subject to variability. Whenever variability is present, somebody must bear it (i.e., become the residual claimant to it). In any exchange, the parties agree how to allocate the variability between them. By guaranteeing his actions, a person bears the variability he induces. Efficiency is enhanced if the party responsible for the variability, whether it be an individual or a firm, is also the party who bears its effects. One attribute of the firm is that it commits, primarily by using its equity capital, to be the primary bearer to the residual it generates.[22] That promise is made contractually and is enforced by the state.

---

[20] Making it easier to know what the parties have agreed to seems to be a major reason for producing the document itself.

[21] The analysis in the text applies to firms that operate within single states. Agreements to form multinational firms must be enforced by some form of long-term relations.

[22] This, in my view, is a function of the firm that determines, among other things, its size. See Barzel (1997a) and Barzel and Suen (1995).

The state itself, however, cannot make such promises, because there is no third party to enforce them, and it would seem exceedingly difficult for them to be self-enforced. This, as stated, is one of the reasons why protectors are compensated primarily by wages. As already mentioned, and as elaborated later, it is inefficient to compensate the provider of adjudication services according to the "quality" of the adjudication; that, however, is what a profit-seeking business firm is wont to do. For that reason, the state is the efficient provider of adjudication services. As we will see later, however, the notion that the state is not a residual claimant does not apply with the same force to a dictatorial regime.

CONCLUSIONS

By the very nature of their function, protectors specialize in the use of violence, which poses a threat to those they are asked to protect. As discussed in regard to collective action in Chapter 7, individuals can be expected to design a mechanism to restrain the protector before he is allowed to specialize. Maintaining such a mechanism is expensive. They can lower their cost of containing him by imposing constraints on him. One constraint is not to allow the protector to be a full-fledged residual claimant to his performance. Although he will then be less motivated to perform efficiently, he will also be less likely to take wild risks of which he will not bear all the consequences because of wealth constraints, nor will he be likely to accumulate a sufficient amount of wealth to finance a takeover. To further increase the protector's takeover cost, he will have only a short tenure. Clients will also restrict the amount of force a protector is allowed to control, as well as his budget and the way it is dispensed. Decentralization of the protective forces, where economical, can serve two functions: first, reducing the power of any single protector and, second, enhancing efficiency by facilitating closer monitoring of the costs and benefits each unit generates.

Although in many ways states resemble firms, individuals' control of their heads of state is more difficult than firm owners' control of their managers. The reason is that the former are subject to the added difficulty that there is no third party to enforce their agreements with the protectors they employ, whereas firm owners have access to the state's enforcement power to enforce their agreements with their managers. One implication here is that the heads of rule-of-law states will be more severely constrained than will the employed managers of firms.

The Emergence of Legal Institutions

9

Legal Rights

In Part I of this book we developed a framework to study the nature of the state. Part II focuses on legal institutions and puts more flesh on the previously described bones of the state. In this chapter, I discuss the relationship between protection and delineation and how the formation of that relationship amounts to the founding of legal institutions. Protection efforts vary in terms of the assets in need of protection and the types of threats made against them. I demonstrate that legal institutions will vary with the threats and the asset types. In order to proceed, legal rights must be defined.

> **Definition.** *Legal rights are the claims over assets delineated by the state as the property of particular individuals or institutions.*

The "assets" in the definition are all-inclusive. They encompass, among other things, physical assets, as well as individuals (owned by themselves or, in the case of slaves, by others), intellectual creations, brand names, and reputations. The enforcement and protection measures that the state provides include the prevention of any kind of uncompensated use of or damage to one's legal assets by other persons. Such enforcement covers, for instance, damage from rape and from copyright infringement. I argue later that the state's delineation of assets can take two distinct forms. In one, the state explicitly agrees to protect certain assets. In the other, the state agrees to protect any assets that individuals register with it, as well as those that individuals delineate in contracts.

Besides the violence-using enforcer, other third parties can delineate and enforce claims over assets. The rest of this chapter is devoted primarily to the topic of protection and delineation by force-using protectors, touching only briefly on delineation by other third parties.

THE PROTECTION FUNCTION

It was argued in earlier chapters that economic rights can exist in the absence of legal rights. One's assets do not need protection unless others are in a position to use them without permission. For an asset that needs protection, then, there is ambiguity about its economic owner. Assets that are not perfectly delineated lie, in part, in the public domain. By providing protection and legal delineation for an asset, a protection specialist reduces the portion that lies in the public domain and enhances the economic ownership over it. Even when protection is provided, however, ownership will not be made perfect, because airtight protection would be prohibitively costly. The assets protected by the specialist, then, will not be entirely immune to theft.

Theft is diverse, and different skills and organizations are needed to prevent it. Protection, too, can take various forms. Besides the explicit, direct form of "sheer" protection by a specialist, which is what is popularly viewed as the only form of theft protection, there can be two indirect forms of protection: (1) self-enforced agreements whereby potential thieves (individuals, organized sets, or states) agree not to steal, and (2) the use of specialists who offer protection simultaneously to potential victims and to thieves.

Theft and, more generally, wealth capture can also occur when the delineation of rights is incomplete. For example, when the boundary separating the holdings of two neighbors is not clearly marked, they may both claim the same attributes, as when they draw from the common groundwater, or take fruit grown on each other's trees. Because theft constitutes a transfer of wealth at a resource cost, the question arises why potential victims do not make prior agreements with would-be thieves to eliminate or at least reduce such costs. I argue that in certain cases such agreements are actually made, though mostly implicitly, but because of their high cost their coverage is not complete, and in some situations such agreements are altogether too costly to make.

Some individuals or sets of individuals have a comparative advantage in theft because they are elusive. When operating as thieves, they cannot count on getting a satisfactory bargain by abstaining from theft in the future. The reason for this is that once they reveal themselves and attempt to form long-term relations, they have little power left with which to enforce any agreements. This seems to be the case with pirates and marauders who choose to remain thieves. Even when agreements can be made relatively easily, if the supply of such thieves is elastic, the gain from agreeing with any particular one will be small, as others are likely to replace him. We can expect only sheer protection, which will increase a thief's cost of theft, to reduce such theft.

Consider now theft by one state of another state's assets. Under certain conditions it is possible for such states to form agreements to prevent or at least reduce theft between them.[1] The more stable the states are, the easier it will be for them to negotiate such agreements. Without such protection agreements, states will need stronger protection from each other.

In the last form of protection considered here, a protector admits the would-be thieves into his jurisdiction and makes them his clients. If they are organized, he (or his successor) may merge with them. Once the protector has more than one client, he may also effect direct agreements among *his clients*, for whom he serves as the third-party adjudicator and the enforcer of their agreements.

PROTECTION AND DELINEATION BY TYPE OF THREAT

To proceed, the relationship between clients and the protectors they employ, as modeled here, must first be made clear. The protection specialists, as suggested earlier, function as salaried employees rather than as the primary residual claimants to their own actions. They are instructed what to do, because on their own they would tend to make only the minimal effort consistent with the task assigned to them. Their employers, then, must evaluate the costs and returns from alternative forms of protection, choose the ones deemed most attractive, and adopt a mix of inducements and instructions for each protection organization to carry out its assignments. Operating on behalf of his clients, a protector will protect the properties that his protection, net of his cost, will enhance in value. I focus mostly on the induced actions of the protectors.

Protection activities fall into two broad categories. One consists of measures used against large-scale marauders, especially the organized armies of other states that can threaten one's entire state. The other consists of measures against small-scale "local" thieves. We consider the two successively, and in a later section I suggest that in both cases

---

[1] As a general rule, agreements between independent states must be self-enforced. There is no third party using force to enforce them. Other entities, such as the Catholic church, however, have occasionally acted as third parties with some ability to enforce agreements between states.

the founding of legal institutions is a by-product of the provision of protection.

PROTECTION AGAINST OUTSIDERS AND THE RIGHTS DELINEATION IT INDUCES

Individuals must instruct the protector what action to take against outside threats and decide on the constraints they will impose on themselves. The information that would be available ahead of time about large-scale threats in general would seem to be insufficient for issuing instructions regarding the protection of each piece of property. Predicting accurately the nature and timing of such threats seems too costly; it seems more economical to deal with each as it arises. It is unlikely, therefore, that clients will give the protector specific instructions how to protect their holdings that are at risk.

It does seem economical, however, to undertake preventive measures before the enemy is at one's gate. Thus, individual owners may be required to fortify some of their holdings and keep weapons and supplies at hand. To ensure performance, criteria for evaluating compliance must be established. Seeing to it that the criteria are met constitutes a delineation of rights by the state. To see this, suppose that owners of big structures are required to fortify them. When the state confirms compliance, or even non-compliance, it indirectly also confirms that particular persons are the owners of particular structures. The organizations in charge of compliance, and in charge of adjudicating disputes regarding compliance, even if indirectly, are in the business of delineating rights.

Individuals' holdings must be delineated for another, related reason. Although, as stated, the protection effort is unlikely to be customized to individuals' holdings, in the long run individuals will seek protection commensurate with the aggregate value of their holdings. As discussed in Chapter 7, assessments and taxes for the purpose of protection are expected to be proportional to the value of the holdings. The state organization in charge of these taxes, then, must engage, here again indirectly, in the delineation and indeed in the assessment of individuals' holdings. The delineation, though, need not be highly specific, because little depends on it other than the tax level itself.[2]

---

[2] In medieval England, a component of the taxation of the nobility was the requirement to furnish armed men when needed. The number of men a nobleman had to provide was proportional to the size of his landholdings.

The protector will have to decide on the appropriate level of effort for different classes of holdings. The values of the holdings must be estimated for that purpose too. Such evaluation may, on occasion, lead to the conclusion that certain properties are not worth protecting, because relative to their value the cost of their protection would be too high. In that case, the state, presumably, simply will not delineate the assets. In turn, individuals will not expect state protection when using those properties. Among the assets a state will choose not to protect, some may be such that it would be too costly for anyone to protect them, and thus they will be abandoned entirely (i.e., placed in the public domain).[3] Other assets may have positive net value to individuals within the state who will protect the assets themselves, and thus establish economic rights over them. To complete the classification, some assets may have positive net value to other states, and therefore we would expect them to be absorbed into those states.[4]

Delineation itself is costly, and this cost must be taken into account in the decision whether or not to protect an asset. Other things being equal, the higher the cost the state incurs in the delineation of an asset, the lower the likelihood the state will protect it. The middle of the ocean would be difficult to delineate, and it is not delineated. The delineation of offshore properties, however, is steadily expanding because of advances in technology.

The state is expected also to be selective in its protection efforts. Protection is not an all-or-none affair; not all assets will be protected with the same intensity. The higher the cost of protection for a particular application, the lower the protector's commitment to protect. Consider the level of protection as a function of the property location. Assuming that the cost of protection increases with increasing distance of the property from the center, we expect the level and intensity of the commitment to protect to decline with distance. Although the bulk of the effort is likely to be expended in the border regions of the protected area, I predict that the closer a client's property is to the border, the fewer of its components the specialist will agree to protect. For instance, the protector may prohibit the construction of expensive structures in the border area,

---

[3] The notions that states control fixed, well-demarcated areas and that their combined holdings are exhaustive are modern ones. For example, until the twentieth century, most of the desert areas in the Middle East were not parts of any state.

[4] The Coase theorem is not operative here. Delineation costs, which are part of the costs of transacting, are positive. Consequently, who owns what matters here.

thus reducing the need for protection there, even if he permits such structures at the center.[5]

PROTECTION AGAINST INSIDERS' THEFT AND THE RIGHTS DELINEATION IT INDUCES

Consider now ordinary theft. Individuals may choose to engage in self-protection against such theft. Alternatively, they may seek specialists with skills in violence to provide the service. In the latter case, because the protector is specialized, the protection he offers will enable his clients to own assets and asset attributes they would not otherwise be able to own. However, we expect him to protect only the attributes with respect to which he has a comparative advantage in protecting. In his agreement (possibly an implicit agreement) with his clients, the protector, presumably, spells out the assets and asset attributes that he agrees to protect. As the specialist here is the violence-wielding protector, the spelling out constitutes a legal delineation of rights.[6]

As in the case of protection from outside aggressors, some properties will not be worth protecting by anybody and may be abandoned, left in the public domain. The rest will be protected. Two questions arise. First, which properties will be protected by their owners, which by a specialized protector, and which by both? Second, in any case, when will agreements between owners and would-be thieves be reached, and when will sheer protection be chosen?

Relative to other protectors, the economic owner of an asset has an advantage in knowing which of its features he values most and which would be most valuable to thieves. He is expected to take part in the protection of those attributes for which his valuation relative to that of thieves is high. He is also expected to engage directly in protection by, for instance, keeping some assets locked up, out of easy reach for thieves. The measures we expect the owner to take are not unlike those the police and insurers tend to encourage.[7]

---

[5] Barzel (1987, pp. 91–3) and, more elaborately, and with evidence, Allen (1991a) offer an explanation of the Homestead Act consistent with the idea in the text.

[6] In the process of providing theft insurance, insurers delineate rights. Indeed, the restrictions they impose, such as the requirement to keep jewelry in safes, also enhance protection.

[7] In Israel, the police require jewelers to keep the doors of their shops locked during business hours. The owners can admit customers only by using remote-control switches to unlock their doors.

In general, the more idiosyncratic are the assets and the owner's knowledge of them, the more costly is their delineation. There are scale economies to be had in delineating generic assets, as all the assets in the class can share the delineation costs. Such economies are not available for idiosyncratic assets. In other words, the owner of an idiosyncratic asset is relatively more familiar with it than others are, and the latter will have more difficulty in evaluating it and determining the optimal protection effort.[8] Therefore, the owner will play a more significant role in protecting the asset. The owner here lacks a legal title, because the property has not been delineated by a violence-using protector. The owner would not choose to protect it unless he could benefit from it, and thus he is its economic owner.

An owner who takes charge of protecting his own property can do so directly by such actions as building fences, installing locks, and hiding valuables. He can do so indirectly by reaching agreements with the would-be thieves to abstain from stealing. Like agreements between states, these must be self-policing, based on repeated interactions. We expect, for instance, that stationary long-term neighbors will make such agreements.[9] Consider two neighbors owning orchards who might steal from each other. It should be relatively easy for them to reach an agreement, because each is likely to be aware of theft by the other. To a third party, on the other hand, the cost of acquiring the same information and verifying it likely would be high. Thus, a direct agreement between the neighbors may be more effective than protection by the state.

Another factor that affects the choice between self-protection and state protection is the ability to evaluate assets. The more idiosyncratic an asset, the more difficult its evaluation by others, and the less the comparative advantage of the state in protecting it. I elaborate on this point later.

The determination of what is worth legal delineation is not constant. I expect that as the cost of legal delineation declines, and as the benefits it generates increase, more assets and asset attributes will be added to

---

[8] There is an element of circularity in the use of the term "owner" here. To avoid it, perhaps I should state instead something like "the person who will eventually emerge as the economic owner," since before we know that he will protect it, and absent legal ownership, the person does not own the asset. Because confusion is unlikely here, I stick with the term "owner" to avoid the much more cumbersome alternative.

[9] Laws against vagrancy induce longer-term relations and thus reduce the cost of protection not only by the state but also by individuals.

the set of properties delineated by the state.[10] By the same token, legal delineation for some kinds of assets is likely to be withdrawn as the net gains from delineation fall.[11]

Neighbors who choose to use specialists still have to decide whether to hire a single protector for both or hire different protectors, one for each of them. In the latter case, each protector will be guided only by his client's interests. It might appear that a common protector would be handicapped by a conflict of interests, but that is not the case. The rights we are dealing with are not well delineated, and the use of individual protectors would be of assistance in wealth transfer and its prevention. As discussed in earlier chapters, a protector common to both could coordinate the agreements he negotiates so as to reduce the incentives for the two to capture each other's wealth. He is expected, among other things, to determine and delineate a boundary that will maximize the value of the property net of the cost of his services. He might also stipulate that the neighbors must fence their holdings. Inspection to determine whether or not the clients are in compliance will then confirm and implicitly delineate ownership.

The common protector might take even more radical steps. Suppose the neighbors are using their properties for grazing, which seemingly would provide easy opportunities for theft. The protector might prohibit grazing and instead restrict the neighbors to farming, as the latter would offer fewer theft opportunities. Once the changes were in place, it might not be obvious that the protector was engaged in protection. Indeed, he might be viewed as an obstructionist, imposing "unnecessary" regulations. In any case, here, too, the protector is engaging in delineation.

[10] Consider a newly established regime. If, as time passes, it becomes stable, we expect that people will become more confident of its stability and will entrust a larger fraction of their agreements to its third-party adjudication. For instance, we expect the laws regarding theft of straying cattle to become tighter, committing the state to more comprehensive protection of such assets.

[11] The state awards rights to patents and copyrights. The expiration of these rights illustrates the withdrawal of legal protection. The increase in the cost of protection relative to its (likely declining) valuation is a possible reason for the withdrawal of rights for both types of properties. As time passes, both the state and right-holders find it more difficult to determine whether or not a patent was infringed; the change with time for copyrights seems slower. The facts in those cases – that the duration of these rights is limited, that it is longer for copyright, and that the latter depends on the longevity of the copyright holder – are consistent with the notion that legal protection is withdrawn when enforcement cost becomes high. Had the sole purpose of the withdrawal been the commonly asserted desire to charge a price – zero – equal to marginal cost, there would have been no reason for the differential treatment of the two.

Because perfect delineation would be prohibitively costly, disputes are still bound to occur. When the parties turn to the common protector for assistance, he becomes a "third party" who must adjudicate the dispute and enforce his rulings.

I defer to later chapters the discussion of two other issues that this section raises. One is that of additional but very different types of properties that are not legally delineated, and yet individuals choose to maintain those properties in their possession. These are properties whose exchange is governed by self-enforced agreements that are not subject to third-party adjudication. The other issue concerns the role that the protection specialist plays in facilitating exchange. By delineating assets, a protection specialist is providing owners the additional benefit of making exchange easier. In the next two chapters we explore the advantages the protection specialist has in facilitating exchange and the limitations he faces in performing that role.

THE PROTECTOR AS THE ORIGINATOR OF LEGAL INSTITUTIONS

I have argued that the protector's employers must instruct him what to protect and must supervise his performance. A similar argument applies to the provision of legal services. If the protector were the residual claimant to his own action, he would be the one who could most *profitably* provide legal services. However, as his clients' employee, he will not directly benefit from providing these services. The protector being the efficient producer of the legal services, his employers are expected to instruct him to provide services such that their value will exceed both the sum of their resource costs and the cost of supervising the specialist. We will see later that the protector's employers are likely also to constrain him to be fair and impartial in operating the legal system he creates. Provided the foregoing proves correct, then it will transpire that in the process of conducting their business the individuals who control the protector will find it useful to establish institutions that will bring about a rule of law.

The discussion in the preceding two sections has brought out the relationship between protection by an employed protector and the rise of legal institutions. The emergence of a force-using protector common to two or more individuals, along with the enforcement mechanism he creates, constitutes the founding of legal rights. The protection specialist has a comparative advantage in establishing such rights. He is a delineator of legal rights because he must delineate what it is that he agrees to protect. When he assumes the role of a third-party enforcer, he must be ready to adjudicate disputes among clients regarding properties he has agreed to protect. He becomes a judge, then, and he must rule whether or not, and to what extent, a client's rights were encroached upon by other clients. In addition, he is a policeman, as he must be ready to police the agreements to which he is a third party and enforce his rulings. The fees he charges for the services he provides are usually considered taxes. This service, as I argue later, has public-good dimensions, and for that reason we expect the tax to be collected through a general assessment. The protector, then, is a tax collector. As we will also see later, the rights he delineates will also facilitate exchange between clients under the contracts he enforces.

PROTECTION AND DELINEATION OF IDIOSYNCRATIC ASSETS

Protecting and delineating idiosyncratic assets differs greatly from protecting and delineating generic ones. In this section I discuss idiosyncratic assets, and in the next I argue that contracts and registrations are especially suited to generic assets. I argue that owners of idiosyncratic assets are likely to have a comparative advantage in protecting them.

Presumably, the protection level an owner seeks for his assets will be commensurate with the highest value they can command. As a rule, the current owner will be the one valuing an asset most.[12] The state or other outsiders can determine at a reasonable cost the value of an asset to others, but not to its owner. To avoid the moral hazard associated with exaggerated value, the level of protection the state will agree to provide will not be in accordance with the valuation asserted by the owner, but rather with the "common" value to others.[13] It will offer little or no protection for the idiosyncratic component. This common value is likely also to be used as a basis for paying the state for protection of the asset (i.e.,

---

[12] The maximizing holder of an asset does not necessarily value it more (but at least no less) than anybody else. The fact that an owner retains an asset does not preclude another individual or individuals from valuing it more. He will attempt to sell the asset only when he expects the cost of discovering such individuals and of negotiating the price in this (possibly bilateral monopoly) situation to be less than the difference between the sale price and his own valuation.

[13] The difference in the value of an asset to its owner and its value to others is an endemic issue in insurance as well.

for taxation) and, if necessary, in case of dispute, to be demonstrated in court.

Somebody other than the state must protect the idiosyncratic component of an asset, and it is the asset's owner himself who is likely to do that. Unless thieves sell such an asset to the original owner, they can gain only the value of the generic component of the asset. When, for example, they steal an heirloom piece of jewelry, all they can sell it for is the value of the gold it contains. Although the owners of assets are not specialized in protection, they are more familiar with these assets than others are, which is likely to give them an edge in protecting them. Given the disparity between the value of idiosyncratic assets to the original owners and their value to thieves, I predict that, per unit of their value to thieves, more resources will be devoted to their protection than to generic assets, and they will be stolen less often. Consider bicycles. Whereas brand-new bicycles are generic, they become idiosyncratic with use. To reduce the chance of theft, people may replace their bicycles later than they would have in the absence of theft, because as bicycles get older their value to thieves tends to decline faster than their value to their owners, who also find older bicycles relatively easier to protect.

The human capital that individuals possess constitutes a rather striking instance of an idiosyncratic asset. The difference between its value to its owner and its value to others is substantial. Its owner can use this capital in the labor market, where he may benefit from it as an independent operator or as a wage employee. He cannot, however, sell this asset in the market. The economic reason for this seems to be that it is exceedingly difficult for buyers to induce performance commensurate with the value of that capital. Such difficulty was clearly evident when slavery was widely practiced. The investment in the human capital of young slaves was modest compared with that of the surrounding freemen, in spite of slaveowners' better access to the capital market compared with that by the bulk of freemen.[14] Moreover, the human capital of captured slaves was largely wasted. Captors who could arrange for sale of the captives to the captives' relatives at low cost usually did that because it brought the highest return. When sold to their relatives (and indirectly to themselves), the freed captives presumably would be expected to pay back the purchase price to their redeemers by operating

---

[14] One reason for slaveowners' better access to the capital market was that they could post slaves as security against loans. Freemen could not post themselves as security.

as freemen within their original communities, where they could more easily put their human capital to profitable use.

Given the low value of one's human capital to others, it is not surprising that the state usually does not delineate legal rights over it.[15] Indeed, the longer the term of an employment contract, the greater the need for the owner of the human capital to use non-state means to enforce it.

DELINEATION BY CONTRACT AND BY REGISTRATION

Legal delineation can take two forms, one direct, the other indirect. As already discussed, the state delineates directly the assets it chooses to protect. I point out that individuals themselves also engage in delineation. They delineate legal rights when they register assets with the state. They also delineate rights, though less directly, when writing contracts that the state tacitly recognizes as legally binding. That recognition, however, is conditioned on meeting prior conditions that the state imposes.

Individuals who write contracts are free to make whatever stipulations they wish. The state agrees to enforce contracts provided they do not violate any law and meet certain conditions such as quid pro quo.[16] A third party need not be present when such agreements are made. In order to adjudicate disputes, however, a third party will have to be provided information sufficient to resolve disputes when they arise. The assets and attributes we can expect the protector to delineate, then, are those that can be delineated in contracts at low cost. Individuals can spell out the attributes of their agreements in sufficient detail even if their exchange is idiosyncratic. But once they spell these out, given that state enforcement cost tends to be lower, there will be no point in employing other third parties to enforce such agreements.

The delineation that contracts provide remains moot as long as there is no dispute. "No dispute" here means that the parties implicitly agree on how the courts would rule on the issues at hand. In that case, then, rights are implicitly delineated.[17] A dispute that brings the

---

[15] Delineation does take place when the courts award compensation in cases of personal injuries.

[16] As indicated later, however, the state may choose not to enforce stipulations – long-term labor obligations being one example – even if they are contractually made.

[17] More accurately, although the parties disagree, the disagreement is not significant enough to go to court over it.

parties to court implies that a contract did not delineate rights adequately, possibly because of changes in conditions after the contract was signed. The ensuing court ruling then will explicitly delineate the parties' rights.

Consider now the registering of assets and of transactions with the state. The state requires the registration of certain transactions and of certain assets, seemingly because in cases of dispute it will then be easier for the state to enforce the agreement. Be that as it may, the registration constitutes legal delineation.

I now turn to the requirement of quid pro quo. Why is a contract not valid unless it meets this condition? Why does the state impose such a condition? A possible reason is that without it the scope for dispute would be likely to expand. People sometimes say things such as "I will give you a million dollars if you smile for me." If any such statement could result in court action, the use of the courts could explode, or flowery language disappear. But given the constraint that the quid must be commensurate with the quo, such difficulty largely disappears. The costs of court services, which the state provides free of marginal charges, are then kept more manageable.

The state also determines which contract provisions it will enforce. Consider the use of the polygraph. Until recently, some jurisdictions in the United States allowed the use of polygraphs in the employment relationship while making the polygraph's readings inadmissible as court evidence. What can explain that exclusionary action? The interpretation of polygraph readings is very controversial. Admitting such evidence in court inevitably would lead to hard-to-resolve disputes, resulting in low yield to legal resources. The inadmissibility eliminates that source of legal dispute.[18]

STATES' RESTRICTIONS ON PRIVATE EXCHANGE

Individuals employ protectors to reduce theft. The act of delineation itself, however, interacts with the probability of theft. Both the ease of matching assets to individuals and the assets' degree of idiosyncrasy will affect their attraction to thieves. Idiosyncratic assets are easy to match to individuals, whereas the matching is difficult for generic assets. The latter are more attractive to thieves; being generic, possessing them does not constitute evidence of theft, and tracing their origin is expensive.

[18] Federal law now prohibits employers from using polygraphs.

Occasionally, state-imposed restrictions make tracing easier. For instance, the U.S. Postal Service charges the full face value for postage stamps, not only in retail sales but also in wholesale lots. Anyone who offers stamps for sale for less than their face value, then, is suspect of theft, or of illegal recycling of already used stamps, which may, indeed, explain the Postal Service policy.

The state has another reason to impose restrictions on private transactions. Individuals who negotiate contracts operate under the state's third-party enforcement. The state's marginal charge for its policing and adjudication services is zero, and individuals will maximize subject to that zero price. I hypothesize that to reduce excessive use of its services, the state will impose other restrictions on contract exchange besides the requirement of quid pro quo. The most severe restriction is to ban certain exchanges altogether. Where conflicts among the transactors are common, and thus where the exchanging parties are likely to become heavy users of the state services, a ban seems attractive. This may be the reason why gambling is often banned, and perhaps why charging interest (usury) is sometimes prohibited. The state can also impose less severe restrictions. Mandating the installation of automobile locks results in an increase in the cost of theft. Mandating the use of standard weights and measures, of state currency to denominate values, and of state registration of certain transactions, such as the exchange of automobiles, makes adjudication easier.[19] Finally, the state may simply leave certain relationships outside its jurisdiction, and whenever such agreements are made, the parties must use other methods to enforce them.[20]

States' restrictions aside, generic assets are more vulnerable to theft than idiosyncratic assets. For this reason, the former require more protection than the latter. To reduce the cost of protection, people may opt to forgo the gains that could be had from standardized production of generic assets that are very expensive to protect against theft and instead produce only idiosyncratic assets.[21] One implication of this argument is

---

[19] The registration of transactions, of course, also facilitates taxation.

[20] Consider the rights over children in lesbian relationships. States in the United States tend to recognize the legal rights of the natural mother, but unless the mother's lesbian partner legally adopts the children, the partner has no legal rights over them. It seems that had the state recognized such rights, it would have become relatively easy for friends, baby-sitters, and other acquaintances of the mother also to lodge claims over the children. The cost to the state of adjudicating such disputes could then have become considerable.

[21] The specimens of one-of-a-kind commodities are identifiable, making them difficult to resell. For example, it is expensive for thieves to try to sell a one-of-a-kind

that if the costs of setting standards were to decline, and thus their use were to increase, the level of theft would also increase. Because, as argued later, the state has a comparative advantage in setting standards, when the cost of setting them falls, I predict that the scope of the state will increase. In addition to that direct effect, it will also increase to better protect individuals from the expected increase in theft occasioned by the increased use of standards.

THE ADJUDICATION OF DISPUTES

No disputes are anticipated at the time rights are delineated. Why do disputes arise, then, and how are they adjudicated? Disputes occur when people make competing claims over the same assets. An individual will concede ahead of time if he thinks his chance of winning a dispute is low. Disputes can arise because of parties' inconsistent estimates of the situation at hand. Each party presumably believes that he has a good chance to prevail. Because there can be no dispute at the time an agreement is negotiated, disputes develop only because of exogenous changes that lead to divergence between individuals' evaluations of their situations.

For instance, a river that has long been used to designate property boundaries may overflow and shift to a new course. Individuals may then be uncertain where the boundaries of their properties lie, and each may err in being too optimistic about the location of the border. As another example, the boundaries between two parcels of land tend to be marks or features on the ground's surface. The valued attributes of such properties may include underground water sources and foliage spanning across properties. The marks on the surface are unlikely to delineate these attributes clearly. There may have been no dispute when the line was first drawn because the value of the poorly delineated attributes was too little to matter. If the values of such attributes should increase, people may overestimate their chances of winning them and choose to compete for them. To the extent that the disputed rights lie under the state's jurisdiction, the parties may take their dispute to court. The settling of the dispute will result in clarifying the ownership of the assets.[22]

high-fashion item, because, other than the buyer of the original, anybody seen wearing it could be identified as the owner of stolen property. Making assets identifiable also raises the cost of forgery.

[22] In the process of settling their disputes, however, individuals expend resources in attempts to gain a larger share of the assets. I hypothesize that when choosing their

Parties will cease to be in dispute if the resolution of a dispute between another pair of transactors clearly applies to their case as well. The legal resolution of disputes is subject to scale economies in the delineation of assets that possess similar attributes. Disputes between different pairs of individuals may arise simultaneously because of changes in general conditions that affect them similarly. The resolution of a dispute can serve as a precedent for other disputes under the common law, and sometimes even expanding the coverage of statutory law. When made public, the resolutions of court-adjudicated disputes become precedents for other disputes, and the state can apply such rulings to similar disputes. The total cost of resolving an entire class of disputes, then, can be just a fraction of what it would have been if each had been resolved individually.

To illustrate, consider a region where the rights to groundwater in tenancy contracts had remained undelineated, as historically such water had been of little value. Because of recurring droughts, the market value of the groundwater has increased. Before new contracts are written to adjust to the change, disputes between tenants and landlords regarding ownership of the water may arise. A ruling on one such dispute, however, can be applied to all the tenancy agreements.

The resolution of one dispute may apply to other cases not only where uniformity of conditions is present but also where the state deliberately creates uniformity by imposing the appropriate restrictions on contracts. Prior to the imposed uniformity, each dispute had to be resolved on its own. Under uniform contracts, the resolution of one dispute amounts to delineating the rights in all similar cases. The parties whose rights are thus delineated are spared the expense of competing for them, and the state is spared the expense of adjudicating them.[23] Thus a state that mandates community property for all marriages denies couples the opportunity to make different contractual arrangements. That saves all couples

---

dispute-settling methods, individuals will favor the ones that will maximize the net value of their properties.

[23] The economies in resolving numerous individual disputes by adjudicating just one of them disappear when the disputes are combined in class-action suits. The disputants in class actions, in resolving their disputes, are expected to spend an amount commensurate with its *aggregate* value. This is a case where internalizing an externality *lowers* joint wealth.

Class action, however, can serve at least one useful function. It allows many small competitors who are harmed by a big one to combine their cases and make it worthwhile to pursue legal action even where no one individually could recover the litigation costs. Thanks to Timothy Dittmer for this observation.

the cost of competing for the rights that might have been disputed, and it saves the state the cost of adjudicating them.[24]

In some cases, the prior existence of the appropriate legal framework works to produce uniformity. In the United States, individuals can establish firms subject to a variety of legal models, such as the cooperative corporation, the limited partnership, and the limited-liability corporation. After choosing a model, individuals are, to an extent, free to modify it. The law under which they operate, however, specifies default terms and thus makes the rights involved clearer and the resolution of disputes easier.

A final aspect of the scale economies to adjudication concerns the care with which rights are delineated. As the number of assets with similar attributes increases, the state will gain further by more clearly delineating rights in the first place. These scale economies are available for the delineation and for dispute resolution by a third party, and, as indicated later, especially when the third party is the state. On the other hand, these economies are not readily available for self-enforced agreements.

PRICING ADJUDICATION SERVICES

How should the state finance its adjudication services? Efficiency considerations call for payments commensurate with the value or quality of the service. Individuals' direct offers would reflect their willingness to pay. Such payments would be efficient where rights were well delineated; they would not be efficient, however, for dispute resolution. In general, individuals are willing to pay for enhancing the value of their property. In the adjudication of disputes, a person might increase the value of his property by inducing the adjudicator to favor him at the other's expense. Such action would consume resources to effect transfer. That is why, in cases of dispute, willingness to pay is not a proper measure of the enhancement of joint value,[25] or, more accurately, why only the combined willingness to pay can measure the enhanced joint value.

We expect the charges for financing dispute-resolution mechanisms to have two components. One is direct, to be imposed on the parties to the adjudication and tied to its expected cost, though smaller than that cost.

---

[24] Allen (1990) suggests that the reason for the commonly observed state regulation of the marriage contract is that it makes it more uniform and thus cheaper to adjudicate.

[25] This may explain why bribes are prohibited.

The other is indirect, taking the form of a general property tax. We consider the two in turn.

The benefits from adjudication depend on the clarity of the adjudicated rights. The more clearly the third party delineates them, the higher the total value of the property. The marginal cost of added clarity is positive, and most likely rising. To maximize the net value of the adjudication, the two should be equated on the margin. It would be desirable to charge each party according to his marginal valuation. By the very nature of the problem, however, together the two disputants have erred in overestimating their gains. As stated, disputes arise only when the parties assess the situation at hand differently. If the parties had known how the property was going to be delineated, and thus its value to each of them, most likely they would not have been in dispute in the first place.

In the absence of side effects, or externalities, seemingly it would be most efficient to charge the parties (or just the plaintiff) a fee for access to the adjudication process – a fee equal on the margin to the cost of adjudicating one more dispute of the particular class of disputes. In that case, a fee equal to the adjudication cost would be in order. Side effects, however, are to be expected here. As mentioned, the adjudication of a particular dispute is likely to have the beneficial effect of reducing the net costs of other disputes. Thus, the expectation is that a fixed fee (or a fee structure) for the adjudication will be set at a level lower than the cost of adjudication and that, given the fee, the parties will decide whether or not it is worth their while to avail themselves of the service.

The property tax, to which we now turn, seems the right instrument for handling the side effects. Because of the public-good nature of dispute resolution, the value of a particular resolution extends beyond the particular case. Therefore, the adjudicator (i.e., the state) is expected to charge the parties to the actual adjudication only a fraction of the real cost of resolving their particular dispute.

The problem of financing dispute resolution is even more acute than that for other public goods. The resolution of a particular dispute benefits other parties in similar situations, because they then cease to be in dispute. Quite often, however, it is not easy even to identify these other parties. The financing problem can be finessed, however, by taking advantage of a property tax where such a tax is already in existence.[26]

---

[26] In Chapter 7, I argued that the proportionate property tax is efficient for financing protection expenditures. I now argue that for the reason here, unrelated to the earlier one, the same tax is efficient also for financing the judicial system.

As viewed here, the tax to finance delineation is to be superimposed on the existing property tax. That tax, as a rule, is proportional to the market value of the properties that an individual holds. Now, as a result of a court ruling on one dispute, the joint value of other holdings that will benefit from ceasing to be in dispute will rise. Because a property tax is already in use, the increase in the value of the particular properties that the court ruling affects will lead to increases in tax assessments and thus increases in tax revenue. This amounts to a seemingly efficient arrangement whereby those who benefit from the precedent will subsidize (through a court fee that is less than the court cost) those who choose to litigate. Because what is produced here is a public good, it is appropriate to finance it by a compulsory imposition (i.e., a tax).

The fact of property taxation combined with the scale economy to delineation can induce the state to increase the delineation of assets, especially generic ones. All specimens of generic goods, obviously, have the same measurable attributes. Court decisions regarding any specimen, then, will apply to all of them. Moreover, given the economy in delineation, we can expect more of their attributes to be delineated than will the attributes of comparable idiosyncratic goods. Better delineation of assets increases their market value. When assessments depend on the market value or exchange value of the assets, their better delineation will increase their assessed valuation and thereby the tax revenue the state will collect. The more generic, or less idiosyncratic, assets are, the higher their exchange value. As delineation is increased and as the legal system improves, we can expect that people will substitute away from idiosyncratic attributes to generic attributes. Such a switch will also lead to an increase in the tax base. A contemporary example of a significant increase in the tax base concerns the increase in women's participation in the labor market. The marketplace component of women's economic contribution is part of the tax base, whereas their contribution as homemakers is not.

Arbitration, as distinct from court adjudication, usually is used to resolve disputes whose resolutions are unlikely to have applications to other cases. Arbitration need not be entirely private; it can fall under state jurisdiction. Parties to contracts often stipulate the use of arbitration to settle disputes between them. When stipulated in a contract, arbitration is subject to state enforcement, because the entire contract is subject to such enforcement. Arbitration decisions, however, do not, as a rule, constitute precedents, and therefore the resolution in such a case does not become a public good, as it usually does when a dispute is resolved in court. For that reason, arbitration decisions are not subject to the scale economy that court decisions enjoy.[27] A direct implication of this argument is that whereas in cases of arbitration the parties will bear the full cost of each case, the fees in cases of legal adjudication will be tied to actual adjudication costs and, on average, will be *less* than those costs.

The fact that the state does not charge for its court costs is another reason why it tends not to delineate idiosyncratic assets legally. The state would not be able to recover the subsidy on court fees, as the resolution of disputes regarding such assets would have no bearing on other cases.

THE LEGAL ENVIRONMENT AND THE PERCEPTION OF IMPARTIALITY

The scale economies in adjudication are applicable only if individuals are able to identify disputes that are similar to each other. A major factor that seemingly makes disputes similar is that of "standards." Individuals' perceptions also have to do with the legal environment. The legal environment is discussed next; the applicability of standards is discussed in the next chapter.

To realize the gains from scale economies to adjudication, people, either directly or on advice of legal counsel, must have the same perception regarding which disputes the state will consider as similar. At least two factors affect such perceptions. One is individuals' awareness of the legal delineation of assets. The other is their trust in the impartiality of legal rulings.

Stable conditions and consistent past rulings make it easier to know what the current rulings are likely to be. In addition, such knowledge facilitates sorting properties into the appropriate legal categories and exploiting the accompanying scale economies. The state will gain, then, from consistent rulings and from adopting policies with a high likelihood of keeping the state stable. It will also gain from operating the courts

[27] See Bernstein (1992), however. Bernstein describes what amounts in practice to local autonomy in the diamond industry. The local autonomy is self-enforced. Dealers who join the association agree to the use of arbitration in case of disputes among them. The arbitration rulings are used as precedent there. Bernstein demonstrates that the rationale for the operation is that state law is not well suited to that industry. Although individuals cannot be prevented from bringing disputes to state courts, they may then lose their standing in the association.

openly and publicizing their rulings. This may explain why rule-of-law states place the particulars of disputes and court resolutions in the public domain.

A similar, though more subtle, effect on the scope of state operations concerns the ease of creating precedents. The easier the creation of precedents, the higher the value of a common legal system. Stable conditions also enhance precedent creation. When conditions become less stable, the value of legal precedent declines. I expect the scope of the state to decline then too.[28]

The creation of an environment of impartiality in legal rulings, also subject to scale economies, will increase the demand for the state's third-party services. A slanted ruling constitutes a transfer, or a "legal" confiscation. I expect people to spend resources both to influence and to avert such transfers. Moreover, if people perceive that the legal system is becoming less impartial, they will transact more of their agreements outside its jurisdiction, lowering the demand for its service. I expect, then, that the state will work to promote impartial adjudication, as well as the appearance of impartiality, or "fairness." The degree of impartiality, however, is unlikely to remain constant. For instance, protectors have discretion in how "arbitrarily" to exert their power (i.e., how much to adhere to the rule of law). The less secure they feel about retaining that power, the smaller their gain from impartiality, and I expect them to use their power more arbitrarily.

The ease of determining whether or not rulings are impartial will depend on how widely rulings apply. The wider the application, the easier it is for people to discern if rulings are impartial. The larger the set of affected individuals, then, the greater the economies in enforcing agreements impartially. The desire to enhance the perception of the fairness or impartiality of legal proceedings is another reason for conducting them in public.

The extent to which the state is a party to disputes is a rather different factor that seems to affect the perception of impartiality. The greater the state's involvement in an enterprise, the more it is a residual claimant to its operations. When subjects have disputes with its enterprises, the state stands to gain by favorable rulings. People will be suspicious of the impartiality of the adjudication mechanism that the state operates

---

[28] Stable conditions are conducive to technical change, and, ceteris paribus, in periods of high growth brought about by technological change, the scope of the state is expected to increase.

(especially in dictatorial states), since it is the residual claimant to these enterprises. When the state spins off enterprises into private hands, it ceases to be a residual claimant to their operations. Subjects who are in dispute with these spun-off enterprises will be more willing then to submit the disputes to state adjudication. The more advanced is the rule of law, the higher will be the state's net income from adjudicating contract disputes. We expect, then, that as the rule of law becomes more advanced, the number of enterprises to which the state is a residual claimant will become smaller.

CRIMINAL JUSTICE

A primary function of civil justice is to extend the state's delineation and policing of rights by issuing and enforcing court rulings. In this section I argue that criminal rulings regarding crimes in which there are victims, and perhaps regarding victimless crimes as well, can also enhance delineation in general.

The state delineates rights by enacting laws and imposing regulations. It classifies violations of the legal delineation as "crimes." Crimes, then, are the violations of the rules the state *has chosen* to impose. Actions not in such violation are not crimes. For example, suppose that for some time person B has been the sole fisherman in a particular stretch of a river, which has made him the economic owner of the fish there. The state, however, then stipulates that anyone who catches fish there can keep them. Even though the stretch has long been under B's control, the state does not choose to assign him legal title to it. Person C, who attempts to catch fish there, then, does not become a "criminal," because the state will not deem his action a crime.

As stated earlier, two factors seem to prevent the state from delineating legal ownership over some of the assets that individuals value. One is the cost of demonstrating encroachment on one's property to a third party. The other is the high cost that other individuals would incur in assessing the value of one's idiosyncratic assets.

To illustrate the encroachment problem, consider rape. Historically the law usually has been clear that rape is a crime that violates the rights of the victim. In most societies in most periods, however, the rape of a wife by her husband was a glaring exception to this rule. One might claim that in societies where wives were the legal property of their husbands, wives did not have rights, and therefore legally husbands could do whatever they wanted. Also, rape within marriage usually was not considered a crime even in societies where wives did have legal standing. However, even in societies that did not recognize their legal rights, wives still must have had certain *economic rights*, and thus the term "rape" still applies.[29] Why, then, had within-marriage rape not been a crime? One explanation is that such rape is extremely difficult to prove in court. To protect their within-marriage agreements, then, the wife in particular, and both partners in general, had to resort to self-enforced methods.

I turn now to idiosyncratic assets. Such assets often are not delineated legally. The state, then, will not classify as crimes any encroachments on such assets or on the idiosyncratic attributes of assets. If there is a decrease in the cost of standardizing what previously was idiosyncratic, we can expect the state to bring these assets more fully under its jurisdiction. Because encroachment on assets that are not legally delineated is not a crime, and encroachment on those that are legally delineated is a crime, we can expect criminal activity to increase when assets are newly legally delineated. This is partly due to the change in the classification of what constitutes "crime." However, as will be elaborated in Chapter 14, a substantive force is also at work here. Thieves are more likely to steal standardized assets than any similar idiosyncratic assets, because, relative to their valuation by their owners, the former are more highly valued by thieves than are the latter.[30]

As suggested earlier, one reason why generic or standardized assets are better delineated than are idiosyncratic assets concerns the scale economies in the delineation of the former. Standards are set up to be applied to classes of assets. In the case of criminal activities, the publicizing of infractions and of penalties is also subject to scale economies, because would-be thieves are thereby apprised of the standards that define the crime and of the penalties they may have to endure. This aspect of crime prevention tends to induce transfer of protection responsibility from individual owners, or even from local protectors, to protectors who are prepared to protect all assets falling under the standard. Only

---

[29] I am under the impression that most societies, even those that seemingly did not grant wives any legal rights, deemed the murder of a wife a crime. Where that was the case, then, it is not true that wives totally lacked legal rights.

[30] Clothing items can be purchased "off the rack" or be custom-tailored. The former are more generic, and their measures, which tend to be standardized, are marked. The theft of off-the-rack clothes can be expected to bring thieves considerably higher sale prices relative to their original market prices than will theft of custom-made items.

the latter will fully internalize the effect of publicizing the criminal proceedings.

A final point regarding criminal justice concerns the net return from theft prevention. There are scale economies to delineating standardized assets, as well as to state protection of a class of assets that are not strictly uniform. On occasion, the cost of protecting a subclass of such assets may exceed its benefits. As a rule, to avoid loss of reputation, the state will honor its implicit obligation to protect these assets. However, where the reputation loss can be avoided, the state may attempt to exclude the subclass from the protected set.

The biblical treatment of gleanings seems a case in point, where the return to protection was low, and the enforcer was able to avoid it without loss of reputation. The case is as follows. The Jewish law prohibits landowners from reharvesting a field in order to recover the gleanings from first harvest. Rather, it requires that the gleanings be left for the poor. A rationale for this stipulation is as follows: The state, presumably, had committed to protect crops. Such protection is most valued as the crop nears maturity. At the time of the main harvest, the return from protection must substantially exceed its cost. The cost of protecting the gleanings is similar to that of protecting the main harvest, but the gain from that protection is rather small. The state, following the Jewish law, however, stipulated that the gleanings had to be left for the poor. In that way it exempted itself from protecting the gleanings, seemingly without loss to its reputation. Moreover, by explicitly granting the poor the right to the gleanings, their incentive to steal from the main crop was decreased, thus lowering the cost of protecting the rest of the crop. The constraint on the gleanings, then, enhances the economic rights to the main harvest.[31]

RIGHTS DELINEATION BY OTHER THIRD PARTIES

Any third party that agrees to enforce agreements must stipulate and commit to what it will enforce and what it will not. This constitutes delineation. The rights delineated by a third party not using force are not legal rights; by definition, legal rights can be delineated only by the state. But the analogous economic role of all third parties, discussed in earlier chapters, applies to delineation too.

---

[31] Jewish law also prohibits the harvesting of field edges. The explanation for the restriction on gleanings applies here too.

Indeed, we expect that like the state, non-state third parties will engage in delineation primarily where there exist scale economies to delineation. For instance, the laws enforced by religious organizations apply generally. Some of these laws relate to agreements such as the marriage agreement, and religious institutions provide their members a common format for this agreement. Consider, in this light, the following hypothetical situation: A new product that affects fertility is developed. A husband and wife, both practicing Catholics, cannot agree between themselves whether or not taking advantage of the new product is in accordance with Catholic doctrine. They go to the church to adjudicate the dispute. The ruling, especially if by a high authority, applies to all Catholics. This is an example where scale economies to delineation are applicable also to third parties not using violence.

Here, too, the main difference between the state and other third parties seems to be quantitative. The state's edge is in delineation of the rights to commodities that change hands often; it engages in delineation where the scale economies to it are most pronounced. Other third parties seldom delineate rights to commodities.[32] The services they delineate tend not to change hands and therefore are not subject to the same scale economies in delineation that commodities are subject to.

PAIRING INFORMATIONAL REQUIREMENTS AND MEANS OF ENFORCEMENT

Adjudication of disputes requires both information and means of enforcement. In this section I suggest that the two are closely related. In general, third parties set both the standards of evidence and the severity of penalties to be imposed. Note that in the United States the standards of evidence required for criminal trials are higher than for civil trials, and the permitted penalties are more severe in the former than in the latter. Criminal conviction requires evidence of guilt "beyond a reasonable doubt" and can bring severe penalties, such as imprisonment or even execution. The information requirement for civil convictions is less rigorous, just a "preponderance of the evidence," and the penalties imposed tend to be less severe, conviction bringing only a monetary fine.

Let us now compare the state's third-party enforcement with third-party enforcement by other organizations; we restrict the discussion,

---

[32] One exception is the practice in the diamond industry described by Bernstein (1992).

however, to organizations that operate within states and are controlled or regulated by them. A major characteristic of non-state third-party enforcement is the relatively low standard of evidence required for adjudication, as in the cases of some religious institutions. Another major characteristic, both in rule-of-law states and in autocracies, is that the state does not allow non-state third-party organizations to use physical force as a means of enforcement.[33] Those who control the physical power tend to prohibit others from the use of such power in their adjudications. Seemingly, both kinds of regimes impose the restriction in order to reduce the chance of a takeover. The reason for restricting the severity of the permitted penalties, which applies primarily to rule-of-law states, is quite different.

In general, individuals agree in advance to be penalized if they violate the rules they have agreed to follow. But as those possessing the power to penalize may abuse it, the individuals that agree to be penalized may also require safeguards against abuse. One such safeguard is that the more severe the permitted penalties, the more stringent the procedures and the higher the quality of the evidence that must be presented. Conversely, the more casual the procedures and evidence a third party employs, the less severe the allowed penalties. To the extent that individuals organize and empower their third-party enforcer, which is the case with some religious institutions, those individuals presumably did not grant their enforcer the use of physical power for enforcement, thus limiting the severity of the permitted penalties.[34] Where casual methods in adjudicating disputes are used, enforcement by the use of force or the threat to use force is not allowed, even if it would be the low-cost method of imposing penalties. This line of reasoning may explain why in rule-of-law states certain "disputes" such as murder or rape are adjudicated by the state, and private organizations are not allowed to adjudicate such cases.[35] This reasoning on why a state may constrain itself, however, does not apply to autocracies.

---

[33] Where the state and the church have been cooperating in the adjudication of dispute, however, the state often has allowed the church to use physical force for enforcing its decisions.

[34] In the United States, the common law prohibits religious groups from suing people for exiting (Posner, 1996, p. 185).

[35] Private police are quite common in many rule-of-law states. Private police, however, possess much less power than do state police. For example, private police "may not arrest people and often have no greater enforcement power than ordinary citizens," "Policing for Profit," *The Economist*, April 19, 1997, p. 27. See also Shleifer and Vishny (1993).

States under different types of regimes tend to use different standards of evidence to adjudicate disputes. Although rule-of-law states do not use uniform standards for all adjudications, they generally restrict themselves to the high end of the range of standards. For instance, in the United States, both in civil cases and in criminal cases, high standards are used. Autocratic states tend to use much lower standards. When the latter prosecute individuals, sometimes for "crimes against the state," rumors often are admitted as evidence. As noted, autocratic states do not allow private adjudicators to use force. The domain these states claim for their courts, however, seems wider than that claimed in rule-of-law regimes, so they tend to adjudicate a wider range of disputes. "Fundamentalist" states, for instance, often adjudicate marital disputes that seldom fall under judicial jurisdiction in rule-of-law states. Moreover, for similar infringements, autocratic states tend to impose more severe penalties on individuals convicted by their courts than do rule-of-law states.

CONCLUSIONS

A protector protecting two or more neighbors is in a position to delineate their common boundaries so as to reduce disputes and thereby maximize the net joint value of their properties. Neighbors may steal from each other, and theft is a wealth-reducing activity. A protector may impose restrictions on the neighbors to induce them to abstain from theft.

It is not economical for protectors to protect "everything." They have to spell out, then, what they will protect from thieves, and what from foreign states. What they agree to protect are "legal rights." Disputes among clients can still arise. Protectors become judges when adjudicating disputes, and they become the police when enforcing their decisions. Thus a protector protecting two or more individuals is the founder of legal institutions.

Adjudication services are subject to scale economies, as rulings can be applied generally when different groups of individuals make similar agreements and their causes of dispute are similar. By imposing standards, by offering standard legal forms (limited-liability company, condominium, and marriage), and by mandating uniformity for some types of contracts, the protector and his clients can better realize these economies. Dispute resolution is a public good, and I expect the fees imposed to finance that service to take the form of a compulsory tax.

Because the rights that delineation enhances lead to increased property values, a property tax is the appropriate tax for the service.

The comparative advantage of violence-using protectors is in protecting contract agreements, especially standardized ones. The protection of idiosyncratic assets falls mostly on their owners. The value of such assets to their owner is difficult for others to ascertain, and thus only the owner knows what the appropriate level of protection is. Moreover, he is likely to have an advantage in protecting them. I predict that to the extent that assets become more generic, the role of contracts, and with that the scope of the state, will increase. Moreover, generic assets are more attractive to thieves than are idiosyncratic ones. I also predict, then, that as standards become more common, so will theft, and so will the state's effort to combat it. In some cases the cost of protection may be so high that the state will impose restrictions on market activities, and even ban certain actions.

10

The State's Enhancement of Market Trade

CONDITIONS FOR LEGAL DELINEATION

In this chapter, probing further into the nature of legal rights, I first ask this: What characterizes assets that are exchanged by contracts, that is, by agreements enforced by the state? To qualify as contracts, agreements must satisfy certain requirements imposed by the state; they must not violate any law, they must involve quid pro quo, and so forth. In addition, in some cases the state may stipulate the registration of contracts and of properties. An agreement that satisfies these requirements is, therefore, a "legal" contract (though not necessarily a written document).

As long as contracts meet these requirements, the state does not take an active part in determining what goes into them. If the state is to enforce what the transactors choose to delineate, the transactors must provide sufficient information to enable the state to adjudicate in case of dispute. In addition, for the third party to be able to adjudicate disputes about the performance regarding an asset that is changing hands, the asset delineated in the contract must be matched to the recipient. The ease of matching will depend on the nature of the asset; matching unique assets is easier than matching generic ones. Among other attributes, the former can be more readily authenticated than the latter. The state may engage in authenticating ownership, but ownership can be authenticated by other means too. In the case of land, an ownership registry that matches individuals to parcels of land is usually maintained by the state. Authentication by a party other than the state also occurs – for instance, where appliance manufacturers serially number the appliances they produce, and then register the buyers. Ownership registration can reduce disputes and help settle them when they occur. The advantage of the state lies in its presumed neutrality. One will find, then, that people use state registry where neutrality is highly valued.

It is important to reiterate the distinction between legal rights and economic rights and to recognize that the presence of conventional legal rights does not necessarily imply that economic rights are well defined. It may appear, for example, that registering land will guarantee that property rights to it (as well as property rights in general) will be well defined. Whereas the state may enforce the rights to land that contracts stipulate, these are not necessarily all the economic rights associated with land. Consider an area where irrigation is essential and water can be pumped from an underground pool. The size of the pool substantially exceeds that of the optimal plot when used for agricultural production. In that case, legal delineation of the various plots does not seem sufficient to allow efficient exploitation of the land. When individuals own the plots they cultivate, it is difficult to prevent them from using the water excessively. Though one would not expect them to eliminate over-exploitation of water, they may reduce the overexploitation by using long-term relations to supplement state enforcement. Such an arrangement underscores the notion that legal delineation by itself is unlikely to yield the efficient outcome.

Alternatively, a single person may own the entire surface area above the pool. The problem with excessive use of the water then disappears. But in that case the land may require more labor services than the owner can supply himself. He can employ others by paying them wages, but that necessarily induces shirking. The employer, as discussed earlier, becomes a third party to his employees. Under this agreement, too, then, the legal delineation of the land is supplemented by the non-state enforcement that the landowner supplies to his employed workers.

What is it that is being registered? A piece of land can be described by its unique location. When the state takes charge of land registry, registering land with the state under a person's name constitutes matching a particular land parcel to a particular person. The registration of various intellectual rights and of brand names automatically yields unique matching, and the registration of individuals (birth certificates, voting lists) consolidates their ownership over themselves. Such registration makes "identity theft" more costly and thus less attractive to anyone who would seek to take on another person's identity to be used in illegal transactions such as drug sales.

Certain specialized resources are needed to maintain a registry. Literacy, lasting written documents, and the capacity for document storage are some of the resources that facilitate record-keeping. Improvements in such bureaucratic attributes tend to facilitate the state's delineation of land and of other assets; these improvements, therefore, tend to increase the scope of the state.

It is problematic to ascertain the ownership of assets that are not easily distinguishable from one another. Some can be made distinguishable: Manufactured items can be numbered serially, and cattle branded uniquely. Both types of assets can be registered under the owners' names. The exchange of such delineated assets is straightforward; the initial owner simply transfers the registration to a new owner. Given that the state maintains registration records, it also performs the registration transfer, thereby facilitating third-party enforcement.

Some commodities are difficult to identify directly. Direct identification of specimens of commodities such as wheat, bricks, or sheets of paper is impractical; the cost of identification relative to their unit value would be too high. Identifying gold is not economical because marks on gold are easy to alter or to obliterate. Such items, however, can be identified indirectly by specifying their locations and describing their generic, standardized attributes. When such a commodity exists at a legally delineated site, its location matches it to a person – the legal owner of the site.[1] The exclusivity of the site's ownership confers the same exclusivity to the commodity located there.[2]

A commodity can be viewed as generic if it is a member of a class that can be sufficiently and economically described in an exchange agreement and if no resources have to be expended to sort among members of the class. Such commodities, then, can be exchanged by a contract that describes their physical characteristics and the locations of their origin and destination. The contract can be executed using the state to ascertain that the provisions of the contract have been met. The state is not necessarily a third party to the exchange of every generic commodity; the exchange can be enforced by some other third party or by a self-enforcing mechanism such as the seller's reputation. For most low-value retail transactions, the use of the courts to resolve disputes is not economical; these transactions usually employ the seller's reputation for

---

[1] This also applies to individuals who live in rented apartments and to tenants renting farms. For the duration of the rental contract, the tenant is the legal owner of some of the property's attributes, especially of the non-built-in contents of the property.

[2] This may explain the intense effort to delineate rights to land (and why the homeless find it difficult to keep any kind of property).

enforcement. When commodities become easier to delineate in contracts, or when the value of easy-to-delineate assets increases, we can expect the scope of the state to increase too.

ROADS AND MARKETS

The state possesses various tools with which it can promote contract trade. In this section, I discuss the provision of public roads and of markets. In the next, I consider the provision and setting of standards.

In order to trade, individuals not only must possess goods desired by others but also must be able to identify each other, communicate their preferences, delineate the goods to be traded, come to terms, and physically deliver the goods. Legal delineation facilitates ownership transfer, but access to the goods and to information about them is not automatic. Trade can be exceedingly costly when such access is difficult. Suppose that B and D have goods desired by each other, but that C's land separates them. They may find it expensive to trade, or even to become aware of the trade potential, unless C cooperates with them. These costs become even higher when the potential traders have to reach across the properties of many owners.

A road that abuts the individuals' holdings will enable them to reach each other without traversing the properties of other parties. Indeed, a road system can connect a vast number of individuals into a single network. As Ellickson (1993) points out, the individuals whose properties abut a road need to secure the cooperation of only the road owner to reach all others abutting it. The larger the number of individuals a road connects, the greater its value to most of them. Until recently, roads were also essential for communication among such individuals. However, the radio and other communication devices capable of leapfrogging intervening properties have greatly reduced the communication value of roads.[3]

A road network is useful for connecting a large number of users. The other side of the coin is the low likelihood of repeated interactions among the users when their number is large. Most of them, then, will choose to trade among themselves by contract. The state has an advantage in providing roads and in adjudicating disputes that arise from use of them. Because it stands to gain from the road system, one can expect the state

---

[3] For the same reasons, the introduction of these means of communication also reduces the value of third-party enforcement by the state.

to obtain easements for it, delineate rights to it, protect its users, and apply its third-party enforcement for adjudicating disputes that arise from using it.[4] In the absence of major physical obstacles, it is obviously advantageous to make roads straight. Securing the appropriate easements is not always simple. The Romans, because of the vast size of their empire, had more to gain from good roads than did their successors, and the Romans did build straighter roads.[5]

Designating a central space to serve as a market is likely to further promote trade. What characterizes a "market" is the free access to it and the common-property nature of its space. Making the market common property brings new benefits and lowers a whole array of users' costs: costs associated with discovering trading partners; collecting information generated by the competition that accompanies centralization; bargaining, as the bilateral monopoly that is apt to be prevalent elsewhere is avoided;[6] protecting against the theft and assault that often result in the absence of such concentrations of individuals (though protection costs may be raised by theft such as that by pickpockets); and on-site resolution of disputes.

The market owner can be expected to work to further these cost-reducing factors, since he will thereby be able to increase the charges he imposes. For instance, the owner may restrict the use of the market to only daylight hours, a restriction that can enhance exclusivity and economize on the cost of protection.

Centralization of trade has another important feature: It makes standardization easier and thus tends to increase trade by contract. Trade by contract is especially valuable to individuals who meet only sporadically, and such meetings take place routinely in marketplaces. The protector, then, is expected to encourage the development of marketplaces. He can gain further by connecting markets to the public road system and helping to regulate the roads.[7]

---

[4] Most modern states provide roads directly. Historically it was more common for the state to require local authorities to provide and maintain roads. The provision of private roads was seldom successful. On the other hand, marketplaces, to be discussed next, were largely provided privately.

[5] As Tim Dittmer has pointed out, the Romans probably also had more power of eminent domain, as well as better engineers.

[6] Both here and in general, an institution with exclusive regulatory power seems necessary to effect competition in the textbook sense. In the case described here, a *single* person or organization has exclusive control over the market. The textbook "market" shares this feature (though it is seldom recognized as such).

[7] After the Norman conquest, England was divided among the king and his supporters. Most towns (i.e., trading centers) became part of the king's holdings, rather

Interaction is the main purpose of public space, and open access accommodates it. Easier interaction, however, competes with privacy. Similarly, whereas the delineation of rights allows exclusive use, markets are valued for enhancing interactions, which tend to be in conflict with certain aspects of exclusivity. Open access puts into the public domain some attributes of the people who occupy the public space. In the attempt to reduce the cost of communication, it causes some rights to be attenuated. These include the right not to be spoken to or not to be looked at without permission.

STANDARDS

In order to delineate an asset or a commodity, it is necessary to measure it. Exhaustive measurement would erase all uncertainty about the asset. Measurement, however, cannot be exhaustive,[8] and alternative ways for characterizing an asset exist. For instance, liquids such as cooking oil or gasoline can be measured by weight or by volume, at a current or constant temperature, and with or without a measure for the amount of impurities. If the measures of different specimens of a commodity are not perfectly correlated, they are not entirely compatible with each other. It is difficult to avoid confusion regarding which measures are actually used in particular agreements. However, if only one method of measurement is in use, people can be more confident as to what the exchange agreement is about.

Exchange is easier to enforce if all transactors use the same method of measurement. The state tends to benefit from such enforcement because, per transaction, it reduces its cost of adjudication, and its tax revenue will increase if the base for its tax is the value of the transactions it enforces. The state, therefore, may stipulate the exclusive use of one particular measurement method. However, then the opportunity to specify alternative measurement methods in contracts is precluded, even where there might be reason to prefer them. The more the flexibility is valued, the less the gain from uniformity and therefore from

than part of the holdings of the tenants in chief who were his supporters. The reason may be that keeping the towns under royal control made it easier to connect towns to the state's communication network than if the towns had been under the control of the individual tenants in chief.

[8] The attempt to fully comprehend an exhaustive measurement would surely exhaust its student.

state-enforced contracts. The less the gain from state enforcement, the smaller the state's scope.[9]

Repeated applications of the same measures and the same underlying units of measurement are what accommodates standardization and produces standardized specimens. Standardized commodities are generic commodities. The more standardized that traded commodities and services are, the easier it is to exchange them by contract. In addition, the availability of currency greatly facilitates exchange in general, and contract exchange in particular. Ease of measure and ease of transfer, as well as wide recognition, are the main attributes of a commodity that serves as currency. The standardized nature of currency reduces the need to use difficult-to-measure commodities that are obtained in exchange only to be transferred to third, and perhaps additional, parties.

Both units of measure and the standardized attributes of currencies are public goods. Once established, they can be applied repeatedly at no added cost. Whereas they are costly to produce, charging for their use, whether or not it is "desirable," is problematic. Standards would not be implemented under the textbook perfect competition. No competitor could survive if he incurred a cost to produce a standard that, given the zero marginal cost of applying it, he would have to provide free of charge. If they are to operate profitably, the producers of standards must be granted exclusive power over them. Uniform standards can be formulated by industry-wide organizations, as is frequently the practice in the United States. Similarly, statewide organizations can issue a uniform currency, and they must have the power to enforce uniformity and collect sufficient fees to cover their costs. For courts to enforce contracts using a standard, there must be an exclusive source stating exactly what the standard is. This ties contract enforcement to the provision of a public good by the state or by its agent.

In the absence of organizations with the appropriate power, providers with some exclusive power may nevertheless privately provide standards and currency. Because no one has full-fledged exclusive power, however, multiple measuring systems and several currencies may have to coexist. However, because, to begin with, property rights to standards are likely to lie in the public domain, resources will be expended in the competition to appropriate them. It is not even clear that the best systems would

[9] The effects of standards on the size of the state are discussed both in the next chapter and in Chapter 12.

eventually prevail. In any case, in numerous instances experience seems inconsistent with the expectation that one system, whether or not it is the best, will quickly prevail. As exemplified by the enduring bewildering multiplicity of units of weight in England, the trend toward using one system is very slow. Absent uniformity, when disputes erupt, the courts will find it costly to determine precisely what the parties agreed to. The difficulty is compounded when, as is often the case, some units of measure are defined in terms of others.

The state may stipulate that it will recognize only certain units used in agreements. That is, the state will not enforce agreements or parts of agreements based on other units of measure. The state may directly undertake, or franchise, the task of establishing uniform weights and measures and issuing a uniform currency.[10] By establishing such units, it lowers the cost of delineating rights in contracts. When exchange parties take advantage of these in their contracts, disputes are less likely to occur, and when they do occur they will be easier to adjudicate. By taking charge of these tasks, the state lowers the cost of trade by contract.[11] It seems that imposing taxes on the use of its services (i.e., on contract exchange) is the efficient way for the state to cover its costs. Note that individuals can avoid the tax by forming other kinds of agreements. Their gain from exchanges they choose to conduct by contract presumably exceeds the tax.

Deliberately making commodities that conform to uniform standards is valuable in reducing the grounds for dispute. The advantage that uniformity affords for commodities such as bricks and for commodity pairs such as screws and bolts, and electric sockets and plugs, is clear.[12] Less obvious, though perhaps not less important, is the greater ease that standardization of commodities brings to contracting. Consider the English

[10] Lane (1977) illustrates the difficulty of maintaining currency standards even by a state. He describes Venice's experience in maintaining a uniform currency in the thirteenth and fourteenth centuries. Venice was extraordinarily stable, and foremost among its interests was accommodating trade. Nevertheless, it issued several not entirely compatible currencies and even used seemingly easy-to-confuse names for them. Moreover, each of the currencies tended to depreciate with the use and clipping of the coins. Compounding the difficulties was the change in the value of silver relative to gold, both serving as bases for its currency.

[11] It is not clear to me what determines whether the state will itself produce standards (or, for that matter, public roads, or any other commodity whose production it finances) or franchise that to private operators. The resolution of this problem does not seem germane to the main concern here.

[12] England's convergence to uniform electric sockets and plugs has also been very slow.

medieval regulations to standardize the capacity of wine containers and to make the width of cloth uniform (Moore, 1985, pp. 132–3) and, as contemporary examples, the stipulated minimum fat content of ice cream and the safety standards enforced in construction. When commodities must conform to standards, transacting in them becomes easier, because the parties and the courts know more clearly what they are expected to give and to receive. Moreover, the more intensive the use of standards, the greater the gain from defining the standards themselves more clearly. As with the identification of commodities, however, the more that diversity is valued, the higher the cost of mandated uniformity. We expect, for example, that as diversity in the width of bolts of cloth becomes more valued, the state is less likely to retain the uniform standard, and thus its scope will become smaller.

One implication of the hypothesized effect of the scale economies to settling disputes is that, ceteris paribus, within a state people will tend to specialize in raising a small number of crops and in producing a small number of products. These crops and products will tend to be standardized, and thus the number of varieties actually produced will be relatively small. The reason is that as standards are applied on a larger scale, contracts become more attractive, and the larger the state, the greater the effect. To illustrate, consider two neighboring independent states initially specializing in two different crops. Because of an exogenous innovation, a new single crop has become suitable for both. As the two adopt the new crop, they are more likely to merge and operate under a single third-party enforcer, since more rulings will then apply to their combined areas. Indeed, they are also likely to further expand the scope of the crop to take advantage of the lowered cost of exchanging it by contract. By the same token, if, in spite of the scale economies to a single crop, a new crop suitable only to part of a state is introduced, that part will be likely to turn into a separate state.[13]

MAPS AND THE DELINEATION OF LAND

The use of maps and the use of standards have a common element. Consider the effect of the invention of maps on the delineation of landholdings, as well as on state size. When land's main attribute is its surface, specifying its location satisfies the delineation requirement. Before maps

---

[13] Medieval Germany seems to provide an attractive testing ground for this hypothesis. It contained many states with populations that seemingly were not ethnically diverse, and its terrain did not have substantial natural barriers.

were introduced, delineation required a description of the physical features of a parcel of land, features that were not easily changeable. The physical features used for delineation could be natural, such as rivers, or man-made, such as hedges and stone fences. In areas where land was identified by its physical features, local enforcement would have been adequate. Individuals would have been aware whether or not others had encroached on their holdings, and neighbors could attest to the borders of different holdings.

In other kinds of areas, where maps would be required to identify boundaries, a more central authority would have had an advantage in the delineation. The introduction of maps was of no great consequence where it was already easy to delineate borders. It was of greater importance where such delineation was difficult, as maps made such delineation easier. Moreover, it is relatively easy to standardize the delineation criteria when maps are used. I expect the scale economies in delineating land and in settling land disputes to favor states that encompass the entirety of such areas, and this implies large states where these areas are large.

Maps by themselves are not sufficient for delineation. Also required is a recognized method of clearly indicating on maps individuals' landholdings, as well as the ability to demonstrate their authenticity to the courts. The latter will be aided by the state's maintenance of such records. The ability to document ownership will make transferability easier as well. Consider areas where the testimony of members of the community was required to confirm ownership. In such areas, the more frequently was a property subdivided or transferred, the greater was the difficulty of proving its ownership. Disputes would have been more likely then. The attempt to reduce the cost of disputes may have been the reason for the rather common practice of prohibiting, or at least heavily regulating, land transfer. The introduction of low-cost documentary proof of ownership may have been the cause for removing the restrictions on ownership transfer.[14]

SCALE ECONOMIES TO STANDARDS AND THE EXPANSION OF THE STATE

States are in a position to mandate standards for the contracts they are ready to enforce. Mandatory standards, however, reduce diversity.

[14] See Ellickson (1993).

Sources of dispute, as well as protection needs, are diverse and often are not easily amenable to standardized treatment. In states that have chosen to merge, we can expect that mandated standards will enhance the delineation of rights where individuals' particular practices in both states had been uniform. On the other hand, where such practices had been idiosyncratic to each of the merging states, the impact of resolving one dispute on the resolution of other disputes will be slight because of the absence of uniform standards. Where uniform standards are imposed, delineation in cases in which use of the old standard is disallowed will be weakened.[15]

For example, in some arid African regions, rights to water sources had traditionally been delineated, whereas rights to land had not. This is not surprising given the vital importance of water there. Some African states have adopted (perhaps at the urging of international organizations) the "modern" practice of delineating land rights to the neglect, or at least partial neglect, of water rights. This alteration seems to have lowered the net value of the combined rights.[16] When legal titles to land in these areas are given to individuals or groups, the chance is high that these new holdings will not coincide with the previous holdings based on water rights. We can expect that people will spend resources to increase their share of the available water, as well as to enhance the value of their landholdings, under the new rules, and also to influence the choices of new rules to their advantage. However, where the value of such arid areas is small relative to land values in the rest of the state, the imposition of the new standard is not necessarily wasteful as long as only *one* standard is adopted.

More generally, the imposition of uniform standards on diverse groups will result in some destruction of wealth and, indeed, may constitute an act of confiscation. Consequently, that tends to be a source of friction or dispute between such groups and between them and the state. The greater the initial diversity, the greater the cost of standardizing the rules. The greater the similarity in the physical resources of adjacent

---

[15] One possible reason for imposing uniform standards is to enhance an objective such as "national cohesion." However, I am unable to analyze such objectives.

[16] The statement is sometimes made that where rights to land are not well defined, neither are property rights in general. As applied to arid regions in Africa, especially those where rights to water are well defined, the assertion is not well taken. There is no reason to single out the rights to land as superior to other rights. In areas such as England and the eastern United States, rights to land are well defined. In these areas the rights to water are only loosely defined, but this is due not to any inherent importance of land but rather to the abundance of water there.

areas, the less the friction due to imposed uniformity, and the more likely it will be that they will become parts of a single state.

States that choose to merge may decide to meld only the practices the groups share, leaving the others to local jurisdictions. This is the rationale behind Riker's (1987) federalist argument, and it constitutes another reason for local autonomy, besides that of the increase in efficiency that autonomy may bring about, as discussed in Chapter 6. The "local" autonomy need not be territorial; for example, different religions or different industries may be given some autonomy.[17] The desire to avoid placing rights in the public domain may explain, then, why states with diverse religious groups often leave the jurisdiction over family law to religious organizations, as has been common in the Islamic world. Local autonomy, however, does not entirely eliminate the potential for friction. Third-party enforcement of agreements that fall within a small locality is confined to the local jurisdiction. Contracting across local jurisdictions on matters of local jurisdiction is not possible then.[18] For example, in Israel only the locally autonomous religious organizations that are approved by the state have the right to conduct legal marriages. Lacking, then, is a jurisdiction for marriage contracts between individuals of different faiths. Such individuals may resort to a self-enforced relationship, but its value may be considerably less than the value of such relationships enforced by the state.

SUMMARY

Although the state takes on itself the responsibility to enforce contracts between private entities, typically it is not aware of their contents until asked to adjudicate disputes surrounding them. Because, as a rule, adjudication is subsidized, the state must discourage its excessive use. It does so by requiring the registration of certain transactions and by imposing such restrictions as quid pro quo, thereby discouraging the formation of dispute-prone contracts.

The state has a strong incentive to encourage the construction of public roads and public markets. It also can benefit from creating standards and mandating their use. Roads are useful not only for transportation but also for communication among people who are otherwise separated by the holdings of others; the roads enable all those abutting

---

[17] Bernstein (1992) discusses autonomy in the diamond industry in the United States.
[18] Other aspects of local autonomy are discussed in Chapter 13.

them to reach one another. Similarly, markets accommodate interactions among all those attending them. Given the large number of individuals involved, their interactions are unlikely to be based on long-term relations. The state, however, can provide them its protection and third-party enforcement of their contracts.

Exchange by contract requires measurement of the attributes of the exchanged commodities. Such measurement is costly, but this cost can be lowered by standardization when applied on a large scale. Standardization also lowers litigation costs, because it makes clearer what parties have agreed on. Standards, as well as the uniformity of currency, are public goods that lie in the public domain unless the state delineates exclusive rights over them. It is also difficult to charge for their use. We can expect the state to participate in the formation of standards and sometimes to mandate their use in contracts. Indeed, the state may require that commodities be produced to uniform standards. Like standards, maps provide for clearer delineation, especially when land is "generic" and can be delineated on a large scale. Mandating standards is not necessarily beneficial, however. For instance, although safety standards in construction make it clearer what the parties have agreed upon, the opportunity to deviate from the standard is forfeited, even when deviation would generate a joint net gain. When states merge, perhaps to take advantage of the scale economies to standards, we can expect that local autonomy will be granted where diversity is highly valued.

II

The Size and Scope of the State

As argued earlier, the size of the state as well as its scope will depend primarily on two sets of scale factors: protection and third-party enforcement. Because I do not have much to contribute to the topic of economies to protection, I touch it only briefly. I then elaborate more fully on the economies to third-party enforcement, arguing that governing on behalf of its clients, the rule-of-law state will pursue activities in which it has a comparative advantage, rather than using sheer "power." The state has a comparative advantage in contract enforcement. State protection is especially useful for impersonal exchange, and for that reason it is complementary to contract enforcement. Contract enforcement is subject to scale economies. In the penultimate section of this chapter, I argue that the reason certain empires were created was to form a large area subject to a single ultimate enforcer in order to take advantage of these economies.

SCALE ECONOMIES TO PROTECTION

The economies of scale to protection seem to affect mostly the size rather than the scope of the state. They consist of simple economies of scale and of the gain from consolidation to internalize what otherwise would be external effects of protection. The dominant scale economies seem to arise in operations against outsiders.[1] One example of scale economies is where a large force can overwhelm a small one at a low cost to the large force. That probably would be the case in a battle where the battleground was in open terrain. Another example is that of a radar instal-

---

[1] It seems reasonable to consider as "outsiders" those individuals who reside beyond the area encompassed by the scale economies to protection.

lation that covers a territory encompassing the holdings of many individuals.[2] Economies of scale to internal protection are also available, but seem to be less extensive than those to external protection. If so, the full effects of the economies to internal protection are likely to be exhausted before those to external protection, and in that case scale economies to internal protection will not affect state size.

Effective protection of one person's property may call for placing protection devices and exerting protection effort on the properties of other individuals. For instance, it may be more economical to protect a property lying beyond a mountain pass by protecting the pass rather than protecting the property itself. Contracting between the owner of the pass and the owner of the property to be protected may be expensive. That cost is likely to be still higher when the lands of many individuals living beyond the pass need protection, especially when exclusion is difficult. These problems, however, are relatively easy to resolve if a single individual (backed by a collective-action mechanism) can arrange for protection of all those significantly affected by the external effects. The larger the area covered by such external effects, the larger I expect the size of the state to be. When conditions change such that a new external effect begins to operate beyond state borders, merger may be undertaken. Merger has its own cost, discussed in Chapter 9.

Internalizing what may otherwise be "conventional" external effects also affects state size. What people own is seldom known with precision. Because it is difficult to delineate the boundaries of their holdings, individuals require protection against encroachment. Sometimes the random effects that increase the cost to one person of protecting himself against his neighbor will reduce his neighbor's cost of encroaching on him. An exceptionally wet winter, for instance, may lead to thick growth in the border area, making encroachment easy and protection difficult. Measures that kept the peace before the onset of the wet winter may no longer be adequate. In such cases, delineating the rights of the two neighbors is especially problematic, and they can benefit from the services of a common protector. The common third party can then delineate their border and adjudicate their disputes more effectively than could independent protectors or a self-enforced mechanism. The rationale that applies to pairs of individuals also applies to pairs of groups. Here, too,

---

[2] When such an installation can serve several states, they can own it in common. It might, conceivably, serve the additional function of deliberately exposing the individual holdings to each other.

disputes arise when the boundaries of the properties of two groups are not easy to delineate, and again a common protector may reduce the net cost of dispute.

The combination of a force-using protector and of a pair of clients, where the former provides the latter with third-party adjudication, is, by the definition here, sufficient to constitute a state. I expect the size of the state to be larger when effects such as those just described extend over many individual neighbors and groups of neighbors. Conversely, where boundaries are easy to draw, as when a cliff separates two neighbors or when a desert separates two communities, individuals and communities will tend to use independent protectors.[3]

Consider the holdings of several individuals who opt for a common protector, but there are independent holdings that lie in the midst of the former. The holdings of the latter constitute breaks in what otherwise would be a unified protected area. Independence-inducing factors in a given area can consist of features, such as dense forests, islands, and steep hills, or of people's activities, such as being nomads. As the number of such factors becomes larger, I expect the size of the protectors who protect the rest of the area to get smaller. Small breaks consist of just a few individuals. Large ones may consist of many independent groups, because their protection may be subject to only moderate scale economies. For instance, for a long period the Alps have been fertile ground for small, independent states. In addition, their existence seems to have reduced the size the surrounding states might have reached had those mountains not been there.

Consider states that lie within large uniform land areas. When the size of such an area exceeds the optimal size for a single state, I expect that states will reach their "optimal" size; the scale economies to protection may already have been exhausted. Moreover, the diversity of the inhabitants of an area may reduce the advantage of including them within a single state. Given the uniformity of the land, such areas are likely to lack protective barriers, and thus they may also lack easy-to-delineate borders. Thus we can expect long-lasting border conflicts among the states in such areas. One example of such an area is the plain covering much of north-central Europe. That may be why, for instance, disputes and border changes between Germany and France, which lie within that

---

[3] Individuals may not be given the option of abstaining from state protection (and from state taxes). In that case, however, the net value of protection to individuals who would have preferred to take charge of their own defense is correspondingly less.

area, have been more frequent than disputes between France and Spain across the Pyrenees.

The initial cost of forming a collective-action mechanism and the degree of success in merging states, along with their collective-action mechanisms, seem also to affect the size of the state, though in a complex way. The desire to take advantage of economies of scale to protection calls for taking prior steps to avoid being run over by the protector. The main prior step here is the creation of a collective-action mechanism. The smaller the size of the group, the easier the creation of such a mechanism. But if the groups forming the mechanisms are small relative to the optimal size for protection, the potential gain from scale economies to protection is large, and so is the potential gain from the merger of individual groups.

SOCIETIES WITHOUT SPECIALIZED PROTECTORS

Taylor (1982) considers states or societies that protect themselves without using specialized protectors "anarchic." Indeed, anthropologists have observed primitive societies with no specialized protection and free of despotic rulers. The existence of such societies, however, does not necessarily contradict the notion of the gains from specialization in general, and from specialized protection in particular. Specialization in protection increases its productiveness. It is attained, however, at the cost of an increased probability that one individual or a subset of individuals – the protection specialists – will take over. It is my contention that the societies with no specialized protector have existed in relative isolation. As long as outside threat is low, the incentive to have specialized protection is also low.

Anarchic existence, however, cannot be a state of equilibrium when several states or societies are located next to one another. The reason is that societies that abstain from specializing in violence render themselves easy prey to those who do; it profits others to specialize in violence and then seize the wealth of the militarily less proficient neighbors. It is true that joint wealth is maximized when *all* abstain from specialized protection. But where all so abstain, it pays for some to revert to specialization in violence. Each predatory group benefits from the existence of peaceful ones. But then the gain to the peaceful groups from avoiding the threat of internal dictatorship by not having specialized protection can be negated by the threat of an even worse alternative. They can do better by having some of their members specialize in protection and then face their adversaries on more nearly equal terms. Groups without specialized protectors are not viable in the long run when not isolated from other groups.

As one example, when Europeans' navigation skills improved so as to give them access to such anarchic societies, most of those poorly defended societies were easily conquered and often wiped out by the European invaders. Taylor (1982, p. 130) and others have recognized that states can emerge in order to counter predatory states. However, they have not recognized the fact that states with specialized protection can emerge in order to engage in predation or to preempt it.

This line of argument generates the following two implications: (1) As stated earlier, societies with no specialized protectors can exist only in isolation. (2) As anarchic societies become less isolated, especially when they become sedentary, we expect them to turn themselves into states in order to avoid being exploited by predatory states, as well as to exploit their less militarily proficient neighbors.

FACTORS THAT AFFECT THE COST OF FORMING CONTRACTS

By the definition here, the state is a third party that uses force to enforce contracts. In earlier chapters I have argued that the state has a comparative advantage in the delineation of assets and in activities that are especially amenable to third-party adjudication and enforcement by violence and thus are amenable to contracting. I expect that as the scale of the delineation of such assets increases, the percentage of delineated assets among all assets will increase, and the scope of the state will increase as well. The extent of the state's comparative advantage in directly supplying services that enhance contract delineation is related to economies to third-party adjudication. The realization of these economies will depend on the size of the state, which comprises the areas where contracts are enforced by a single, ultimate enforcer. I pursue these arguments further in the remainder of this chapter.

As spelling out an agreement in detail becomes cheaper, the advantage of third-party enforcement increases. The reason for this is that it then becomes clearer what it is the third party should enforce. The greater the demand for carrying out such activities within a state, the greater the gains to the state from third-party enforcement. Conversely, when it is difficult to delineate assets or activities in detail, the value of self-enforced relations increases, and the advantage of state institutions declines.[4] There are several factors that can facilitate contract delineation but do not significantly affect the ability to make agreements based on self-enforced methods.

I first consider three factors that affect the ability to produce a contract document: the invention of writing, the availability of writing materials, and a common language. The invention of writing allowed oral contracts to be replaced with written ones. Written documents reduce the role, and the value, of memory and are especially valuable for complex transactions and for transactions that span long periods.[5] All agreements must be authenticated. In the case of a written contract, the main adjudication requirement is the availability of the document itself. In the case of an oral agreement, reliance on memory requires a third, neutral party aside from the would-be adjudicator. It is hypothesized, then, that the invention of writing, assuming it was exogenous, increased the scope of state operations. Indeed, it seems that all the large states that existed in antiquity emerged after writing became available there.

Turning to other effects of literacy, Ellickson (1993, p. 1367) points out that its development led to a change in land tenure from the right to use (usufruct) to perpetual ownership and transferability. Writing also made the use of standard forms cheaper; these could be copied from one contract to another. While memorizing a standard form is also cheaper than memorizing idiosyncratic agreements, memorized unwritten agreements do not seem as amenable to improvement and to adjustment to new conditions as are written ones. Thus, we expect the state to expand its operations when cheaper writing materials are developed and cheaper ways of writing emerge. The introduction of printing is a prime example of a cheaper way of writing; it also reduces the cost of providing standard forms. Similarly, conditions for territorial expansion are more fertile

---

[4] Legal delineation is costly, and the state must raise taxes to finance it. It seems that, as a rule, clearer delineation also facilitates taxation. I do not pursue this identification problem, however.

[5] Before written documents became common, it was essential to memorize contract terms. Children, whose life expectancy exceeded that of adults, were often made witnesses to oral contracts. In that way the effective life of the contract was extended. In some societies, those young witnesses to the ceremony of finalizing the contract were spanked. The purpose of that custom apparently was to etch the contract event into their memory. That practice illustrates the difficulty encountered when oral contracts had to be used. The smashing of a valuable glass, a part of the Jewish marriage ceremony, may be another way of imprinting the memory of the contract on those witnessing it.

when people across state borders have a common language. By this argument, the rise of bureaucracy would be a *cause* of the large state rather than its *effect*.

A second set of factors that affect the cost of contracting concerns the substance of contracts. Among these one can count the evolution of more effective arithmetic (Arabic versus Roman numerals, the introduction of a symbol for zero) and of superior accounting methods. I expect the exogenous improvements in these factors to have expanded state operations. In addition, improvements in methods of communication, such as the emergence of mail service, of the telegraph, and of fax, have made contracts more explicit and easier to effect. We can expect the scope and size of the state to expand as these methods improve. Finally, of vital importance for contracting was the introduction of standard weights and measures, which state regulation greatly enhanced.

Standards not only clarify contract specifications but also facilitate the production of homogeneous commodities and their classification into homogeneous sets. As product homogeneity increases, the cost of contract specification falls, because the same measurements can be applied to a large number of items. In addition, contracts themselves can be made more concise by referring to the generic commodity. Under self-enforcement, on the other hand, the transacted product must be measured and described separately for each transaction.

Two factors that seem to contribute to homogeneity are irrigation and the production line. Irrigation reduces the variability of agricultural crops that once depended on rainfall, and the production line increases the uniformity of manufactured products. I expect the effects of the advancements in irrigation and in production-line operations to interact positively with market size and therefore to enhance the scope of state operations. Decreases in certain measurement costs as well as in methods of classification promote contracting. One example of this was the development of better methods for measuring the specific gravity of crude oil. Adjusting for the specific-gravity differential allows turning a diverse set of oil varieties into more commensurate ones.[6] As the cost of measuring

---

[6] Home mortgages provide another example. Single-family homes are idiosyncratic, and mortgages on such homes are idiosyncratic too. Local mortgage bankers have a great deal of control regarding to whom to lend and thus great influence on the default probability. The idiosyncrasy of mortgages is an impediment to the securitizing (i.e., bundling into homogeneous groups) of mortgages to accommodate their sale in the wider capital market. The securitization of mortgages in recent decades

specific gravity decreased, transacting crude oil by contract became easier.

As state operations expand, it becomes advantageous to promote or induce each of the foregoing factors – for example, to invent writing and to improve accounting methods and the production line. In order to test this part of the theory, it is essential to ascertain whether or not changes in such variables are exogenous.

Exogenous changes in economic conditions can also affect the profitability of contract exchange as compared with self-enforced agreements. Consider the effect of the plague – the Black Death – on the formation of agreements. In the fourteenth century the effects of the plague on the human and animal populations in medieval Europe and elsewhere were disastrous, but it was harmless to land. The plague decimated the labor force, and the value of labor relative to the value of land increased. Labor services are more difficult to delineate and to contract for, and their exchange requires a greater degree of self-enforcement than does the exchange of land. Thus the plague reduced the value of third-party enforcement. We can expect that each major bout of the plague, therefore, would have reduced the scope of state operations.

AGREEMENT FORMS AND THE EXPANSION OF THE STATE

Throughout history, and to this day, substantial amounts of trade have taken place between people residing in different states that have not honored contracts made by their residents with the residents of other states. The trade between China and Europe during the Middle Ages, for example, was conducted without state-enforced contracts. In any trade, the buyer has to spend resources to evaluate the merchandise the seller offers. As discussed in Chapter 5, as the distance between the original producer and the final consumer increases, the merchandise is likely to pass through more hands, rendering the evaluation problem more acute. If the original producers travel with their merchandise, which in the past they often did, the merchandise does not change hands often. The

has been accompanied by allowance for the issuers, such as mortgage bankers, to charge a rather generous service fee. That fee terminates with default. Having the issuers absorb the bulk of the effect of default facilitates securitizing, as net of the effect of (idiosyncratic) default, mortgages are quite uniform and relatively easy to bundle.

potential for specializing, however, is thus forsaken.[7] Alternatively, shippers or merchants can transport the merchandise. In that case, the ultimate user obtains merchandise through intermediaries rather than directly from the original producer.[8] The producer's reputation, then, is unlikely to be carried all the way to the user of his output. Instead, there is a need either for a chain of reputations or for the ability to ascertain cheaply the quality of the traded commodities each time the merchandise changes hands. The commodities and services traded without state-enforced contracts are likely to be limited to those that can be traded profitably by at least one of these methods. Such commodities are likely to constitute the bulk of the trade between independent states that do not honor each other's jurisdiction.

The loss from forgoing trade in commodities that could be readily traded by contract is bound to be large.[9] As states better accommodate contract trade, more such trade will take place. Because the state is the third-party enforcer of contract trade, the larger the state, the greater the opportunity to realize scale economies to contract trade. As the cost of producing commodities that can be readily traded by contract falls, provided the cost of shipping is not high, I predict that states will attempt to expand the reach of their contract trade.

Expansion can take two forms that are not mutually exclusive. A state can expand its scope by internally using its third-party enforcement more intensively, as well as by increasing its size by "interacting" with other states more intensively. I focus on the latter. The interactions among states can be peaceful, such as making agreements with each other, while not necessarily merging. Alternatively, a state can interact with other

---

[7] When merchants travel with their merchandise, they underutilize their skills in trading. Security problems during travel, endemic throughout much of history, required those traders also to acquire skills in violence, further reducing the opportunity to develop and use their skills in trade. Such failure to specialize is part of the costs of transacting, as defined here. This is a dramatic illustration of how significant the costs of transacting can be.

[8] Similar considerations apply to commodities whose production requires a number of intermediate steps. A commodity can be owned by one person throughout its production or can be exchanged from one intermediate step to the next.

[9] The economies that long-distance contract trade offers share some major features with the economies of containerizing. The use of sealed, large-size containers allows, say, a parts manufacturer to ship an entire load to be assembled across the globe without need for handling the parts at each shipping juncture. Prior to the use of such containers, shipments were made in relatively small containers, each handled individually at every juncture along the way – from factory to truck, truck to train, train to ship, and so on.

states by extending its enforcement mechanism beyond its current geographic boundaries. Expansion, too, can be effected peacefully by agreement among states, or it can be violent (or by threat of violence), with one state conquering and annexing others.

PEACEFUL EXPANSION

One form of peaceful interaction among states is a voluntary merger. Examples include the merger of England and Scotland, the merger of some of the independent states in Iberia that became Spain, and the merger of the cantons that compose Switzerland. Such mergers unify two or more third-party enforcement mechanisms. The cost of merger was discussed in Chapter 9 in conjunction with the consolidation of legal rights. Other problems of merger and reasons why mergers are rare are discussed in the next chapter. Here I turn to other forms of interaction between states.

Treaties between countries specify the means by which contracts between citizens or residents of different countries will be adjudicated and enforced. Such treaties produce an outcome similar to that of merger, though weaker in terms of the ease of contract enforcement. Being self-enforced, such treaties require long-term relations between the states. I expect treaties to be prevalent among rule-of-law states. As a rule, these states are stable and can rely on repeated interactions to enforce their agreements. The more entrenched their rule of law is, the less their need for a full-fledged merger. Indeed, the more likely development is that an integrated state will fragment into a set of independent states bound by treaties. The recent movement toward the separation of Quebec from the rest of Canada seems a case in point.

A state can also expand the reach of its third-party enforcement mechanism by establishing "beachheads" or trading outposts in other states, either peacefully or by the use of force. Outposts are created more or less automatically when one state permits citizens of another state to take up residence. Such arrangements then allow citizens in one state to trade *by contract* with their fellow citizens living as aliens in other states. Many city-states such as Tyre, Carthage, Athens, and Venice, as well as more modern empires such as England and Portugal, maintained such outposts, typically operated by citizens of the home country. The arrangement, however, can be viable only if the expatriate citizens sufficiently value their home-state citizenship. This last condition requires self-enforcement; such arrangements often were supplemented by self-enforced agreements giving those who ran the outposts a stake in the wealth at home. For instance, young men who expected eventually to inherit their family businesses were attractive candidates for manning the outposts.

Building on the foregoing discussion of the scale economies to contracting, in the next section we consider the emergence of city-states with no hinterland, and in the following section the onset of the industrial revolution.

THE CITY-STATE

City-states possessed two fundamental features that I believe to be closely related: their reliance on trade and the advanced state of the rule of law that prevailed there. The first was almost inevitable. With little or no hinterland, the residents of city-states could not produce all the food, fibers, and other land-intensive commodities they needed; they had to trade to get them. Throughout history, so far as I can determine, *every* city-state was ruled during much of its existence by a constitutional governing body. When ruled by a king, he invariably had to deal with a council that had substantial control over him. I contend that without the availability of third-party contract enforcement, city-states would have found it too costly to secure the commodities they needed.

In order to conduct contract trade beyond the borders of one's own state, one must have access to some method of enforcement. As already mentioned, a common practice by city-states was the use of an intermediate link – the outpost. The outpost's personnel, obviously, had to deal with the city-state on the one hand and with the outpost's surrounding area on the other. Consider first their relationship with the city-state. Some outposts were established in previously uninhabited areas, manned by citizens of the city-state. That arrangement enabled the citizens of the city-state to ship commodities to, and receive shipments from, fellow citizens at the outpost. Being subject to the same third-party enforcer, they were able to trade under enforceable contracts. When the outpost was located far from the city-state, the gain from conducting trade by contract was bound to be considerable. On occasion, outposts became independent of their city-states, but as long as they continued to operate under the rule of law, as they usually did, they were able to form agreements to trade by contract. The relationship between England, a rule-of-law state, and its dominions, largely populated by emigrants from the British Isles and their descendants, is an example that commenced with a relationship of the first kind that eventually evolved into the second kind.

Completing the long-distance transactions required trade between an outpost and its surrounding area. Although outpost residents maintained trade and legal ties with their home state, they also had to trade with citizens of the states surrounding them. Without an appropriate treaty, such trade was not amenable to contract trade and had to be largely self-enforced. The use of non-state third-party enforcement, or of self-enforcement, however, was not too costly there. The transactors were neighbors who could readily form long-term relations. In any case, even if transactions were conducted on a caveat-emptor basis, the traded commodities had to be measured only once.

Trading outposts could be established near existing foreign states or within them. The outposts of the Phoenician city-states typically operated in new, uninhabited areas. Carthage, for example, was such an outpost founded by Tyre. Establishing outposts that operate within existing states, although at the mercy of those states, can facilitate forming long-term relations with local trade partners. Such an outpost, obviously, would be operating under a treaty between the local state and the colonists' home state. The Venetian colony in Constantinople during the Middle Ages probably was the most famous outpost that one state maintained inside another. It might seem that such colonists could extend their relationship by submitting to the authority of their host state, thereby accommodating contract trade with subjects of their host country. But then they would cease to be under the authority of their home state. At least one of the relationships would have to be self-enforced.

EXTENDING THE STATE BY FORCE AND
FORMING EMPIRES

A more radical solution to the problem of trade across a state's current border is to extend the border. One method of "extending" a border is to conquer a neighbor, and perhaps ultimately to build an empire. By subjecting the new territory to the conqueror's law, the entire territory becomes amenable to contract trade. Many city-states, at one time or another, acquired empires. For example, for centuries Venice had vast holdings in the eastern Mediterranean. The industrial revolution, as I shall suggest momentarily, substantially increased the value of trade by contract, and as a result, the value of an empire. Still, empires seem to have benefited greatly from contract trade even before the industrial revolution.

A whole variety of trades can benefit from contracting. Among these, the extension of credit seems the most important. By itself, credit is unlikely to be extended extensively, if at all, under self-enforcement. Forming a contract-enforcement mechanism, which allows the credit transaction, seems to be of great value. It is significant that in Rome and Venice, two major pre-industrial long-lasting empires, the rule of law was maintained to a very high order. I now discuss some aspects of holding an empire in conjunction with the industrial revolution.

A major change brought about by the industrial revolution was the standardization of products. The products that many individual workers produced in factories were considerably more uniform than those produced under less centralized methods of organizing production. One famous example of uniformity is in the production and assembly of guns. Before the industrial revolution, guns were custom-made, and the parts of each gun would fit only that gun. Under the factory system, the production of parts that formerly were custom-made was standardized, and the new parts were interchangeable.

Standardization reduces not only the cost of production but also the cost of trading by contract. To the extent that specimens of commodities are made to the same specifications, contracts can simply list the specifications, just as futures contracts do. Alternatively, the contracts can stipulate that the traded commodities have to meet the quality of the accepted standard specimens, or perhaps that they have to be of the same quality as specimens delivered in a previous period.

Such commodities can be traded by contract wherever contracts are enforceable. Absent contracts, a chain of intermediaries, each with a high level of reputation, can effect trade. Alternatively, the specimen can be inspected with each transfer. Finally, the producer or an intermediary can transport the commodity in person to the consumer, reducing the number of transactions to one or two. Contract trade largely eliminates the need for such arrangements. Contracts, however, are routinely enforceable only within a state (i.e., within the jurisdiction of a single third-party enforcer).

As argued, pairs of rule-of-law states can relatively easily reach agreements to extend contract enforcement across their borders. This has been taking place between the United States and Canada. Although subjects of one of these states will be more hesitant in signing contracts with subjects of the other than with subjects of their own state, in rule-of-law states this discrepancy seems small. Not so when only one state or neither of them is subject to the rule of law.

The advantage of contract trade increased dramatically with the advent of the industrial revolution. In the wake of that revolution, the need for uniform raw materials for mechanized production intensified, as did the need for more homogeneous labor services. As raw materials became more uniform, exchanging them by contract became cheaper. The increased opportunities to use contracts may explain why the industrial revolution was dominated by rule-of-law states.

An industrial, rule-of-law state may wish to extend the advantage of contract trade beyond its own borders. It can do so by conquering a non-rule-of-law state with which trade would be advantageous and then imposing on that state its third-party enforcement mechanism.[10] Although two such countries probably would have traded with each other before the conquest, the conquest will expand the scope of the trade to include contract trade in the newly emerging industrial commodities. Before the industrial revolution, England operated a trading outpost in India via the British East India Company. During that revolution, England converted India into a crown colony. The Dutch handled Indonesia and the Spice Islands similarly. Although within-empire trade often was enhanced by protectionist policies, the advantage of trade by contract accommodated by empires seems to have been the main force for the high volume of such trade.

Conquest, of course, is not free of cost. As is obvious, the more powerful the state targeted for conquest, the higher the cost. It is not surprising, then, that whereas industrialized European countries colonized Africa, they only established outposts in China.

Let me emphasize that I am not asserting any direction of causality among the industrial revolution, imperialism, and uniformity of raw materials, though my hunch is that imperialism was the effect of the other two. But perhaps the causality had its source in the empires emerging and enhancing the value of uniform raw materials used in industry and in the uniform output produced.

The desire to expand the range of exchange by contract is not the only reason for imperialistic policy. Another reason, seemingly more

[10] Lenin held the view that imperialism is an inevitable step in capitalistic development. I concur with Lenin's view that the two are closely related, though I do not consider imperialism "inevitable." Lenin also claimed that imperialism would be capitalism's last gasp before its collapse. The title of his book, *Imperialism, the Highest Stage of Capitalism*, captures the essence of that claim.

prevalent historically, is the prospect of loot, or the military leaders' pleasure. However, the empires that emerged when the purpose was trade differed radically from those where the objective was loot.

Rule-of-law states are geared for contract trade. I expect them to expand primarily in order to extend their trade by contract. Despotic regimes, on the other hand, tend to discourage trade, and we expect them to conquer mostly for loot. With despotic regimes, the expected duration of the imperialistic domination is short, or, more precisely, will last for the amount of time required to extract loot yielding the maximum net present value. I also expect their rule to be harsh, in order to reduce the chance of rebellion, and the conquered countries to remain poor. If the purpose of the conquest is trade expansion, I expect that looting, when it takes place, will be relatively mild and brief. Moreover, I expect the duration of the rule to be relatively longer, with the conquering country introducing third-party enforcement as part of a rule-of-law regime.[11] I predict that in this case the volume of trade between the conqueror and the conquered will increase, and as time passes, the general level of wealth of the *conquered* country will increase as well. In fact, the post-conquest rule of law in such conquered countries often seems more advanced than it was before the conquest. These distinctions between the types of conquering states may explain why the British rule of their empire, or the Venetian rule of theirs, was relatively benign compared with that of the Spaniards in America or of Napoleon and of Hitler in their mostly European empires.[12] More generally, we expect a positive correlation between the rate of growth in income in colonies and the level of the rule of law in the imperialist state.

SUMMARY

Part of the scale economies to protection would seem to be due to the ability of a single protector to more efficiently protect neighbors than could separate protectors. The reason is that the former is in a position to draw easy-to-defend boundaries among his clients. The advantage

---

[11] Consistent with this argument is the observation that the long-term colonial powers that replaced marauders in Africa drastically reduced the slave trade.

[12] The treatment of the two parts of Germany after World War II provides an instructive comparison of what happened between Russia and East Germany on the one hand and what happened between the Western allies and West Germany on the other.

such a protector has, and the size of the state, will be less where natural boundaries exist.

As emphasized earlier, contracting is subject to scale economies, as are delineation and enforcement by the state. Factors that facilitate contracting, then, are likely to enhance the scope and scale of the state. The inventions of writing and of printing, along with increasing literacy, are among the factors that contributed to the replacement of oral contracts by the much more effective written ones. Improvements in accounting and arithmetic made contracts, especially written ones, more powerful. Finally, the expansion of irrigation and of industrial production was conducive to product uniformity, which is also amenable to contracting.

Contracts are enforceable only within states or between states that agree to honor one another's contracts. Treaties facilitated the latter kind of trade. Rule-of-law states are likely to sign and honor such treaties. The larger the state or the trade-agreement area, the larger the area that can benefit from contract exchange. State expansion seems to be the most effective way to effect contract trade when treaties are absent.

States can expand in various ways. Many of the ancient city-states, as well as some more modern states, established trading outposts. Their purpose was not only to enhance their trade in general but also to allow trade by contract. Trading between citizens of a single state enables them to use their state to enforce their contracts and reduce the need to use other means of enforcement. The greater the distance involved, and the greater the number of steps between producer and consumer, the greater the advantage of contract trade.

The most drastic form of state expansion is by conquest. A state that conquers others is in a position to impose its contract-enforcement mechanism on the conquered states. All the residents of such empires are subject to the same final enforcer, whereas before consolidation of the empire they had to enforce their trade by other means. It seems plausible that this was one of the main reasons for the formation of the British Empire. That empire covered a vast area in which all trade could be enforced by contract. Because England produced a large volume of standardized commodities, and probably imported large volumes of standardized raw materials, its gain from forming a trading empire was considerable. Indeed, its colonial subjects, though denied political independence, similarly benefited from the trade by contract.

PART III

The Character of the State

12

Merger and Local Autonomy

In this and the next three chapters I discuss four topics that will elucidate the character of the state and promote further understanding. The
order of these chapters is arbitrary. They concern problems that earlier
chapters raised indirectly, but were not integral parts there. I begin with
autonomy and merger.

It appears that small states should be able to avoid being captured by,
and forced to pay tribute to, larger ones by voluntarily merging in order
to mount a unified defense. Yet historical examples of voluntary merger
are few. In this chapter, I argue that the prevailing ideas related to the
advantages of merger are ill-conceived. I then explore conditions leading
to merger, concluding that considerations of trade and its enforcement,
not cooperation for military defense, are the factors that drive merger
agreements.

WHY POOLING MILITARY STRENGTH IS INSUFFICIENT TO EXPLAIN MERGER

Individually, small states make tempting prey for larger, more powerful
states. The combined military powers of small neighboring states,
however, may exceed that of a threatening large state. The small states
can do well if they can pool their forces. If merger between states were
easy to arrange, it would be of great value. Cooperation, however, is
always problematic; each party can gain the most from the cooperative
enterprise by keeping its own contribution to a minimum. This difficulty
is relevant to the pooling of military forces. Agreements among states
must be self-enforced, and the temptation for a free ride is bound to be
strong. One method of reducing the chance of a free ride is by merger,

where the individual states submit to the combined power of the newly merged state.

The literature does not deal with this problem directly. Rather, several explicit and implicit assertions regarding different forms of pooling military powers are commonly advanced. It is almost universally implied that each existing state, whether small or large, has already solved the problem of harmonizing the interests of its various component groups and that it can put forward a unified effort. It is further implicitly asserted that by merging, the states involved could solve the incentive problems encountered when they attempt to cooperate.

The other side of the coin is the assertion that a mere treaty among states will not do, since the participants cannot be relied on to perform. Riker (1987) clearly subscribes to the view that merger is superior to an agreement. He states (p. 18) that "federalism is a constitutional form of gathering several governments together to take action, mostly military, that would be *impossible* for the governments separately" (emphasis added). Treaty partners, indeed, seem constantly to bicker about each other's effort, and it is easy to find examples in which the signers of a treaty failed to keep their promises, as well as instances in which one would even join forces with their original common enemy.

This line of reasoning, however, contains two related non sequiturs. One is that the mere existence of the state solves the incentive problem. The other is that by voluntarily merging, the previously independent states will become a *unified* large state. Large states, presumably, had been costlessly unified. If by merging, small states can become unified large states and thus enjoy the advantages of size, it then becomes a major puzzle why history is rife with instances of small states becoming prey to large states. And why were voluntary mergers so few? Contemporary Switzerland and Spain resulted from voluntary mergers, as did Great Britain. It is not easy, however, to extend the list.[1] Moreover, as I now argue, it is not an accident that the originally independent Swiss cantons, the independent states in the Iberian Peninsula, and the pre-merger England (including Wales) and Scotland that participated in those mergers were all governed by rule of law. In the next two sections I iden-

---

[1] There are many historical examples of mergers, but upon examination, few prove to have been voluntary. The merger in 1938 between Germany and Austria clearly was not voluntary. The unification of Germany and that of Italy in the second half of the nineteenth century are more difficult to classify. Prussia dominated the unification of Germany, and Italy's unification followed a great deal of fighting.

tify conditions under which a merger is not incentive-compatible and circumstances under which a merger is likely.

DICTATORIAL MERGERS AND TREATIES

Who will control the state created by a voluntary merger?[2] The individuals currently controlling a state that is contemplating merger presumably will be vitally interested in the answer to this question. The answer seemingly will depend on the character of the candidate states. Consider first the case in which all the would-be constituent states are dictatorships. I argue that independent dictatorships are unlikely to merge in order to form a single dictatorship. The reason is precisely that offered in Chapter 8, where I argued that the heads of independent military forces within a state would be unlikely to support one of their number who attempted to become a dictator. Unification would reduce the number of dictators to one. As one of the rulers became sole dictator, what would be the fate of the other original dictators? It might be plausible that each dictator who relinquished his full dictatorial power would nevertheless retain his following, and at least part of his organization. But then he would pose a threat to the new dictator, who in turn might fear that he could be eliminated. Although the chance that the merged dictatorial state would be saved from any enemy would be higher, all the original dictators, save one, might not live to see that.

The emergent sole dictator might be willing to commit to treat the other dictators well. However, given the record of discontinuity for most dictatorial regimes, it would be difficult for any of those desiring to become sole dictator to credibly commit to treat the others well. It is highly implausible, then, that the other dictators would agree to merge and let one assume sole dictatorial powers.

Is it a necessary outcome of a merger of dictatorial states to be ruled by a single dictator? Or could such states merge without becoming subject to one dictator? Could not the founding dictators of the merged state rule it collectively? They could, for example, form a council to run the merged state. Then the original dictators would have to continue to maintain control of their power bases within the merged state; otherwise, any one of them who gained control of the combined power would

---

[2] By Riker's definition of a federation (1987, pp. 74–5), the federations formed voluntarily by states make up a subset of all federations. As suggested later, it seems more desirable to confine the definition of "federation" to states that have merged voluntarily.

be able to become a sole dictator. The agreement, then, might take the form whereby each of the original dictators would have veto power over decisions by the merged council. In practice, each would have a real veto power by retaining control over the military force he brought into the bargain. Moreover, none of them would be likely to agree to yield real authority to a central adjudicating body; dictators have little to gain from ceding such authority. Because the central body would not have any independent decision power, the agreement would not turn the individual states into a single state. Indeed, the possession of independent decision power is part of Riker's definition of a federation. What might emerge, then, would be just a treaty between states, not their merger.[3]

Are rule-of-law states more inclined to merge voluntarily than are dictatorial states? Consider, first, rule-of-law states that emerged from small groups of individuals and the underlying collective-action mechanisms, as discussed in Chapter 7. The more entrenched the collective-action mechanisms of a small group, the less threatened are group members from internal takeover. Such groups may broaden their membership and merge their protection organizations with those of other groups in order to take advantage of the scale economies to protection (and other economies in state-level operations). The merger of such groups has some advantages, as well as costs (Chai and Hechter, 1998). Rule-of-law states (i.e., groups with collective-action mechanisms and specialized protectors) might be no less reluctant to let go of their individual powers than are dictatorial states. As small states merged to become larger ones, wealth-transfer problems likely would become more acute, especially if the states were relatively homogeneous internally, but differed significantly from each other.[4] Each of them, if given state power, could gain at the others' expense. Each would attempt to protect itself against expropriation, as well as against takeover by one of the other states, by stipulating that their collective-action mechanisms be merged as well. Like individuals forming a collective-action organization, the individual states might implement procedures such as supermajority voting that could significantly reduce the prospect of confiscation.

---

[3] The merger between Syria and Egypt in the 1960s, supposedly creating a single state called the United Arab Republic, did not provide for a unified military. The two ruling dictators retained their powers, and the union quickly petered out.

[4] If variability is measured by the statistical variance, then the variability of the merged group is necessarily greater than the average variability of the constituent groups. This is true even if members of each of the groups are randomly drawn from the same population.

States that attempt to cooperate must be wary of each other, even when they limit themselves to forming military treaties. Whoever controls the power may attempt to take over. Such wariness is dramatically illustrated by the military cooperation among the city-states of classical Greece (ca. 500–449 B.C.) to fight the Persians. According to Durant (1939, p. 236), "the Greeks . . . committed the folly of dividing the command among ten generals, each supreme for a day."[5]

RULE-OF-LAW REGIMES, MERGERS, AND TREATIES

Because of their greater credibility, rule-of-law states are able to merge more easily than dictatorships. As a rule, such states will have existed for a long time and presumably will have accumulated satisfactory records. For the same reason, they tend to have success with treaties to protect themselves against outsiders. Why, then, would rule-of-law states ever merge? One reason is that rule-of-law states may seek not only to enhance their protection but also to *expand their trade*. A protection treaty will not serve that purpose as well as will a merger. The ability to trade by contract and have contracts enforced by the state greatly facilitates trade. Strictly speaking, contract trade cannot traverse state borders. States can gain the full benefit from contract trade only if they unify their third-party enforcement.

A state, whether dictatorial or governed by rule of law, is characterized by its ultimate third-party enforcement power. Third-party enforcement, of course, is a necessary condition for contract trade. Whereas rule-of-law states thrive on contract trade, dictatorial states tend to discourage such trade, or, at best, tolerate it. States can expand their contract trade by merging.[6] The value of the merger will depend on the nature of the current trade and the potential trade between the participating states. The more the trade between them is amenable to contracting, the greater their gain from contract trade. Rule-of-law states will tend to merge when their valuation of such trade increases. For instance, when one state begins to develop an industry producing highly standardized goods subject to low transport cost, the advantage from

---

[5] Citing Plutarch's "Aristides" as his source, Durant (1939) proceeds to state that "they were saved by the example of Aristides, who yielded his [one-day] leadership to Miltiades."

[6] Conquest can serve the same purpose. In Chapter 11, I hypothesize that rule-of-law states acquire empires in order to enlarge their contract-trade territory.

accommodating its contract trade with other states increases, and the gain from merger increases.

Federation is the form of governance that seems most appropriate for rule-of-law states wishing to merge.[7] We expect the federal authority to be controlled by the members of the federation. We also expect these to maintain control of the military force[8] and to form a unified legal authority to allow them to trade by contract within the entire domain of the federation.

The evolution of Switzerland to what it is today closely conforms to the foregoing expectation of how states will merge. As already mentioned, in the second part of the thirteenth century three freemen states, or cantons, formed a federation to defend themselves against the Holy Roman Empire.[9] The number of cantons in the federation continued to grow until 1815, when it reached its current size. When the cantons merged, they established rules to minimize the chance of transfers among themselves. Two major features have distinguished Switzerland throughout its history: (1) the firm rule of law that governs it and (2) the substantial local autonomy of the cantons. Of all contemporary rule-of-law states, Switzerland is the only one that evolved, essentially uninterruptedly, from a voluntary beginning.[10] The Swiss, as noted before, have maintained considerable local control over their military institutions. To the best of my knowledge, the Swiss military has always been composed of militias, and from early on they fought in formations composed of soldiers from the same localities. Moreover, Swiss soldiers possessed or were provided with personal weapons that they kept in their homes.

---

[7] Switzerland, the United States, and Canada were formed as federations. The Swiss federation was formed by independent states. In the United States and Canada, the colonial period was already characterized by reliance of the states and provinces on the English law, which facilitated the creation of a unified legal system.

[8] According to Riker (1987, p. 75), in "the American government under the Articles of Confederation, . . . national officials were by one constitutional device or another forced to defer decisions on some national questions to the organs of constituent governments." In addition, there was the guarantee "of the perpetual existence of the constituent governments such that they are enabled to maintain themselves (in the selection of officials, etc.) independently of the national government." And he says that "the framers of the Constitution divided authority over the militia in specific detail; in more specific detail, actually, than they divided any other authority" (p. 159).

[9] I did not encounter information on the role of trade in the merger.

[10] One might claim a similar status for the United States, in spite of its emergence from English colonies.

In merger, as in marriage, some partners are preferable to others. For example, a rule-of-law state is less likely to merge with a dictatorial state than with another rule-of-law state, and dictatorial states are even less likely to merge with each other. The reason dictatorial states are unlikely to merge has already been stated. Neither is the "mixed" merger a likely one, for two reasons: (1) The rule-of-law partner or partners would fear being taken over by the dictatorial partner, since dictators find it difficult to commit not to take over. (2) The legal institutions in the two differently governed states likely would differ greatly. Such states, then, likely would deem the costs entailed by merging their legal systems too high.

As an alternative, they might pursue a treaty. A treaty, of course, is not worth much unless the parties to it are likely to abide by it. The more prone a state is to break its promises, the less attractive it is as a treaty candidate. One's track record seems to be the best indicator by which to estimate future performance. The agreement must be self-enforced, and the better a regime's past record in meeting its treaty obligations, the more attractive it is as a participant in a proposed treaty.[11] In order to secure others' support, then, a dictator would have to demonstrate his willingness to reciprocate. One immediate implication is that a new dictator who has no track record is less likely than a well-established one to be invited to participate in a treaty. The latter, of course, must have an acceptable record, and where participation in treaties is valued, we can expect an effort to compile such a record.[12]

Consider now the internal operation of a treaty. Its members presumably will monitor one another to ensure cooperation. Their main tool for enforcing compliance is expulsion from the treaty. Members will be concerned with future performance rather than with past record per se. A record of stability seems to be the clearest predictor of future performance. In order to qualify, dictators would be expected to encourage orderly succession. Orderly succession, however, would require a mechanism separate from the dictator to bring it about. A dictator could create such a mechanism by giving up some of his power. The dictator, then, would be introducing a rule of law. The introduction of additional

[11] The German Hansa was one of the most enduring and most powerful treaties ever made. Of its some 180 members, only one was autocratic; all the rest were rule-of-law city-states (Dollinger, 1970).

[12] One possible reason that most Italian city-states of the Middle Ages maintained their rule-of-law institutions may have been to demonstrate that they were trusted allies to others in the face of powerful states posing constant threats to them.

elements of the rule of law would similarly enhance stability and therefore the good standing of his state with the other treaty states.

Earlier, in a single-country dictator model (Barzel, 2000a), I suggested
that outside danger is a major inducement for introduction of the rule
of law. The main force there is the increased cost of facing the emerging
threat from the outside. I argue that the wealth of a dictatorship that
turns itself into a rule-of-law state is likely to increase rapidly. It can
devote some of the additional resources to defense. Here the context is
of independent small dictatorships newly facing a large dangerous state
in their neighborhood. The introduction and furtherance of a rule of law
can help the small states strengthen their defensive alliance and make
them more secure from the threat posed by the large state. It will also
tend to perpetuate itself, as well as to enhance the wealth of both rulers
and subjects.

Not every rule-of-law state is an attractive merger candidate for every
other. Disparity in wealth seems an impediment to merger. In general,
the return to the poor from stealing from the rich is likely to be high.
The state uses the police to protect property both from its own residents
and from outsiders. Sometimes it also "bribes" the domestic poor not to
steal the property of the rich. Both forms of protection are costly. It seems
easier to deter theft by bribing one's own poor than by bribing subjects
of other states. The existence of a boundary, however, reduces the cost
of preventing would-be thieves from entering a state; it creates a "gated
community." It also reduces the cost of deporting such suspects who have
already entered. One of the major intended effects of merger is to
increase individuals' mobility in order to increase specialization and
trade. That, however, will also facilitate the mobility of undesirable elements. To the extent that the wealth distributions of the states merging
with one another are similar, merger per se does not seem to exacerbate
the problem. But if the wealth disparity across states is large, individuals in the rich states become attractive prey for individuals from the
poor states. If the disparity is large enough, such theft problems may
negate the other gains from merger.[13]

---

[13] The European Union delayed accepting poor countries as members until they could
reach an "adequate" income level. Moreover, both before and after poor countries
were allowed to join, the union chose to subsidize them substantially. In that way,
the incentive that the residents of poor countries had to move into the more pros-
perous category was reduced. Johnsen (1986) offers a closely related argument
regarding the potlatch custom of the native American people of the Pacific
Northwest.

More generally, a political border makes it easier to isolate a country from certain external effects that subjects of other countries might introduce, such as additional forms of crime, or the transmission of communicable disease. The greater are the adverse effects that the opening of a border may bring about, the less is the gain from merger.

LOCAL AND CENTRAL JURISDICTION

Consider now the functioning of a federal state. How will the jurisdiction of a federal system be divided between the federal level and its constituent units? The general principle of such division, expounded in Chapters 6 and 10, is that rights that can be clearly delineated locally should be assigned to the constituent units, and those that cannot should be assigned to the federal level. Interstate trade and patents are obvious cases belonging to the latter category. National defense is another; a threat from a foreign state typically affects more than one unit within the federation, and rights to the effects of defense effort are difficult to delineate if conducted at the level of the individual unit. On the other hand, regulations such as zoning will have virtually no spillovers across the borders of the units, and therefore there is no advantage in granting jurisdiction over them to the federal authorities. Indeed, in the case of zoning, even the constituent units of the federation would seem to be too large for that function, and jurisdiction over it can be granted to units at a still lower level.

In many cases the classification is not clear-cut. Various modes of transportation, for instance, vary greatly in terms of the territories they traverse. To the extent that one can isolate freight operations that seldom ship goods outside of individual units or counties, we would not expect that jurisdiction over them would be granted to the federal authorities. Other freight carriers organized to operate throughout the entire country may nevertheless carry a significant fraction of their shipments locally. If those operations were placed under federal jurisdiction, virtually all disputed rights would be encompassed within that authority. Administering such a jurisdiction, however, almost surely would be overly bureaucratic and inflexible. It might not effectively handle local matters, then. On the other hand, placing those activities under local jurisdictions would result in capture attempts, because some issues would inevitably spill over the borders of the local jurisdictions. It does not seem that rights could be clearly delineated in that case.

Deciding on the best jurisdiction for such activities, then, is a matter of weighing the advantages and disadvantages of the wider jurisdiction compared with the narrower ones. The notion that there is a trade-off here is capable of yielding refutable implications. One such implication is that as the level of spillovers increases, due, say, to improved navigability of a river traversing more than one constituent unit, the jurisdiction of the local units is predicted to shrink, and that of the wider unit, perhaps the federal one, is predicted to expand.

LOCAL AUTONOMY

As discussed in earlier chapters, the state, as a rule, is likely to be a contiguous geographic entity. The territories of the constituent states that combine into a federation or other form of union are then likely to be contiguous.[14] The individual constituent states will tend to retain some autonomy within the system. Presumably, prior to the merger there would have been some local autonomy within each of the constituent states, such as with regard to zoning, and such autonomy likely would be retained.

Local autonomy, however, need not be based solely on geography, as discussed in Chapter 6. Autonomy might be given to ethnic groups or religious orders that are spread across local political units. Similarly, trade or civic groups might be granted some autonomy. The less the potential for spillover of rights of an operation, the more likely it will be granted autonomy. We expect that in order to minimize such spillover, the jurisdiction will coincide closely with the reach of the effects of the operation.[15] Consider times and places where different religions have coexisted in a state and individuals have interacted in religious matters, such as marriage within their religion. In these situations we expect that the religions would have been granted autonomy regarding their religious practices. To the extent that the binding force of the religions declines, however, we expect the state to reduce the local autonomy of the religious organizations. This is because under the new conditions of waning

---

[14] Three non-contiguous states were formed during the twentieth century: Pakistan, which was composed of East and West Pakistan; the United Arab Republic, which was composed of Egypt and Syria; and Germany, consisting of its main, western part and of East Prussia. The three pairs, however, were connected by water. In any case, none lasted very long as a unified state.

[15] Tullock (1994) provides an extensive and mostly normative discussion of the spillover problem.

religious efficacy, rights cease to be well delineated under the religious jurisdictions.

Local autonomy might also be given to various military or semi-military forces. The military forces that operate in a state perform various operations, some of which are quite separable from others. The operations of the coast guard or the border patrol are largely independent of those, say, of the air force. We expect that when the advantage of integrating a particular force with any of the others is not large, that force will be organized independently of the others. This can apply even to the relationship between the air force and the navy.

SUMMARY

Small states are attractive prey for large states. They can make themselves less palatable by merging with one another, thus becoming larger states. Yet, historically, voluntary mergers among states have been rare. In this chapter I have argued that small dictatorships are unlikely to merge and form a single large dictatorship. The new dictator could not commit not to harm the others. All the others could expect to find themselves losers under the merger and thus would not agree to it. Even a merger subject to government by a committee of dictators would be unlikely to succeed, as no one would relinquish control of his power base to the central authority.

Merger is problematic even for rule-of-law states. Merger does not guarantee internal unity; indeed, it makes certain kinds of transfers easier. Before they merge, then, we expect rule-of-law states to make elaborate arrangements to reduce transfer opportunities, as well as the chance for dictatorial takeover. Switzerland is the prime example of a successful federation, but except for perhaps the United States, the list cannot be easily extended. Switzerland is distinguished by the local autonomy of its cantons. In the process of merging, the originally free cantons made sure that their local autonomy would be preserved.

Treaties, which must be self-enforced, offer an alternative to merger. Past behavior seems to be the main indicator whether or not a state is a desirable treaty partner. Here, too, rule-of-law states have an edge, because they tend to be more stable and more reliable than dictatorships. The latter can choose to relinquish some of their authority and move toward a rule of law in order to qualify as treaty partners.

13

The Distinction between "Legitimate" and "Criminal" States

As pointed out in earlier chapters, the state is neither the only organization to engage in delineation nor the only one to use force to enforce rights within what is conventionally viewed as its territory. Other organizations operating in the same territory can act similarly. The medieval Catholic church, for example, delineated certain religion-related rights and sometimes was allowed to use force to enforce them within states that it did not control. States sanction, or at least tolerate, some of these organizations. In this chapter, I focus on criminal organizations operating within the state, but banned by it. They resemble the state in that they, too, delineate rights and forcefully enforce them.[1]

As argued in Chapter 6, the state and criminal organizations can be viable side by side only if they differ in the kinds of power they use. The state seems to have a comparative advantage in the open use of arms and in the use of heavier weapons such as armored cars. Criminal organizations' advantage is in the covert use of arms, and they tend to use small, easy-to-conceal weapons. States can neither easily overpower criminal organizations nor effectively compete with them in their domain.

The two enforce different kinds of agreements; criminal organizations enforce primarily agreements that the state prohibits. They also differ in the ways they adjudicate disputes. Criminal organizations are unlikely to hold their trials in public and probably are less fussy than the legitimate state in the quality of evidence they require. We can expect transactors, then, to be more selective in the agreements they bring to criminal organizations for enforcement.

---

[1] Vigilante organizations sometimes use force for certain types of enforcement. As a rule, they are not "criminal," but neither are they fully endorsed by the legitimate state. Interesting as this kind of organization is, however, I do not discuss it here.

THE RATIONALE FOR CRIMINAL ORGANIZATIONS

The existence of criminal organizations is no anomaly. It is *implied* by the existence of the state. Making protection foolproof would be prohibitively costly.[2] One factor that contributes to the costliness of uprooting criminal organizations (as well as unorganized criminals) is the high cost of acquiring information relevant to criminals' behavior. Enforcers need information about their subjects' activities to know where to apply their enforcement power. They cannot credibly threaten criminals with state power unless they can identify them, and the state must incur costs to become informed about who is engaged in prohibited or "criminal" activities. Because there seem to be no significant scale economies to identifying criminals, the state will not eradicate all criminal activities.

Realizing they will not necessarily be caught and punished, individuals may perceive that they can gain from activities the state proscribes. Criminals are diverse, and they can be organized in various manners. Some operate independently. Some operate as teams, using self-enforcement to enforce agreements. Finally, still others, on whom we focus in this chapter, are organized in teams to engage in lines of activity that the state prohibits and, within their operations, use force for third-party enforcement.

As is obvious, the main lines that criminal organizations pursue involve circumventing the activities the state constrains or bans. These include activities such as holding and trading in weapons and narcotics. Criminal organizations' comparative advantage arises from the fact that they do not face competition from the enforcement power of the state.[3]

To better comprehend the nature of criminal activities, it is imperative to inquire, first, Why would a state that seeks to maximize subjects' wealth ban or regulate *any* activity? Is not imposing the appropriate taxes more efficient than imposing constraints and bans? In general, the

---

[2] I have shown (Barzel, 1982) that sellers do not find it economical to measure and sort commodities to the point where buyers will refrain from further choosing; between them, they sort more than they would cooperatively. The rationale behind that statement is the same as that behind the conclusion that a state that provides protection at the joint wealth-maximizing level will not prevent all theft.

[3] According to Durkheim, in order to maintain their cohesiveness, all groups deliberately criminalize certain fringe activities. Wealth maximization is the hypothesized reason here behind making certain activities criminal. The two objectives, however, are not necessarily mutually exclusive.

full delineation of any commodity or any activity would be prohibitively costly. Therefore, in any transaction, some attributes are left in the public domain. The direct delineation problems, however, do not seem to capture the main issue with weapons and narcotics. Delineating them does not appear to be more difficult than delineating many legal commodities. Moreover, even where delineation is prohibitively costly, the state need not resort to a ban; it might simply refrain from delineation of such goods.

The use of some goods, however, tends to generate negative side effects (or externalities),[4] and sometimes the exchange of a good is prone to dispute, thus requiring excessive use of the state's legal resources, which are not marginally priced. It might seem that the state could simply impose taxes at the rate needed to take care of the external effects, or at least to mitigate them. The state, indeed, imposes significant taxes on some commodities, most notably, in this connection, alcohol. Taxes, however, lose much of their regulatory appeal if the rates at which they are imposed diverge significantly from the side effects they are intended to counter.

Although it is relatively easy to set taxes that will account for the side effects due to the "average" individual, there are two related reasons that for some individuals the side effects will significantly deviate from the average. One is that different individuals generate different effects. Consider guns, for example. One of the side effects is their use in robberies. Suppose that a tax on guns is imposed at a rate equal to the average side effect. Such a tax would be excessive for those using guns for self-defense, and it would be too low, and thus an insufficient deterrent, for those using guns for crime. Setting tax rates for individuals commensurate with the side effects they induce clearly would be prohibitively costly here.

The second reason for the discrepancy between the external effects and tax rates, actually an extension of the first, is that some individuals are able to evade taxes altogether. When the side effects are substantial, the appropriate tax rates must be high, and so will the gain from evasion be high. Evasion is an especially attractive territory for criminal organizations, which can effect it on a large scale. Moreover, the existence of legal markets in such commodities raises the cost of detecting evasion; when a commodity is banned, anybody observed to own or trade it is identified as a violator of the law. The state may then conclude that the

---

[4] Weapons also have military uses and can be used against the state, which is another reason to regulate and ban them. This applies especially to military assault weapons.

gain from banning the trade in, and sometimes the use of, guns and narcotics will exceed that from taxation. Not bearing the burden of the side effects of their action, individuals may wish to acquire prohibited commodities such as narcotics. The state not only does not enforce contracts for trade in banned commodities but also spends resources to deny individuals ownership over them. People who possess banned commodities are their economic owners, even though they lack legal title to them. Denied legal rights to them, trading in them is more costly than if they were legal.

Consider the trade in narcotics, which the state bans. Individuals who wish to acquire them may be concerned about enforcement of the terms of their transactions. Long-term relations with sellers are likely to be costly here. Criminal organizations such as the Mafia are characterized by the possession of physical power. Like the legitimate state, they can use their power to enforce agreements. They seem to have a comparative advantage in creating at least a rudimentary enforcement mechanism to delineate certain rights and are expected to use it to delineate rights in banned goods.

The state enforces contracts by fining and imprisoning violators. Criminal organizations seldom operate openly. They use violence in contract enforcement. Their most economical method of enforcement is to inflict bodily harm; incarceration is hardly a viable option to them. This distinction apart, the character of their delineation action parallels that effected by the state, and individuals who trade in narcotics are likely to use their services.

When a criminal organization such as the Mafia delineates rights, it also facilitates trade in the delineated commodities. For example, it helps delineate the quantities and qualities of narcotics. It enforces the buyer's agreement to pay and the seller's delivery of the agreed commodity. It also adjudicates the parties' disputes. This enhancement of economic rights over banned commodities is of exactly the same nature as the enhancement of economic rights over legal commodities brought about by the legitimate protector's enforcement.

Though these organizations are illegal, they rely heavily on their brand name, especially on "honor." Like the legitimate state, they can gain by adjudicating disputes impartially.[5] The more that people believe that the

---

[5] In legitimate states, the creation of long-term relations is handled primarily by the collective-action authority, not by the protectors. It appears that in criminal organizations such separation is less pronounced.

enforcers adjudicate disputes impartially, the higher the demand for their services. Last, but definitely not least, like the state in its relations with other states, these organizations use force or the threat of force to make transfers to themselves, such as their "protection" against broken windows and the like.

There are two implications of this argument: (1) As suggested by Gambetta (1993), who describes various illegal transactions that the Sicilian Mafia guarantees, criminal organizations with adjudication and enforcement power will emerge as a consequence of government prohibition of legal trade. The argument in earlier chapters implies that such organizations are most likely to emerge where they can create rights over *tradable commodities*. Where price controls are imposed, or when the possession and exchange of a commodity are banned, we can expect illegal or "black" markets to be organized. The emergence of organized crime in the United States during the prohibition of alcohol is consistent with the hypothesis. Crime (such as rape) that does not involve tradable goods is less likely to attract organized crime. (2) A reduction in the world price of a banned commodity produced outside a given country is expected to increase the level of activity of organized crime in that country. Because the commodity is banned, we expect *organized* crime to be involved in its trade. The reason for the increased activity is simply the increase in the quantity of the commodity demanded because of its lower price. The amount of resources used in providing it locally can be expected to increase. As is obvious, it is unlikely that this amount would be observed directly. On the other hand, I predict that the level of legal action against organized crime will be higher too, and that can be observed.

THE SCOPE OF ORGANIZED CRIME

As just argued, criminal organizations that use force for enforcement can profit by delineating rights to commodities and to activities that the state regulates or bans. These organizations meet the definition of the state adopted here, and therefore are "states." The soundness of the definition is underscored when it is noted that under certain circumstances many conventional states permit and even promote precisely the same types of activities that other states normally tend to ban and thus indirectly delegate to criminal organizations. The hypothesized condition for the state's tolerance or even promotion of activities that are usually banned is simply that the side effects of these activities are "exported."

Consider the maritime "flags of convenience." Some countries that have virtually no fleet of their own impose only lax shipping regulations and are eager to attract the registration of foreign ships. The owners of those ships seek that registration because they wish to avoid the stiffer standards of their home countries. The individuals placed at risk when ships operate under flags of convenience are not, as a rule, subjects of the countries providing the flags of convenience. Similarly, some countries offer virtually unregulated corporate registration, primarily to foreigners.

Another rather striking example is that of gambling. Most countries ban gambling. Some countries permit it provided that the gamblers are foreigners.[6] The activity is clearly branded as undesirable; these countries do not permit their own citizens to engage in it.[7] Yet they seem to feel that it is just fine to make money out of it as long as the gamblers are foreigners. The reason seems to be that the negative side effects in this case are borne by the foreigners.[8] Monaco and the states of Nevada and New Jersey permit gambling, but most of the gamblers there are tourists, not residents. The perpetrating states are no different from criminal organizations in terms of these activities. For that reason, the latter organizations are no less qualified to be considered states. The circle, indeed, seems closed. Apparently, within the United States, large numbers of members of the Mafia reside in the same neighborhoods. It is said that the Mafia prohibits drug dealing in these areas.

Criminal organizations have a comparative advantage in another kind of activity as well. Consider the distinction drawn in Chapter 10 between assets such as land, which can be directly identified by the courts and

---

[6] Alan Wykes (1964, app. 2) states that as of 1964, Cambodia and Egypt had gambling casinos that were open only to foreigners. Apparently, at least until quite recently, the Philippines and Korea also permitted gambling to holders of foreign passports only.

Regarding another service, I hypothesize that Swiss citizens may not be permitted to maintain the kind of secret bank accounts permitted to foreigners. Thus far I am not aware of the facts in this case.

[7] The families of individuals who sustain substantial gambling losses can become destitute and become a burden on the state. This may be a reason for the ban. Bingo is unlikely to impoverish anyone and is routinely permitted. State lotteries are common, but they impose heavy taxes on participants. In addition, gambling on state lotteries on a large scale is expensive, because the costs of buying a large number of tickets and of checking the outcome are not trivial. They are not likely, then, to impoverish many of their patrons.

[8] One apparent reason why some states allow foreigners to gamble, but do not allow the sale of narcotics to them, is that the resale of narcotics to citizens is easier than resale of gambling services.

matched to its legal owner, and assets such as generic goods, which can be assigned only because their locations identify their owners. A stolen asset of the latter type can be readily disposed of at a price near its market price. The prime example of such a commodity is cash, which thieves can enjoy almost at its nominal value.[9]

The return to thieves from theft of identifiable assets is low, because those assets can expose their holders to the police and consequently tend to fetch low prices in the open market relative to their value to their legal owners. Consider the theft of expensive automobiles. Thieves can disassemble cars and sell their parts without too much fear of detection, because disassembly transforms them into generic parts not easily traced by the police. Because eventually the parts have to be sold individually, however, the net revenue from sale of the parts tends to be only a fraction of the value of the original car in the legal market. Thieves tend not to use a stolen car as a car (rather than dismantling it) partly because of the higher risk of being caught. And, of course, the state will not protect the thief (or his buyer, even if unaware that it was stolen) from a new thief (Gambetta, 1993). However, a criminal organization, having the ability to enforce rights, may act like a state and deter "secondary" theft by protecting the assets of its own subjects. Such an organization, then, may be able to enhance the value of stealing what otherwise would seem to be well-delineated assets.

This last point also applies to war loot. Identifiable assets that once were owned by people in a country that has been conquered can be turned into legally owned, identifiable assets in the conquering country.[10] The Nazi lootings of the museums in the countries they conquered exemplify such theft.

As in the case of the legitimate state, the enforcement of agreements by organized crime must compete with that by other third parties and with self-enforced agreements. The steadier the relationship between the suppliers and the buyers of banned commodities, the lower the cost of self-enforcement relative to enforcement by the criminal organization. If, for example, a drug dealer has the economic rights over a particular

---

[9] Thieves enjoy full nominal value only with coins. Paper money is not strictly generic; the serial numbers on the bills are unique and sometimes are used to identify stolen ones.

[10] This also applies to "plain" theft when the stolen goods are sold across state borders, especially when the states do not cooperate in the prevention of such activities.

street corner, he is better able to form long-term relations with clients than is a dealer who has no constant base of operations. The latter, then, is more likely than the former to become a customer of a criminal organization.[11]

As a final point regarding the scope of criminal organizations, consider their relationship with revolutionary movements. The press often publishes stories about revolutionary movements that cooperate with, or act like, criminal organizations. Is there a reason to expect the two to act alike or to be tied to each other? For whatever reasons, some revolutionary movements form organizations that possess coercive power and operate within states. Some quickly take over the state (Castro in Cuba). They become "regular" states then. Some are quickly crushed and disappear from the scene. Some others, however, continue to operate within states for long periods without taking it over. This is especially common in occupied countries or among minorities, such as the Basques, who perceive or at least portray themselves as oppressed. These organizations can use their military power to establish enforcement mechanisms and to adjudicate contracts. They are equipped, then, with the enforcement machinery needed for organized crime and therefore have the potential to be low-cost operators in illegal markets. It is not surprising, then, that these organizations often gravitate to such activity or are lured into it.[12]

THE BOUNDARY OF THE CRIMINAL STATE

At equilibrium, there is a balance of power between the state and criminal organizations, each with activities in which it has a comparative advantage. The borderlines between the two sets, however, are unlikely to be well defined. There is no single ultimate enforcer within that gray area. The jurisdictions of different enforcers are likely to overlap in part, and disputes can be expected there. The greater the area over which the two organizations dispute each other's power, the greater the weakening

---

[11] Because either form of activity is illegal, it may be interrupted by the state. The proposition in the text, then, must be subject to the effects of such interruption.

[12] Terminology seems to play an important role in the operation of revolutionary organizations. They claim to represent the "oppressed" and conclude that taking something from the "oppressor" is not a "crime," but rather a "just" act. Conversely, the "legitimate" state often characterizes these organizations as "terrorist."

of rights resulting from the existence of more than one power-backed third-party enforcer in the same area.[13]

As an example of poorly delineated rights, consider a person who signed a contract and now perceives that he is about to become a loser under it. Suppose that a criminal organization offers to intimidate his partner, so that he can wiggle out of his contractual obligation. The rights under the contract turn out to be poorly delineated because of the absence of a single ultimate jurisdiction over the particular area. Had the victimized transactor been aware ahead of time of the difficulty of enforcing the contract, he would not have signed it. Rather, he would have chosen not to make any agreement, or else would have made one to be enforced by some other means.

Although there must be a balance of power between the state and criminal organizations, their absolute amounts of power will differ significantly. Stability in the relationship between criminal organizations and the state within which they operate requires the latter to be stronger than any of the former. Otherwise, either the state will disintegrate and cease to exist or the strongest criminal organization will take over the state and simply become the state. The continued existence of criminal organizations, then, requires the existence of the state.

At equilibrium, criminal organizations cannot compete with the state by delineating rights to commodities or activities that the state chooses to delineate; they can be effective only where the state chooses to deny delineation. As just argued, criminal organizations are expected to engage in some rights delineation. The asymmetry between such organizations and the central protector that gives meaning to the notion that only the latter is "legitimate" is basic, however, not in how the protector acquired his status but in the types of activities he engages in.

SUMMARY

By the definition here, a state is characterized by the existence of a central authority using violent means to enforce agreements within a given ter-

---

[13] Does the Sicilian Mafia make a positive contribution to the well-being of Sicilians, or does it make their lot worse? The reasoning here suggests that where the Mafia is the sole enforcer of rights, its contribution might indeed be positive, though it is likely to take for itself a large fraction of the net gain. Where it competes with the state, its operations result in costly transfers. Those who claim that the Mafia's contributions are positive seem to focus on the activities in which the Mafia has exclusive rights. Those who claim that its contributions are negative seem to focus on the gray area.

ritory. Criminal organizations, as is evident, meet these criteria, and thus are "states." On the other hand, they are not usually viewed as "legitimate" states. They are considered illegitimate because they specialize in activities the state proscribes and defines as criminal. These are the activities in which they have a comparative advantage. The state spends resources to prevent criminal acts, but it would be prohibitively costly to completely eradicate them, and some will occur, including those effected by organized criminals.

One reason the state prohibits certain activities is that they entail undesirable side effects. Individuals who do not bear the burden of the side effects of their actions may wish to engage in the banned activities. Their net valuation of these activities can be enhanced when they use criminal organizations to enforce their agreements.

Criminal organizations operate side by side with legitimate states. Although the legitimate state is necessarily more powerful than the criminal one, their powers are in balance; at equilibrium, the former does not find it worthwhile to eliminate the latter. The boundaries between their jurisdictions, like all boundaries, are never well delineated. Rights in such no-man's-land lie in the public domain. Making agreements there, whether enforced by the state or by criminal organizations, is difficult, because neither enforcer can then guarantee enforcement.

14

Power, Violent Conflict, and Political Evolution

Power plays a curious role in economists' attempts to formulate a theory of the state. North (1981) and Olson (1982), two of the more prominent economists who have written on the state, do not give power much of a role. North, for instance, initially brings up the importance of power. In summarizing his discussion, however, he does not even refer to power, but rather states that the ruler is subject to "a competitive constraint and a transaction cost constraint" (p. 28). Olson (1993) introduces the notion of the power of a "roving bandit" who, like the dictator I have discussed (Barzel, 2000a), turns into a "stationary bandit." But neither he nor I have explored the role of power itself.

Umbeck (1981) seemingly was the first modern economist to construct a model of the state that starts from a "primitive" beginning. In his model, "might makes right"; individuals' power determines everything. Power is also the central force in the accounts of many historians and political scientists. I concur with Umbeck that individuals' power determines the initial distribution of wealth, but the picture changes as Umbeck's model is extended to accommodate specialization.

Individually, specialized protectors have more power than others do. When power is delegated to specialized agents, others must deal with the problem of preventing the agents from taking over and becoming principals themselves. However, physical power, along with other personal attributes, such as cunning, that individuals possess, will predominate only until cooperation emerges. Given the trade-off opportunities between wealth and power, then as wealth is accumulated, sheer physical power will quickly recede to share or even yield center stage to the power that organizations control. I focus in this chapter on two issues related to power. One is the role of uncertainty about the parties' relative powers in inducing violent dispute and the factors contributing to that uncertainty. The other concerns the effects that violent disputes engender.

POWER AND THE THREAT OF USING IT

In modeling the emergence of the state, Umbeck assumes that there exists a set of unspecialized, equally skilled individuals.[1] He also assumes an absence of scale economies to the use of power, and he assumes that everyone is perfectly informed of its distribution. He shows that under his assumptions, an equal distribution in this case, the distribution of individuals' power determines the distribution of wealth. Moreover, because the effect of the use of power is known in advance, there is no need to use it, and nobody does. Rather, power functions as a credible threat.

Umbeck's empirical observations are derived from the California gold rush, and they fail to refute his implications. At that time, neither the military forces nor the legal institutions of the United States government had a significant presence in the area where gold was discovered, and miners had to create their own institutions. Umbeck points out that the individual miners all carried guns and asserts that they were similar in ability. His informational assumption seems reasonable under those conditions. Moreover, the gold rush did not last long, and the mining of individual deposits was too brief to allow the gold-seekers to form agreements based on repeated interactions that would have been necessary to reap the gains from specializing.

Personal power loses its dominant status when economies of scale to protection are present and individuals collaborate in the use of power. Emerging in its stead, as discussed in Chapter 12, are methods of organizing power and institutions to contain it. The focus here is on the methods that societies adopt to protect themselves from the power of their specialized protector and on the development of rule-of-law institutions. In such an analysis, factors other than the sheer power possessed by individuals and organizations at a point in time gain importance. These other factors, in turn, affect the accumulation and distribution of power.

I assumed earlier that two arguments enter into an individual's utility function: expected material wealth and personal safety or longevity. Power is often considered an end in itself (i.e., an argument in the

---

[1] See also Skogh and Stuart (1982).

individual's utility function). Indeed, it is often stated that power is the sole objective of rulers and of states. That assertion seems highly implausible. As long as power is not the *sole* argument in individuals' utility functions, people will not maximize it.[2] More importantly, when power is not the sole argument in the utility function, taking the desire for power into account does not change the argument here. In addition, whether or not power enters into the utility function, it is a means of acquiring wealth and of preventing others from capturing one's own. Individually and collectively, individuals will maintain and advance their power as they would any wealth-enhancing activity.

As Umbeck emphasizes, the possession of power does not mean that it will be put to use. Power can be used to conquer or simply to loot. Regarding the former, state B may be more powerful than its neighbor, state C. Still, B will not necessarily conquer C. If there are diseconomies to governing the two together, B may choose not to initiate a fight, for its wealth and probably its power would decline if it were to take over C. Although the two states are not equal in terms of power in this case, there is a balance of power between them. Turning to looting, fighting is not a necessary condition for it. Fighting will not occur if C admits it is weaker and agrees to pay tribute to B. C's potential for resistance, however, constrains the size of the tribute B can extract.

People spend great amounts of resources to accumulate and maintain power. Because the potential use of power as a threat is easy to overlook, its importance is often under-appreciated. Two questions regarding organized power arise: (1) What determines how much power a state will amass? (2) What are the conditions under which power will be used? The first was addressed in Chapter 10 as part of the discussion of the limitations on third-party enforcement. We now turn to the second.

UNCERTAINTY ABOUT RELATIVE POWER

As in Umbeck's model, here power can be used as a threat, but not exclusively so. Under the condition of costless information, individuals know

---

[2] It may seem unfair to fault historians, or even political scientists, for being loose with language when stating that individuals maximize power, thereby implying that this is the only argument in the utility function. In their discourse, however, that assumption is not innocuous. Those scholars often follow through, in that they ignore trade-offs between power and other factors. If significant trade-offs are available and are taken advantage of, the implications that the model that assumes no trade-off generates are likely to be refuted.

when a balance of power exists or what the difference in power is. The possession of such knowledge seems to be a sufficient condition for them not to use power. Viewed from a different angle, under the condition of costless information, rights are well defined, and no resources will be spent on capture.

Given the many dimensions of power, however, collecting information on relative amounts of power is costly. Individuals differ in terms of the various aspects of power, such as strength, speed, stamina, cunning, and intelligence, and the degrees to which they possess these are subject to continual changes. Moreover, when people cooperate, their coordination, motivation, and ability to enforce agreements also become important features of the power they accumulate. Given the complexity of power and its continual changes, people must spend resources to determine not only the extent of others' power but also the extent of their own. The need to economize on the cost of information implies that people are unlikely to become perfectly informed of the distribution of power. Therefore, they are also unlikely to be certain whether or not a balance of power prevails or what the true difference in power is. As shown by Landes (1971) and Gould (1973), uncertainty is a source of conflict. When the uncertainty is about power, the conflict can easily become violent. Conflict here can be internal, between a protector and his clients, or external, between states.

An outbreak of conflict, as in a decision to go to court, is not the result of uncertainty per se. Rather, it results from a particular configuration of random "errors" such that the parties overestimate their power relative to each other. Because such errors are random, conflict is not predictable. What is predictable is that as the magnitude of the sum of the errors increases, the *uncertainty* about individuals' or states' relative power will increase, and for that reason the probability of a conflict will increase. I first discuss the causes for internal conflict and then turn to war between states.

INTERNAL CONFLICT

As long as subjects can control their specialized protector, a balance of power between them and the protector, and among themselves, is expected to prevail. Stable conditions are conducive to the preservation of the status quo and of the information underlying it. We can expect the clients to maintain control over the protector so long as conditions remain unchanged. Conditions do change, however, such that one side or the other may perceive that the balance of power has shifted significantly. As a result of a significant change favorable to him, the protector may perceive that he has become strong enough to capture full power. If he gains such control, he can confiscate subjects' wealth.

The situation is symmetric in that the change could favor the subjects. When their power increases, they may try to wrest concessions from him, especially if he has done so to them in the past. But their behavior is unlikely to be symmetric to that of the protector, in that they will not wish to get rid of him; their objective is rather to control him.

In any case, none of this jockeying for position, by itself, necessarily must lead to the use of violence. In each case, if the sides assess the situation in the same way, the side that perceives itself to have become weaker may accede to the other's demands. Errors in estimation, however, are inevitable. Still, even if they assess the situation differently, as long as neither side overestimates its power significantly, they will not be expected to resort to violence. On occasion, however, such parties will overestimate their power. Violence can erupt when each side, simultaneously with the other, estimates that it has the upper hand and can expect to win, or, more accurately, when the sum of the two estimated probabilities of winning sufficiently exceeds unity.[3]

People, however, are likely to be aware of the predicament, akin to the "winner's curse," that uncertainty can entail. We can expect them to take deliberate action to lower the uncertainty. They can reduce the chance of violence by making it easier for each to assess the other's power. This may explain, in part, why medieval English rulers were itinerant. By traveling with a complete entourage and visiting in turn each of his most powerful nobles, the king and the nobility could more readily assess one another's power. The increased accuracy of their estimates reduced the chance for conflict.

Under certain conditions, voting is another method of *revealing* power. As mentioned in Chapter 4, when votes are allocated in proportion to individuals' power, an actual vote constitutes a revelation of power. The vote reduces the error in assessing power, reducing the chance of conflict.[4]

---

[3] Violence can also erupt when they agree on who is stronger, but not about the extent to which the war cost to the stronger would be less than the payment he is trying to extract from the weaker.

   The sum has to exceed unity by a finite amount, because the parties will not use violence unless their estimate of their combined gain from the use of violence, net of the costs they incur, is positive.

[4] Thanks to Timothy Dittmer for this observation.

The balance of power is a function not only of its current state but also of its expected path and variations therein. Suppose that a balance of power between two individuals exists at a point in time, and the one stronger at that moment may perceive that over the long run he will remain stronger. He may also expect, however, that for some brief intervals the balance will be disturbed and that he will temporarily lose his edge. He may fear that during one of those lapses the other individual will overpower him before he can regain his strength. As Weingast (1994) suggests, the stronger person, during his time of strength, may take preemptive action even though under the current conditions the value of the use of power may seem negative. The more evenly balanced the powers of two individuals are to begin with, the greater the chance of a violent conflict. The reason is that even a moderate divergence in their perceptions of their relative powers may suggest to one or the other that the time is right to gain dominance.

WAR

Pairs of states not at war with each other and not actively preparing to go to war presumably will perceive that there is a balance of power between them. They will have to reevaluate each other's power after any change occurs, but they will not go to war unless the balance is upset. The basic reason for war between states, just as for internal violent disputes, seems to be a change in conditions that leads to the adversaries simultaneously overestimating their power relative to each other.[5] When they consider going to war, given the cost of winning, the notion of "winner take all" does not apply. To see that, suppose that a change occurs such that state B now perceives itself to be slightly more powerful than its neighbor C, whereas previously C was slightly more powerful. B can now win a war with C. The cost of war is positive, however, and the *net* value of the loot or tribute B can extract is going to be slight.

Returning to the estimation of power, consider what seemingly is a common historical occurrence: brief outbreaks of fighting between states. Brief as these skirmishes usually are, they may enable the adversaries to

---

[5] Another reason sometimes offered for why people go to war is simply to maintain readiness, to keep honing their fighting skills; to be optimal, such training may call for real fighting. The rationale for such fighting is a bit shaky, however. If the opponent is feeble, there is not much to learn from fighting him. If he is not feeble, is not fighting him too dangerous?

sharpen their assessments of each other's capabilities. With such additional information in hand, the adversaries may quickly come to terms.[6] When they agree in their estimations of their powers, the expected loser is likely to agree to pay tribute to the expected winner, and such payments, indeed, are also quite common in history.

THE ENFORCEABILITY OF AGREEMENTS BETWEEN STATES

Consider a state that admits to being weaker than another and is agreeable to paying tribute to the latter. A self-enforcement mechanism, however, must be available to enforce such an agreement. In its absence, the parties may be unable to avoid costly fighting. Negotiating successful self-enforced agreements is difficult. Still, it is not impossible; the more predictable is a country's behavior, the easier it is to form a self-enforced agreement with it.

The predictability of a country's behavior will depend on at least five major factors, all of which directly or indirectly relate to the collection of information: (1) how long the ruling regime has been in power, (2) the ease of collecting information about it, (3) the extent of the rule of law, (4) under a dictatorship, the dictator's background, and (5) the rate of change in military technology.

The first three factors are general, the fourth is relevant to dictatorships only, and the fifth applies only to violent conflict. The effect of the longevity of a regime is straightforward. A regime that has just emerged from overthrowing its predecessor has no history, so there is little to draw on to predict its behavior. As it continues to stay in power, others will accumulate information about its conduct. Then predictions about its conduct will become more reliable, and the chance that it will be involved in a violent conflict will be lowered.

---

[6] This line of reasoning may explain two otherwise puzzling biblical episodes, both associated with the emergence of King David. In the war of succession between David and King Saul's heirs, at one point the two armies faced off. Rather than commence fighting right away, the generals sent two small elite units to fight each other, or, as they stated, "Let the young men now arise, and play before us" (Samuel II, 2, 14). Only after that engagement ended in a draw, thus failing to reveal whose force was superior, did the two armies begin to fight.

A few years earlier, an Israelite army had faced a seemingly superior Philistine army. There, too, they chose to engage in a preliminary small-scale fight – the famous confrontation between David and Goliath (Samuel I, 17). That one had a more decisive outcome. Using a slingshot, David hit Goliath and then slew him, thus presumably demonstrating the superiority of the Israelites' force. The Philistines promptly ran away.

The more difficult it is to collect information about a state, the more difficult it is to come to terms with it. For example, it is costlier to obtain information about the conduct of migrating nations than that of stationary ones. Even if regimes of the former type are stable, it may be difficult to learn about their strength and behavior. War between them and stationary neighbors is more likely, then, than war between stationary neighbors.[7]

Regarding the third factor, how entrenched the rule of law is, the more secure the control of the collective-action organization over the state, the more predictable is the behavior of the regime. Moreover, rule-of-law regimes tend to be stable, and thus agreements among them based on repeated interactions are more likely than under dictatorial regimes. We can expect that the frequency of wars among rule-of-law regimes will be low. This is not because rule-of-law regimes are inherently peace-loving, but rather because of their greater stability. We can expect the frequency of wars to be greater between pairs of countries only one of which is governed by the rule of law, and still greater between countries neither of which is governed by rule of law.[8]

Turning to the fourth factor, consider individuals who once were dictators' subordinates and were able to exploit their positions to usurp dictatorial power for themselves. There are two subordinate positions or offices that are likely to provide their incumbents a springboard from which to overthrow a current dictator and acquire dictatorial power for themselves. One is that of military commander, and the other is that of a court politician. The uncertainty confronting such a military commander seems quite different from that faced by a politician. After seizing power, it is plausible that the former, being more adept in military tactics and technology than the latter, would be more likely to initiate military action. The military commander would also be more likely to dream up military schemes to try to surprise his enemies. On the other hand, after becoming dictators, former court politicians are less likely to come up with plans for military adventures on their own. Neither would they be inclined to let their newly acquired generals loose to experiment with military innovations, because that might give the generals leeway to grab

---

[7] The same rationale applies to the difficulty that potential victims encounter in reaching agreement with thieves or pirates who prey on them.

[8] There have been no wars among rule-of-law states at least since the beginning of the twentieth century. The medieval Italian city-states, however, frequently fought with each other, in spite of being governed by rule of law. Perhaps the culprit there was the regimes' instability (in spite of the typically rule-of-law governance).

power for themselves. Dictators who have risen from the military, then, are more likely to generate uncertainty regarding the prospect for war than are those who have risen from the court, and the probability that war will break out under their rule correspondingly increases.

The fifth factor, the rapidity of changes in military technology, seems to have a significant effect on the predictability of a county's behavior. However, the possibilities here are too numerous and too complex for me to attempt to offer any useful predictions. Among the factors that seem to impinge on predictability is the degree to which the military innovations themselves are on the conservative side, and similarly for the ways they can be used. Moreover, in terms of predictability, offensive innovations seem to have different effects than defensive ones, and each mode benefits from its own level of secrecy. I am unable to tease out testable implications from these factors and must reluctantly leave this issue entirely unresolved.

Although when dealing with each other, sovereign countries have no third-party enforcement mechanism to resort to, they, like individuals, can negotiate self-enforced agreements such that each will perceive that the other will believe that it would lose from violating the agreement. Once self-enforced relations are in place, the parties can take steps to enhance them. For instance, each of two neighboring states that have signed a non-aggression agreement may unilaterally remove trees from its side of the border to make it more difficult for it to attack the other by surprise. A sovereign country can also demonstrably abstain from developing certain kinds of weapons, and perhaps develop others as joint ventures with partners with whom it wishes to avoid war.

Success in implementing self-enforced agreements is far from being guaranteed. The difficulty of reaching an agreement may itself be indirectly a reason to go to war. Even two countries that agree in their estimates of their relative powers may still decide to go to war. A weaker country will do well to concede and agree to pay tribute to the stronger. However, because the tribute agreement may not be enforceable, the weaker country may fear that it will be taken over even if it concedes. Indeed, as already mentioned, conquerors have often violated the conditions of surrender that they have stipulated. Certainly a country that is perceived by both sides to be the weaker is expected to lose. Still, it may choose to defend itself, because the chance it could win is still positive, and the stronger country might choose not to spend the resources needed for conquest.

THE AFTERMATH OF WAR

What is the nature of dealing with the spoils of war? I focus on the winner's viewpoint, which is sufficient, because the discussion entails the implications for the loser. How will winners exploit losers? And how will winners divide the spoils of war among themselves?

It might appear that winners would cash in by simply extracting in each period the maximum difference between the gross income that losers can produce and the minimal value of resources necessary to produce that income.[9] That amount, however, is not automatically known, and resources must be expended to determine it. Because of the cost, the determination will not be perfectly accurate. Mistakes, both in overestimation and in underestimation, are expensive. Errors in overestimation will result in the winner trying to extract more than the loser can deliver, thus harming or even killing the goose that lays golden eggs. Underestimation will result in direct income loss. Seemingly more serious is the fact that it will undermine the security of the winner. In order to produce to their capacity, individuals must receive the right to the residual of their own effort. This means they must be granted some autonomy. Occasionally there will be large positive residuals, providing losers with sufficient resources to defy the winner.[10] The winner can largely avoid these problems by directly supervising the inputs of the individuals in the conquered country (i.e., colonizing it and enslaving its subjects, as a dictator may do with his own subjects after taking over). That policy, however, will yield a smaller total output than would be produced if the latter were producing to their capacity. I predict that the longer the colonization lasts, and the more the conqueror is governed by rule of law and thus geared for trade, the more autonomy he will grant the conquered. When colonizing is not economical, the winner may loot what he can, destroy what might become menacing in the future, and retreat.

Dividing the spoils of war will have two major effects: to increase the disparity of wealth as well as the disparity of rights among subjects. In general, even those remunerated primarily by wages must receive some

---

[9] This is essentially the same problem as that of a dictator attempting to extract the maximum amount from his subjects, as briefly discussed in Chapter 5.

[10] Elsewhere (Barzel, 2000a) I have discussed means available to dictators to maintain their security while giving clients some leeway. The argument also applies to relationships between conqueror and conquered, and it is especially relevant for empires created for trading purposes.

reward tied to performance in order to induce performance. The wartime leader presumably assumes the role of residual claimant to the outcome of war to a greater degree than do other combatants, and all combatants more so than non-combatants. The successful war leader, then, is expected to emerge greatly enriched, and the other surviving combatants as more enriched than non-combatants.[11] In addition, when slaves constitute part of the spoils of war, as long as the slaves are not sold to other countries, the winners become slaveholders.

Consider a state that has won a war and that prior to the war was a free society with equal-standing citizens holding comparable amounts of wealth.[12] Successful wars are likely to greatly reduce the egalitarian character of such societies. As just asserted, inequality among the original citizenry is likely to increase substantially as a result of successful war. Moreover, although the political rights of the citizenry may be well protected, the slaves they acquire, besides being poor, will not share in those rights.[13]

Wars have been fought continually. Consequently, at any point in time a large fraction of the world's population may have been enslaved or turned into colonial subjects. Elsewhere (Barzel, 2000a) I have discussed forces that propel autocratic states toward a rule of law. I argue that defensive wars, and other shocks, tend to reverse the trend and induce autocratic rule. Shock due to the ensuing realignment of power within a country is likely to raise the costs of completing various contracts and thus weaken the rule of law. The more severe the fighting, and the more drawn out the war, the stronger the effect. Moreover, in the aggregate, war impoverishes the combatant states and therefore makes them weaker and more vulnerable to states that have remained neutral. Although the winner is expected to get richer and thus more powerful, a deviation from the expected outcome can weaken even the winner. The celebrated

[11] It is significant that in contemporary rule-of-law states, opportunities for successful military leaders to get rich arise primarily *after* they have completed their military service.

[12] The model here admits slavery prior to the beginning of cooperation. However, it seems that slavery would have been rare then. Independently operating individuals may choose not to hold slaves because of the threat slaves pose to their masters' lives.

[13] Such a post-war state of affairs seems to correspond to those in classical Athens and in Norman England. Both countries were, to a degree, "democracies." In both countries, freemen had full political rights, though their wealth distribution was uneven. Side by side with those freemen, however, were slaves, or serfs, very poor and with little say in the conduct of the affairs of the state.

lament "another such victory and I shall be ruined" describes a situation that seems quite common.

SUMMARY

It is evident that "might makes right," but power can determine wealth distribution at the individual level only until cooperation in its use commences. Before they allow specialists in the use of power to emerge, individuals who create a collective-action mechanism will first amass sufficient power to control the specialists under most circumstances. As long as conditions remain stable, there will be an equilibrium, or balance of power, between the two parties. Small changes favorable to the power specialists may allow them to enhance their positions, but not to take over.

By itself, disparity in power between parties does not mean that power will be deployed. As long as the parties are well informed of their relative powers, they will settle their affairs by the threat of the use of power rather than by its actual use. People, however, are never certain how much power others and even they themselves have. Violent conflicts can result when the parties err in excessive optimism about their own power. A conflict between the protectors and their controllers will take the form of civil war. Conflict can also occur externally between states: a "regular" war.

Whereas war is not predictable, in that it is induced by random errors in estimation, if the size of the error is reduced, the probability of war will decrease. Parties can reduce the error by making their power more transparent. They can engage in activities such as conducting military exercises in full view, and removing objects useful for hiding offensive equipment. Wars, obviously, do occur. They have two major effects, besides the destruction of life and property. They tend to increase wealth disparity, enriching primarily the winning combatants, and they tend to reduce the rule of law. The reason for the latter is that war disrupts economic life, and individuals tend to default on their contractual obligations. The increase in the rate of default reduces the value of contracting in general.

15

The Time Path of Change under Dictatorships and under Rule-of-Law Regimes

I have argued (Barzel, 2000a) that people create institutions in order to prevent confiscation and use "checks and balances" to enhance the viability of those institutions. Severe shocks tend to upset the checks and balances and increase the probability that one individual or another will be able to usurp power and become a dictator. In that paper I also described some of the features of dictatorships and the conditions under which those regimes can evolve into rule-of-law states.

In this chapter, I first explore the notion of shock and the paths its effects can take, followed by an inquiry into the distinction between mild and severe shocks. I then compare, along two main dimensions, dictatorial regimes and regimes governed by rule of law. First, I ask how an outside threat will affect each of the regimes. Second, I examine how the two regimes differ in terms of (1) the rights held by the head of state, (2) the state's participation in enterprises, (3) the extent to which legal rights are developed in the state, and (4) the distinction the states make between legal rights and economic rights.

THE EFFECTS OF SHOCKS

At any point in time there is a balance of power between protector and clients. Each particular balance will determine what actions the protector can take, as well as the size of his reward. A shock upsets such a balance and, more importantly, increases the level of uncertainty in the assessment of power. As a rule, the damage caused by a shock is not evenly distributed across states, nor is it within a state.

Generally, a shock is anything that causes a change in the balance of power and the uncertainty associated with it. Natural disasters such as floods and earthquakes tend to inflict great damage. These were seldom predictable in the past, and mostly they are still unpredictable, and thus are "shocks." Shocks can also result from sheer errors, accidents, or even the spread of a new religion. A large fraction of *severe* shocks seem to be man-made. By the model here, civil wars and external wars are the primary causes of shocks, and wars can also be the effects of shocks. Although civil war is endogenous, its outcome, like the outcome of an external war, is unpredictable, and thus constitutes a random shock.

Suppose that the shock is the overflow of a river. Suppose further that the overflow impinges primarily on the work of the collective-action organization by, say, making its assembly more difficult. In that case the power of the collective-action mechanism becomes weaker relative to that of the protector. In general, shocks tend to alter the balance of power. As long as a shock does not endanger the collective-action mechanism, I define it as "moderate"; if it is sufficient to destroy the mechanism, I define it as "severe." Shocks occur continually, and viable institutions must withstand at least some. I first consider shocks that do not lead to destruction of the collective-action mechanism.

Even moderate shocks will affect the relationship between the protection specialists and the collective-action mechanism. As emphasized throughout this book, airtight control over the protector would be prohibitively expensive. The agreement, perhaps implicit, between the protector and his employers does not cover every contingency. The protector's employers, then, cannot distinguish between the effects of random shocks and the effects from shirking and other forms of substandard performance. Thus they allow the protector some discretion and will punish him only if his actions exceed certain bounds. The more severe the shocks, the wider the boundaries and the greater the protector's degree of discretion.

To illustrate the effects of shocks, consider the relationship in medieval England between the protector (i.e., the king) and the barons. On several occasions the king is known to have accused individual barons of treason. The rest of the barons may have had difficulty in determining whether or not a conviction was an unbiased finding of treason (typically based on evidence of contacts with foreigners). On his part, the king may have accused a baron unjustly in order to get rid of an adversary and confiscate his property. In general, it is difficult to tell which distribution a single draw comes from, but such a determination becomes easier with increasing sample size. In the case here, the king might get away with, say, one or two trumped-up cases. In other words, the king had some leeway to take "arbitrary" actions. But if he brought too many such cases, his barons might conclude that he had stepped over the line. They might then attempt to rein him in.

What might precipitate the arbitrary action? When the king benefited from a moderate wealth gain (due, say, in the case of the English kings, to a successful war that expanded his personal holdings in France), his ability to resist the collective force of the barons increased too. In this illustration, the king's wealth gain is an example of a "mild" shock, a straw that does not break the camel's back.[1]

Returning to the general case, consider a shock that adversely affects the collective-action mechanism. If the effect is clear to all, the mechanism controllers may concede greater control or even complete control to the protector. As a rule, I expect shocks to increase the level of uncertainty in the assessment of power, since the errors in estimating relative powers will become larger and more frequent. The greater the uncertainty about the new internal power alignment, the greater the chance a civil war will erupt. In case the specialized protector wins, his relative power is likely to increase, and there is an increased chance he will become dictator. I consider as "severe" those shocks that result in the destruction of the collective-action mechanism.

A shock can upset the balance of power within a state or between two states. The chance that each of a pair of states will then perceive that it will gain from fighting the other will also increase, and then war will become more likely. Losing a war can weaken the power of the collective-action mechanism relative to that of the protector, and there, too, the protector may take over. The ruler who emerges is likely to gain enough power to destroy the existing collective-action mechanism.[2]

I expect dictators who wish to stay in power, and who are not inclined to trade wealth for power on a large scale, to eliminate the collective-action mechanisms within their countries and in the countries they take over and to prevent new such mechanisms from emerging. Thereby the threat faced by dictators that they, too, could be overthrown would be reduced. Absent a collective-action mechanism, individuals can do little to get rid of an emerging dictator. True, individuals can erect new

---

[1] It seems to me, however, that the civil insurrection of the barons that ended with the Magna Carta was the consequence of two major defeats (severe shocks) the king had suffered in France in the preceding decade.

[2] The emerging ruler might well be the old one. Nevertheless, such rulers, even if previously committed to the rule of law, are prone to become despotic.

collective-action mechanisms, or renew the old ones. The new ruler, however, possesses the means to drastically raise the cost of effecting collective action. The more thorough the destruction of the existing mechanism, the more difficult the creation of a new one.[3]

I now offer a scenario featuring a sequence of events that can lead to dictatorship via civil war. Consider a state that has been functioning harmoniously, subject to the rule of law. A racial or religious difference that was innocuous in the past begins to gain in importance. Such a difference can come to the fore when, for example, major decisions must be made by vote and a majority forms that attempts to confiscate some of the minority's wealth. As a result of the rift, the forces within the collective-action mechanism that initially were unified can become divided. A protector who previously was under the control of the collective-action mechanism may attempt to take advantage of the rift and align himself with one of the factions. It seems that the weaker faction needs the protector more than the stronger one and thus is likely to offer him better terms. He is likely, then, to team up with the weaker faction. Together with his new allies, he may be stronger than the other faction. He and his allies might then overpower their opponents.

The protector and the faction with which he allies himself are not necessarily "friends." Each knows that the other may first "use" it and then, when it ceases to be of use, "betray" it. When they reach their agreement, the new allies will make whatever arrangements each believes will best protect its own rights. They also perceive, among other things, that the balance of power between them can be maintained. However, the chance is high that an internal power struggle will disrupt that balance. If the outcome favors the protector, his allies may belatedly discover that the assurances they extracted were insufficient. If the outcome favors his allies, the protector may find that after he has done his job they will get rid of him. Nevertheless, at the time they made the agreement, both sides perceived the gamble as worthwhile. Of course, the balance of power between the parties may not change much, and they

---

[3] Some of the regimes that now govern the former satellites of the Soviet Union and the states that constituted that union are autocratic. Some are governed by the rule of law. Consider the destruction of the collective-action mechanisms that initially existed there. That destruction was accomplished over a longer period of time in the states of the Soviet Union than in its satellites (the Baltic states are not strictly part of the pattern, as they were annexed to the Soviet Union in 1940 and were occupied by the Nazis during most of World War II). This difference in those amounts of time may explain, in part, the current difference in governance between the two sets.

may choose to keep their agreement and continue to cooperate after subduing their adversaries.

SPECULATIONS ON SOME TWENTIETH-CENTURY EVENTS

The distinction between conditions that generate mild shocks and those that generate severe shocks (i.e., between conditions that lead to shocks that weaken the collective-action mechanism and those that destroy it) allows an interpretation of some relatively recent events that otherwise might seem puzzling. Compare the Nazi takeover of Germany or the Communist takeover of Russia with the takeover of Chile by Pinochet. The first two takeovers occurred in countries with very short histories of constitutional institutions.[4] On the other hand, Chile had experienced many decades of constitutional rule before the Pinochet takeover. It seems highly plausible that a well-functioning collective-action mechanism existed in Chile prior to Pinochet's takeover, whereas the control mechanisms were very weak in Germany and in Russia. The revolutionary forces in those two countries were able to overcome such mechanisms relatively easily and, after securing power, were able to demolish them.[5]

In Chile, in 1973, Pinochet took over from President Allende. Although Allende was the legitimate head of state, having won election in 1970, many suspected that he intended to seize total power and become a dictator. I hypothesize that the Chilean collective-action mechanism was activated to install Pinochet as dictator when fear of Allende's motives became acute.[6] I venture that the controllers of the collective-action mechanism effected a two-step procedure. The first was to remove from the Chilean political scene the elements viewed as a threat to the rule of law. The second was to restore the constitutional regime. Pinochet

---

[4] The Nazis initially came to power by constitutional means. However, the constraints to keep them within the constitutional framework were totally inadequate. That may have been due partly to the weakening of the rule of law after World War I, and perhaps in part to the conquerors' harsh policies.

[5] It does not seem an accident that both countries banned organized religion. Had organized religion remained legal, it might have posed a threat to those regimes. It seems that in Communist Poland, the Catholic church did indeed tend to undermine the regime.

[6] The question whether or not Allende attempted to acquire dictatorial power is still hotly debated. The argument here hinges not on the validity of that claim but on the notion (which may be difficult to verify) that such suspicions were held by the collective-action mechanism.

was given substantial dictatorial powers to perform the first. However, those powers most likely were somewhat restricted in scope. They clearly were restricted in duration. My evidence for the presumed restriction on the actual duration of Pinochet's rule is what transpired to be an enforced and thus seemingly enforceable constitutional amendment to limit his term. When Pinochet's term came to an end, he was *forced* to give way to a legitimately elected government, and was allowed to compete for office. The fact that Pinochet did not postpone the elections, which dictators are wont to do, is what convinces me that an effective collective-action mechanism existed in Chile at that time.[7] The collective-action mechanisms in existence in Russia and in Germany were at best weak. Whatever internal powers existed in those states were not sufficiently strong to force out Lenin or Stalin or their successors or Hitler after they became established in power.[8] Thus the lack of rule-of-law institutions in Germany and in Russia led to severe shocks, while the existence of rule-of-law institutions in Chile allowed for the shock to be more mild.

THE STAYING POWER OF THE RULE OF LAW IN ITALIAN CITY-STATES

The line of reasoning applied here may help to explain the persistence of the rule of law in the city-states of medieval Italy. Note first that almost all those city-states either were continuously governed by the rule of law

[7] There is no reason to think that Pinochet himself had ever been sympathetic to preservation of the rule of law. It also seems plausible that, even today, various elements in the Chilean military and elsewhere are not sympathetic to the rule of law and may favor returning full power back to someone like Pinochet. In any case, love for the rule of law is not a sentiment that can be taken for granted, and those with collective-action power are not expected to act on the basis of such sentiment. Rather, those with such power are expected to take steps to ensure that the rule of law will prevail.

It seems that as of the summer of 2000, the agreement to exempt Pinochet from prosecution was not enforceable.

[8] Fascist Italy presents an interesting intermediate case. Mussolini usurped power in Italy in 1922, some four years after World War I. Prior to that, Italy had been governed by rule of law for several decades. My interpretation of the ensuing events is that the war weakened, but did not demolish, the collective-action mechanism in Italy, and Mussolini himself had to submit to such power at least to a minor degree. That may explain why Italy was not ruled nearly as dictatorially as was Germany or Russia. It seems that Mussolini was less constrained than Pinochet, but more than Hitler or Lenin. Although he ruled longer than Pinochet, his rule was much less ruthless than that of Hitler or that of Lenin and Stalin.

or seesawed between the rule of law and dictatorial rule. What are often described as dictatorial dynasties in those cities seem to me to have been cases of serious weakening, but definitely not collapse, of the rule of law. Probably the most famous dynasty that was considered dictatorial was that of the Medici, who were the main power in fifteenth-century Florence. By and large, however, even at the height of their power, the Medici had to abide by various decisions of the elected council of Florence.

Many of the Italian city-states were taken over at one time or another by neighboring city-states, some more than once. The conquerors seemingly did not demolish the collective-action mechanisms of the conquered cities. A possible explanation for such treatment is as follows. By and large, a rule-of-law regime is less threatening to its neighbors than is a dictatorship. A conqueror who had taken a neighboring city but did not plan to retain it may have wanted to maintain the rule of law there so as to be able to more easily conclude treaties with it in the future than if it had become autocratic.[9] Thus, when the occupying forces left a conquered city, the liberated city was able to quickly return to the preconquest rule of law.[10]

COMPARING THE EVOLUTION OF RULE-OF-LAW REGIMES WITH THAT OF DICTATORSHIPS

How do dictatorial regimes stack up against rule-of-law states? Whether governed by a dictatorship or by rule of law, an internally stable state not seriously threatened by another is under no pressure to alter its policies. Inertia, however, will affect the two regimes very differently. Dictatorships tend to stagnate. A dictator, if he wished, could strike deals with his subjects to develop profitable new projects that would enrich both sides. However, subjects who were allowed to accumulate new wealth might use it to try to depose him. Because, to begin with, a dictator is very rich, even in a very poor country, his gain from change would be relatively modest, hardly worth the risk.

In a rule-of-law state, the inertial effect is that the state's current growth will tend to maintain its course. Under the rule of law, a *steady* course implies *growing* wealth. As rule-of-law states are becoming pro-

[9] The Western Allies' imposition of a rule of law on their defeated World War II enemies can be similarly explained.

[10] In note 12 I argue that in those cities, individuals with the ability to seize power often did not find doing so worthwhile.

gressively richer, they are likely to become stronger, better able to avoid falling prey to others. Indeed, because rule-of-law states tend to grow faster than dictatorships, then as time passes, the balance of power between the two will shift in favor of the former. Although a rule of law can be dismantled by internal upheaval, the longer the rule of law is in existence, the smaller the chance it will be upset, because changes are continually being made to strengthen it.[11] As new steps in the process of strengthening the rule of law are undertaken, newer steps may become less costly to implement. In addition, some potential arrangements for safeguarding the rule of law are subject to scale economies and become feasible with increases in wealth. Countervailing forces, of course, are continually emerging. Presumably, using their collective action, individuals will attempt to prevent such forces from gaining the upper hand.

Consider now the effect of a serious, but not imminent, outside threat. The institutions in a rule-of-law state will already be inducing a high rate of income growth and, with it, an increased ability to face adversaries. I would not expect such a threat to that state to cause a change in institutions. In a dictatorship, on the other hand, the dictator facing such a threat can gain from changing his institutions. In his pursuit of personal safety, he forgoes a great deal of potential personal wealth in order to reduce the threat from within. The threat from the outside, however, compromises the dictator's safety. He can gain by devoting more resources to defense and assigning a higher priority to income growth.

A dictator might achieve income growth by attempting to meet his subjects' demand for third-party adjudication. Individuals will not demand that service unless the dictator is properly constrained. An *absolute* dictator, however, cannot commit to abstain from confiscation and thus cannot provide that service. A dictator's offer of third-party enforcement for his subjects will be accepted only if he relinquishes some of his power and institutes safeguards that can be trusted to prevent him from confiscating his subjects' gains. A dictatorship that turns itself into a rule-of-law state, then, is likely to experience rapid income growth. The recent spectacular income growth that followed the easing of restrictions on rights to private property in Communist China

---

[11] The chance that a well-established rule-of-law state will turn into a dictatorship is not zero, however. One striking example of such a reversal is that of ancient Rome. After several centuries of rule of law and internal peace, civil strife became common, and in 44 B.C. Julius Caesar turned Rome into a dictatorship.

testifies to the speed at which such a policy change can yield significant results.

As per-capita income rises, the state will become better able to amass the resources necessary to fend off the outside threat. Indeed, individuals would have much to lose from foreign conquest, and thus they will be better motivated to participate in the defense effort. Therefore, a dictator faced with an outside threat can be expected to ease the restraints on individuals, strike deals with them, and even create a mechanism that will tie his hands somewhat, so as to enforce the deals. He must also provide third-party adjudication and continue to enhance its status.[12]

The strange mix of authoritarianism and rule-of-law elements in Singapore seems to fit the foregoing characterization. When, in 1965, Singapore became an independent state, it already possessed rule-of-law institutions. Those had been introduced during the 140 years of colonial British rule in the Malay Peninsula, of which Singapore was a part. After Singapore's transition from British crown colony to independent state, Lee Kuan Yew was elected its first prime minister, and his party continues in power. Singapore, however, is small and shares a border with what is now called the Federation of Malaysia – a much larger and poorer state. Rapid economic growth has been vital to Singapore's effort to amass the power necessary to prevent being run over by Malaysia. In spite of some repressive actions, by and large Singapore continues to be governed by a relatively high degree of rule of law.

LEGAL RIGHT VERSUS ECONOMIC RIGHT IN THE TWO REGIMES

Agreements by contract delineate legal rights and are subject to state enforcement. Other forms of agreement are enforced by alternative

---

[12] Earlier in this chapter I discussed the aftermath of war between Italian city-states and offered an explanation why the winner often allowed the loser to retain its collective-action mechanism. Cities recently having been freed from conquest seem ripe for takeover from within. I now offer a reason why individuals in position to usurp power in such cities seldom attempted to do so, allowing their cities to restore constitutionality. Numerous constitutional city-states existed in Italy during that era. Any city, including newly freed ones, had such cities as neighbors. The newly freed cities had to face the steadily increasing power of their thriving neighbors. To avert the threat, they had to readopt a constitutional regime and accumulate wealth quickly. A dictator would not have fared well under those conditions.

enforcement mechanisms, thus enhancing economic rights but not legal rights. The distinction between the two kinds of rights looms large in the comparison between rule-of-law regimes and dictatorial ones.

Consider first the residual claimancy in an absolute dictatorship. As pointed out earlier, the *absolute* dictator is the *sole* residual claimant to the income of his state. Wealth is necessary for acquiring power, and virtually anybody is capable of converting wealth into power. Examples of such conversion might include devoting resources to building muscles, learning how to move without being detected, acquiring machine guns, and securing the cooperation of others in the use of power. If no subject is allowed to accumulate wealth, physical or human, none can acquire power. A person whose gross income can finance only the amount of consumption needed for sustenance cannot accumulate wealth. A dictator is sure to remain absolute, then, if he prevents his subjects from earning any income in excess of such amounts. If a dictator were able to fix each subject's income at the subsistence level, he would become the claimant to the entire residual income his state could generate.

Absolute dictatorship, however, is not a state of affairs that can be attained in reality. The cost incurred by even the most ruthless dictator in preventing subjects, among which would be supervisors and policemen, from controlling some of the residual income would be prohibitive. Rather, a dictator will attempt to keep his subjects' residual income low and maintain some control over its use. He will do so by structuring individuals' rewards to consist primarily of a steady subsistence component, while avoiding projects and discouraging activities that would generate highly fluctuating incomes. To the extent that some individuals may nevertheless earn high incomes, we can expect the dictator to channel it toward non-threatening uses, such as expensive but easy-to-monitor residences.

The distinction between a dictator's management of income variability and that under a rule-of-law regime suggests an operational measure of the rule of law. This measure is the share of the income variability associated with protection that the protector bears in the territory he protects. This share is high in dictatorships and gets lower as the rule of law becomes more secure.[13] For instance, we expect a dictator to grant

---

[13] It seems difficult to measure accurately the share of variability the protector bears. But compare the medieval English kings to contemporary American presidents or American chiefs of staff. When England fought France on French soil, the

less autonomy to local police than will a rule-of-law state. This measure of the rule of law, or of the deviation of a state from dictatorship, is operational.

In Chapter 4, I drew attention to a fundamental difference between the rule-of-law state and the firm. The difference is that the former is not, and the latter is, the residual bearer of its own actions. The dictatorial state *shares* with the firm the characteristic of being the residual bearer of its own action. As stated, a truly absolute dictator would bear the *entire* income variability of his state. If such a dictator were to undertake a new enterprise, he would become its sole owner. He would not be inhibited in his pursuit of profitable action the way the employed protection specialist is in a rule-of-law state; rather, his motivation parallels that of the sole owner of a firm.

A dictatorship and a firm nevertheless differ significantly, but the difference lies elsewhere. Unlike a firm, the absolute dictator's state must be *totally* integrated, horizontally and vertically. Because the dictator cannot personally specialize in everything and be everywhere at once, he must delegate some responsibilities. But delegatees who do not bear any of the residual will shirk, presumably totally. The dictator's only way out is to relinquish some of his dictatorial powers and allow other individuals to bear some of the variability of their actions. This, of course, means a step in the direction of a rule-of-law state. Still, by and large, we would expect that dictatorial regimes would directly operate large fractions of the enterprises in their states, while heavily regulating most of the rest. Putting the "means of production" in the hands of the state (or, euphemistically, "the people") is a common trait of dictatorships, whether or not they declare themselves "socialist."[14]

Hereditary monarchy has dominated much of human history. Where do such monarchies lie vis-à-vis the comparison between dictatorships and rule-of-law regimes? Among contemporary states, some of those

---

territory gained became the English king's personal possession, and the territory lost was his loss. On the other hand, the bulk of the gains or losses from wars fought by the United States becomes translated into lower or higher taxes. The share of the president or chief of staff in that change of wealth is minute (even if it may significantly affect his personal wealth).

Taylor (1982) defines as anarchic those societies with no concentration of power. In those societies, because no one specializes in protection, there are no protection specialists to bear the income variability.

[14] Wittfogel (1957) provides a plethora of evidence of autocratic regimes, and especially "hydraulic" regimes, that retained ownership of the bulk of the resources in their states.

with the strongest rule-of-law regimes are hereditary monarchies, especially those in northern Europe. On the other hand, numerous monarchs have been despots. I contend that in spite of the existence of rule-of-law monarchies, the origin of hereditary monarchy necessarily lies in dictatorship.

In Chapter 8 we considered the constraints that we expect subjects to impose on the protectors they employ. Among these is their length of service, or tenure. The shorter the tenure, the less the opportunity for a protector to take over the regime. A protector who has the right to bequeath his status to his descendants, or, for that matter, to anybody else, necessarily has a great deal of control over his operations. I hypothesize that subjects will seek to retain such control, and thus I do not expect them to grant their protector the right to select his successor. Consequently, if we observe a protector who possesses such a right, we have to conclude that he, or one of his predecessors, acquired the right *by force*. If this argument is correct, then all hereditary monarchies, including the contemporary constitutional ones, must have originated as dictatorships. By this argument, then, the existence of a hereditary monarchy is sufficient evidence for the prior existence of a dictatorship.[15]

Among contemporary rule-of-law states, Switzerland is distinguished by its republican origin. From its very beginning, late in the thirteenth century, Switzerland has lived entirely without hereditary rulers.[16] Its leaders, civilian and military, all have had limited tenure. Similarly, during a long existence as an independent state from about A.D. 600 to A.D. 1797, Venice likewise was a republic, clearly shunning hereditary rulers. The doges were appointed for life, which often was quite long, but after A.D. 800, Venice did not allow sons to succeed their fathers.[17]

Dictatorships and rule-of-law regimes differ, of course, in many other ways. I now compare the two in terms of the following additional dimensions: (1) the extent of the legal institutions they can be expected to

---

[15] In 1830, after gaining its independence from the Netherlands, Belgium's rule-of-law institutions imported a king whose regime was to become hereditary. That contradicts the prediction in the text.

[16] Apparently, the nobility that existed in Switzerland was not a significant force in Swiss political life.

[17] The papacy is an interesting, more idiosyncratic case. The pope is appointed for life, but does not have the right to appoint a successor. The celibacy requirement makes the danger of appointing sons to the post less acute. Indeed, celibacy may have been prescribed to prevent the emergence of hereditary rights within the church.

create, (2) the extent to which they encourage or discourage substitutes for the state's third-party enforcement, and the differences in the constraints they impose on such arrangements, (3) their methods of controlling the protection resources, and (4) the size and scope that each state will tend to reach.

Legal Institutions

I do not expect the legal institutions developed by dictators to be as extensive as those developed by rule-of-law states. Dictators are the primary residual claimants to the incomes of their states, and most of their subjects do not own much. Given their subjects' poverty, there is not much room for disputes among them that could be economically settled by legal adjudication. Moreover, subjects would be reluctant to seek legal recourse in their disputes with dictators. The reason for this is that because of the nature of the beginning of their rule, dictators will not have developed a reputation for impartiality. Thus the demand for the services of legal institutions in dictatorial regimes will be low. In turn, the dictator's incentive to invest in the legal structure is weak. Thus, we can expect, for instance, that standard legal forms, as well as uniform weights and measures, will be less developed and less widely used in dictatorships than in rule-of-law states.

Substitutes for the State's Third-Party Enforcement

As meager as we expect the legal institutions under dictators to be, by the model here, substitutes for such institutions will be more meager still. The reason for that is the threat such institutions pose to the dictator. The gains from getting rid of the leader will be radically different in the two regimes. A subject who attempts to assassinate the head of a rule-of-law state is likely to be penalized even if he succeeds, lowering the incentive for such action. Only by destroying the bulk of such a regime's power could a person gain from killing its leader. By contrast, a subject who is able to get rid of a dictator can expect a substantial gain; his chance of becoming the new dictator is high. Dictators, obviously, will try to reduce their opportunities for being liquidated.

One method of getting rid of a dictator is by revolt. A pre-condition for revolt is the existence of a collective-action mechanism. Its function would be to prevent a free ride by those who would benefit from the revolt, but would let others bear the cost. For example, tight-knit groups incur relatively low costs in forming collective-action mechanisms. Such a mechanism can threaten the dictator directly; it also will facilitate wealth accumulation by subjects.[18] Subjects can use their wealth to gain power, which may explain why dictators are so vigorous in trying to uproot "profiteering." The existence of these capabilities, then, threatens dictators indirectly as well. Thus we expect dictators to discourage the formation of collective-action mechanisms and to eliminate existing ones. Subjects' freedom to form substitute organizations, then, will be more constrained under dictators than under rule-of-law regimes.

Another substitute for the state's third-party enforcement is organized crime. However, I am unable to determine unambiguously how organized crime fares under one regime as compared with the other. Dictators presumably impose more restrictions on their subjects than do rule-of-law regimes, and thus organized crime should have more profitable opportunities under the former than under the latter. But given the relative insecurity of dictators, organized crime threatens them more, and they are expected to make greater efforts to suppress it. The net effect on organized crime, not easily measurable in the first place, is indeterminate. Similarly, although we expect dictators to suppress more vigorously the possession and trading of weapons, no definite prediction seems possible regarding such suppression under dictators relative to that under the rule of law.

There is, nevertheless, one major force pulling toward a lower level of organized crime in rule-of-law states. Such states are characterized by a high level of contract trade and by the arrangements made to facilitate it. Among these is a greater effort, and the use of more refined market means, to induce equating costs and benefits. Therefore, effects that potentially would be external and would be regulated in dictatorships are more likely actually to be priced in rule-of-law states. Because such states need fewer regulations, we expect the scope for organized crime there to be less.

Consider now non-organized crime. Regulations, which are more common under dictatorships, induce such crime (as well as organized crime). In contrast, the production and trade of generic goods that are easy to exchange are expected to be higher under rule-of-law regimes

---

[18] Perhaps for this reason, during some periods in history, some minorities were able to accumulate large amounts of wealth.

than under dictatorships, and these are especially attractive to thieves. It does not seem possible, then, to determine under which regime the level of such crime would be less.

Control of the Protection Resources

The heads of the protection services and others near the centers of power threaten the safety of dictators more than they threaten the heads of rule-of-law states. As just stated, a dictator's murderer may well become his successor, whereas the murderer of the head of a rule-of-law state is likely to be severely punished. Only a full-fledged revolution will replace a rule-of-law regime. We expect dictators, among other things, to give less leeway to their generals than rule-of-law regimes will give to theirs.

The charismatic leader whose comparative advantage is in irregular military activities holds a curious position here. Some legendary figures are found in this category. Part of the lore surrounding them consists of descriptions of how the military bureaucracy clipped their wings and frustrated them in the performance of their patriotic duty. In rule-of-law states we can expect, indeed, that the support such charismatic leaders "deserve" will be stinted. They are unlikely to pose a threat to the regime as long as they are held back somewhat. In dictatorships, except for the occasional very successful leader who himself becomes a dictator, the fate of such figures is likely to be more tragic. They are expected to emerge almost exclusively during revolution. If they do not become heads of state, however, the emerging dictators are likely to eliminate them after the revolution because of fear of their popular support.[19]

The Size and Scope of the State

I expect a dictator to be more aggressive than the rule-of-law regime he replaces in expanding the boundaries of the state. This is because subjects are unable to restrict the dictator's power, whereas, as argued in Chapter 8, I expect subjects to restrict the power of protectors under their control. Seemingly attractive war ventures that would not be undertaken by a rule-of-law regime for fear of the power of its own military are likely to be undertaken by a dictator.

---

[19] Leon Trotsky, seemingly one of the more charismatic leaders of the Communist revolution in Russia, was shoved aside by Lenin and murdered by Stalin.

As discussed in the earlier comparison between the state and the firm, I expect the scope of the dictatorial state, which is the residual claimant to its own actions, to reach deeper than that of a rule-of-law state, because the latter does not assume residual claimancy to its actions. A person who manages to overthrow a rule-of-law state and become a dictator, then, will become the primary residual claimant of the income of his state and will run all, or at least the bulk, of its enterprises. On the other hand, because under a dictatorship the subjects do not bear the residual of their actions, their incentive to produce to their ability is muted, and the *total* income of the state, not to speak of subjects' income, will decline as a result of a takeover by a dictator. The low per-capita income in dictatorial states is not due to "inefficiencies" but rather to a deliberate choice by the dictator.

SUMMARY

Shocks, such as from natural disasters or from war, tend to upset the balance of power between states, as well as that between protectors and the collective-action mechanism that controls them. Shocks allow whoever has gained power relative to others to strengthen his position and benefit from taking "arbitrary" actions. To the extent that all perceive the effects of shocks similarly, the adjustments will be smooth. One of the effects of shocks, however, is to make the assessment of power more difficult. When people reach inconsistent estimates of their relative powers, the chance for violent dispute increases.

I define a shock to be "moderate" when, despite the effects of the shock, the collective-action mechanism is able to maintain control of the protectors, and "severe" when the disruption is so severe that protectors perceive that they can usurp power and become dictators. We expect that a protector who succeeds in usurping power will become a dictator. He will then attempt to uproot the existing collective-action mechanisms, for they pose a threat to his rule.

In general, dictatorial regimes tend to be more stagnant than those governed by the rule of law. The reason for this is that economic growth requires initiative and goes hand in hand with individuals' accumulation of wealth. Such accumulation is a threat to a dictator. For that reason, dictatorial regimes tend to discourage contract trade, and consequently such trade is likely to better flourish under rule-of-law regimes. Yet we expect the ratio of contract trade to trade enforced by other third parties to be higher under dictatorships. This is because other third-party enforcers tend to threaten dictators more than they threaten rule-of-law states, and thus dictators will tend to discourage trade enforced by them even more severely. We expect the dictator, then, to become the primary residual claimant to the bulk of the projects in his state. These are conditions under which the state is likely to stagnate.

A not-quite-imminent outside threat is unlikely to lead to significant change in the policies of rule-of-law states. A dictator facing such a threat, on the other hand, may conclude that he would become safer if he allowed some internal growth, for such growth would generate resources that could be used to defuse the threat. Internal growth requires subjects' cooperation, and subjects will cooperate only if the dictator can credibly commit not to confiscate their gains. Such a commitment implies that the dictator will relinquish some of his power, and that will constitute a step toward the rule of law. Thus, a dictatorship threatened by a non-imminent outside threat is likely to progress toward the rule of law.

16

Recapitulation and an Epilogue

In this book I am attempting to model the emergence of the state and follow its development, primarily when it evolves toward the rule of law. In the model I develop, all individuals, including the Hobbesian king, are assumed to be maximizers. As they begin to socialize, they first do not allow members of the society to specialize in the use of violence, in order to avoid dictatorial takeover by such specialists. However, when threatened by outsiders, they will allow such a specialist to emerge to help protect the members of the society, but only after they form a collective-action mechanism that will be able to control the specialist. The emergence of a specialized protector who adjudicates disputes and enforces his decisions defines the state.

The enforcement of agreements is a major feature of the model. The reason is that in only a subset of all agreements has the state a comparative advantage in enforcement; other agreements will be self-enforced or enforced by other third parties. The determination of which agreements the state will enforce and what fraction of all agreements it will enforce will determine the scope of the state.

Underlying this book is the methodology of the economics of (not well defined) property rights or of (positive) transaction costs, which by my definition is its dual. It models a world that radically departs from that underlying the Coase theorem, where economic property rights are (somehow) everywhere well defined. Institutions, including the state, are superfluous in such a world. Such an idealized world cannot exist, however. Indeed, there is no niche in reality where property rights can be fully and costlessly delineated.

The model's onset is at a time that precedes any voluntary social interactions. Individuals lived then in a Hobbesian "state of nature." Those who survived obviously were able to keep at least some of what they gathered and hunted. Over those commodities, then, they had economic rights. They had to protect what they got, and thus they incurred transaction costs (as the term is defined here). Moreover, they did not yet engage in exchange, because the costs of effecting it were prohibitively high.

As time passed, individuals gathered information about one another and discovered opportunities for exchange. With exchange came within-group specializing. I hypothesize that such groups did not allow their own members to specialize in the use of violence as long as other groups did not seriously threaten them. In that way they reduced the danger of dictatorial takeover. When threats from the outside did arise, they allowed such specializing. However, they first created a collective-action mechanism with sufficient power to prevent a takeover by the specialized protector. They also established procedures for decision-making. Those included, for certain issues, a unanimity or near-unanimity voting requirement of the appropriate set of individuals. The state that emerged specialized in the use of violence and provided ultimate third-party enforcement. The emergence and functioning of such states are the main topics of this book.

The need to contain the specialized protectors is never-ending. When subjects control their protectors, we expect them to impose constraints, such as on the length of service and on their budget. In addition, we expect subjects to pay wages to the protectors, rather than allowing them to retain the spoils of war. The reason is that when paid wages, they will have less chance of amassing the resources needed for a takeover.

Individuals have another way by which to reduce the chance for a takeover. This is to divide protection forces into units that are largely independent of each other. One example, from the United States, is the substantial autonomy the army, the navy, and the air force have and the loose central command over them. Added to these is the existence of the marines, another independent force that substantially duplicates the other forces in its capabilities. Each of the individual commanders then has control over only a portion of the military. Moreover, I argue that they are unlikely to allow one of them to become a dictator. Such separation of forces may be advantageous also in placing responsibility at a more "local" level.

Protection specialists must delineate what they will protect as well as what they will not. The violence-using protector (i.e., the state) takes on itself the task to protect the assets and asset attributes it delineates.

Specifying what it will protect constitutes legal delineation, whereby the state endows individuals with legal rights over assets. I assume, though, that perfect protection as well as perfect legal delineation would be prohibitively costly. Legal rights, too, are never delineated perfectly.

Exchange requires agreements, and agreements must be enforced. Initially, all agreements must have been self-enforced, relying on long-term relations. Increases in the extent of social interaction enabled third-party enforcement without the use of force, by elders for example, to emerge. When the state emerged, it provided third-party enforcement by using its ability in violence. Third-party enforcement plays a major role in organized societies, even though it must ultimately rely on self-enforcement.

Even where state enforcement is available, individuals tend to employ other third-party enforcers to enforce some of their agreements. These enforcers include religious and ethnic organizations, business firms, and, for agreements between states, treaty organizations. The larger the fraction of all agreements that the state enforces, the larger its scope.

The state's comparative advantage has several characteristics. Because enforcement by the state requires territorial continuity, it has an advantage in enforcing transactions that are subject to territorial scale economies. Related to this, it has an advantage in enforcing agreements that are similar to each other, because the adjudication in one case can apply to all the others. This is a basic feature of the common law. Because of the state's edge in enforcing similar agreements, the state's scope tends to increase as commodities become more standardized, which occurs when production processes generate more uniform output and as more standards are set.

As more commodities become standardized, the scale economies to state adjudication increase, and the advantage of expanding the domain of the state's ultimate enforcer increases as well. This force may explain the rise of rule-of-law empires, most prominently that of the British Empire. The British Empire seemingly got much of its impetus from the industrial expansion in England. The existence of a single ultimate enforcer accommodated trade by contract over the vast territory the empire encompassed.

The state enforcement of contracts substantially (though not entirely) accommodates anonymous trade. As the identities of the transactors become less important, it becomes possible to use a single violence-using enforcer for a chain of trades, instead of using a different non-violent third-party enforcer for each trade in the chain. A similar, though more subtle, force applies to the transfer of commodities by contract within a vertical production process, as compared with their within-firm transfer where the firm performs the third-party enforcement.

Standards and a uniform currency are public goods, and states often take part in producing them. In turn, as these are enhanced, contract trade and, with it, the scope of the state tend to increase. As mentioned earlier, the judicial rulings that apply to many similar cases also constitute a public good. This, seemingly, is a reason why the state subsidizes adjudication services. Given the subsidy, however, individuals tend to overuse the service. I predict that in order to curtail such overutilization, the state will restrict or even ban activities that are likely to induce litigation even if they do not have spillover effects.

States differ from firms in the way they use force to enforce agreements. The two forms of organization also differ in the way they are compensated for the services they provide. Firms or, more accurately, firm owners are the residual claimants to their activities, whereas rule-of-law states are not such claimants to their own activities. Where there are no externalities, firms are likely to be more efficient than the state. Given that the state will undertake various activities, it can increase its efficiency by assigning to local authorities those activities whose effects are largely confined to the local level. This, indeed, also applies to the military, providing a motive, besides the creation of independent power centers, to give certain units such as the border patrol local autonomy.

As just stated, individuals in rule-of-law states tend to assume the residual claims over activities that take place in the state. On the other hand, in dictatorships, the dictator tends to assume the bulk of the burden of the variability in the outcomes of activities in the state. The reason that the dictator does so is to reduce the amount of resources individuals command and thus the chance of revolt. Because in dictatorships most individuals are not given the chance to become residual claimants to their actions, their incentive to operate efficiently is stunted, and the dictator who has such an incentive is necessarily mired with a bureaucratic organization. I expect his state to be stagnant and to trail rule-of-law states in economic growth.

EPILOGUE

I have attempted to contribute to an understanding of the forces that have led to the emergence of the state and have affected the course of its evolution. Although I abstract from many of the features of the modern state, it is tempting to try to use the model to predict the course the state will follow. Does it tend toward a full-fledged democracy, a single-world state, the anarchy some consider ideal, or (God forbid) a theocracy?

Such questions themselves are very old, of course, and opinions vary regarding both the likelihood of the various outcomes and their desirability. Over the course of history, many have envisioned the ideal state, though the nature of the ideal, or "utopia," varies from one visionary to another.

The approach here allows us to say very little about the utopias. In the visions that tout utopias, they seem to emerge by magical power and then continue to exist indefinitely. Perfection needs no tinkering, and those models tend to be static. Even Hobbes's model is static in that the transition from his brutish "state of nature" to a monarchy is attained in one leap and no rebound. Once there, things are expected to stay as they are, as no forces for change are present.

Two major exceptions to the static view of the ideal state are the vision of Plato and that of Marx. In the *Republic*, Plato delineates conditions that would lead to the emergence, or rather the return to, the philosopher-king. Marx points to evolutionary forces that would culminate in a classless society. Once reached, however, those utopias, too, become static. Although Marx's model is evolutionary, the evolution ceases when it reaches the stage of the classless society.

The model in this book is also evolutionary, but unlike that of Marx, it never reaches a final state. Rather, the model produces a state that evolves indefinitely. In this sense it is Darwinian. It is Darwinian also in that it does not "strive" to an "ideal" or even to an ultimate form. The notions of continuing evolution and of "survival of the fittest" provide a wedge for determining where the state is headed. Fitness here is clearly correlated with wealth, and in turn, the model suggests that the rule of law is conducive to the enhancement of wealth.[1]

My guess is that the quite general strengthening of the rule of law in the past few decades will continue.[2] History, however, is replete with

---

[1] Evolutionary game theory allows for the existence of two same-species populations, each in a distinct and stable equilibrium. However, it arrives at the conclusion that when the two compete head-to-head, the "better fit" one will win (Dawkins, 1989, pp. 218–20). "Better fit" closely corresponds to less dissipation (i.e., greater wealth).

[2] As might be obvious, I personally hope that the rule of law will continue to advance.

instances of the demise of rule-of-law institutions. One reason given for such demise, or at least such decline, has to do with the effects of the supposedly increasing level of rent-seeking (Olson 1993).

As is well understood, the cost of avoiding transfers that are likely to occur in the future, but whose particular beneficiaries cannot be identified in the present, seems low. Individuals are likely to form institutions that will discourage future transfers if faced with a decision whether or not to allow such transfers. But the cost of discovering future transfer opportunities is incurred in the present. The farther in the future the opportunities for transfer, the costlier their discovery in the present. Because, in addition, the farther in the future such transfers themselves, the smaller their present cost, the chance is low that the organizers of institutions will attempt to prevent all such transfers from occurring. Therefore, as time passes, more and more transfer opportunities are expected to emerge, and when they emerge the beneficiaries are likely to be particular individuals.

The evolution of common-stock corporations provides a striking illustration of the problem and a hint as to why preventing transfers in the political sphere is so difficult. When corporations are newly created, especially if a chief executive is also the majority stockholder, they seem to operate most efficiently. As corporations "mature," ownership tends to become dispersed and divorced from management. Under decentralized control and separation of ownership and control, managers have stronger incentives to effect transfers to themselves. What looks like "rent-seeking" becomes common then. Corporate owners often take steps to stem the tide, and a corporate takeover may further rejuvenate the organization. Plugging all holes, however, would be too expensive, and not all wealth-capture opportunities will be eliminated. The "rent-seeking" opportunities that seem to exist, then, reflect the (constrained) best that can be attained, and thus their wastefulness is more apparent than real.

A similar scenario seems to apply to rule-of-law institutions. Entrenched positions make a reorganization more difficult than the founding of the original organization where there were no such positions. One underlying reason for the greater difficulty of reducing transfer in the state than in corporations is that whereas corporations are subject to third-party enforcement, the central institutions of the state are not. Additionally, the rule-of-law institutions often are subjected to shocks, such as civil or external wars, that increase the difficulty of reducing transfers in the political sphere.

The contemporary rule-of-law states, with the possible exceptions of England and Switzerland, all started with established interests and transfer opportunities in place. Moreover, most of the older rule-of-law states, including England and Switzerland, at one time or another went through major upheavals. Transfer opportunities are inevitable under such circumstances, and it is not surprising that the behavior viewed as "rent-seeking" is rampant. Reform is difficult because it is a bootstrap operation that must cope with the prevailing conditions, rather than starting from scratch. Occasionally some of the capture opportunities will be eliminated, but much of the time, given the system as it is, the cost of eliminating the "waste" will exceed the gain (as discussed in the section on rent-seeking in Chapter 5). The existence of transfer opportunities, then, does not imply the existence of waste.

Contemporary democracies clearly offer opportunities for change, and we do observe powerful forces toward change, both within and outside of mainstream political parties. When a state is successful in equating marginal costs to marginal benefits all around, the opportunities to manipulate the system to effect transfers are few. The greater the existing transfer opportunities, the more powerful I expect these forces to be. A major factor that has to be held constant here is the stability of the rule of law. Stated more operationally, ceteris paribus, the greater the current opportunities for transfer, the more likely is a *radical* change in government. The more stable and more entrenched is the rule of law, however, the less likely is a radical change.

Among all long-lasting rule-of-law states, Venice holds a remarkable and unique position on three counts: (1) The circumstances of its beginning: Until around A.D. 600, the Venetian lagoon contained several villages governed by the rule of law. Their population was small, living almost a "state-of-nature" existence in terms of its wealth. Around A.D. 600, the villages merged and right away formed rule-of-law institutions. Thus it became a rule-of-law state right when it emerged. (2) The longevity of Venice: Venice lasted as an independent state for twelve centuries, much longer than any other rule-of-law state. It was undone by Napoleon in 1797. (3) The stability of Venice: During those twelve centuries, Venice was never taken over by a foreign conqueror, nor was its government ever overthrown by a civil war.

That combination of circumstances meant that the original setting in which those individuals presumably organized so as to minimize transfer opportunities was then carried forward under the most stable conditions. Stability, however, was a far cry from stagnation there; it was accompanied by a smoothly working mechanism to adapt to new conditions and to take advantage of the accumulated experience. Indeed, Finer (1997, book II, p. 1016) states that until the eighteenth century, the government of Venice was the best in the world.

The constitutional history of Venice reveals a continuing effort to prevent a takeover by the doge and to reduce the opportunities for transfer. The effort to prevent transfer had two major components: (1) the measures taken to prevent the emergence of political parties, which would have been accompanied by resource-consuming competition for political spoils, and (2) the effort to prevent resource-consuming competition for governmental positions, especially that of doge.[3]

Preventing the formation of political parties may appear antidemocratic. Among rule-of-law states, however, Venice was not unique in the desire to prevent, or bypass, such formation. In England until the eighteenth or early nineteenth century there were no parties in the modern sense of the term, and in the debate on the American Constitution the idea of banning parties was prominent. Venice's uniqueness is in being successful in this regard. Although Venice did lack political parties, it was open to political debate within and outside its aristocratic voting institutions. Likewise, it had a most highly developed rule-of-law governance.[4]

Venetians were rewarded immensely by their city's lasting high degree of rule of law. First, they enjoyed the benefits of being spared from

---

[3] In 1268 Venice made an extraordinary arrangement for the selection of a new doge, an arrangement that was retained until the last days of the republic. As described by Brown (1895, pp. 150–1), it consisted of a series of steps to select competent electors who then were to choose the doge. At each step in the process of selecting the electors, a number of individuals would be selected, and then *randomly* winnowed. Only after eight(!) such steps was the final set of electors established. They then elected the doge by a supermajority.

One indication of the strength of the Venetian institutions is the fact that the doge was Venetian and served for life. In contrast, the podestas, the managers of the rest of the constitutional city-states in medieval Italy, were always outsiders and served usually for six months only. Continuity in the podesta's position and familiarity with the city he managed were sacrificed, then, presumably to reduce the chance of a takeover. Venice was secure enough in its control over its indigenous chief executive to accommodate a much greater continuity in his performance.

[4] The treatment of its Jewish population testifies to the high level of the rule of law in Venice. Once granted the right to stay, the Jews were never expelled from the state of Venice (indeed, not until the Nazi takeover in World War II). Neither were they subjected at any time to mob killing. They were confined to the very crowded ghetto and were heavily taxed, but they benefited from full protection of the law.

foreign conquest and occupation, as well as from civil war. Second, and obviously not independently of the first, Venice became very rich. For much of the past millennium, on a per-capita basis, Venice seemingly was one of the richest countries, if not the richest country, in the world. This held true not only when Venice was the gateway to the trade with Asia but even after discovery of the sea route to the silk and spices of Southeast Asia, which greatly reduced Venice's locational advantage.

Unfortunately, Venice's success story and the stories of other successful rule-of-law states provide no useful guide for formulating policies to achieve similar results elsewhere. Much of Venice's good fortune was due to fortunate circumstances. Early in its history, because of its poverty, Venice did not constitute an attractive prize for conquest, and its hard-to-penetrate lagoon made it easy to protect even when it became fabulously rich. Equally important, the rule of law became more entrenched with each century of undisturbed constitutional existence. The wry English lesson that it is easy to grow a beautiful, lush lawn by "just taking good care of it for three hundred years" is as applicable and as useful here.

The rule of law is governed by an unfortunate asymmetry: It takes no time at all to demolish, but a long time to establish. This seems highly applicable to the current relationship between China and Hong Kong. It should take a long time to establish a high degree of rule of law in Communist China, but the one existing in Hong Kong could be demolished in a wink.[5] We can hope that China will not choose to dismantle Hong Kong's rule-of-law institutions. Indeed, other rule-of-law states have a strong interest in pressuring China to maintain Hong Kong's rule of law, because they will gain from the added stability. Moreover, it seems highly likely that China's own growth can benefit significantly from the continuation of Hong Kong's institutions. But, ultimately, we must *know*, or, rather, our maximizing model dictates to us, that the individuals in power in China will do what they view as best for themselves, and a rule-of-law island in their midst may not necessarily be seen as best for them.[6]

---

[5] The transformation of Japan from an autocracy to a rule-of-law state is one of the greatest success stories of the second part of the twentieth century. It is worth recalling, however, that after World War II the American occupiers *imposed* (at least in part) the rule of law on Japan.

[6] This paragraph was formulated in 1996.

References

Alchian, Armen A. (1987). "Property Rights," in *The New Palgrave Dictionary of Economics*. New York: Norton.

Alchian, Armen A., and William R. Allen (1977). *Exchange and Production*, 2nd ed. Belmont, CA: Wadsworth.

Alchian, Armen A., and Harold Demsetz (1972). "Production, Information Costs, and Economic Organization." *American Economic Review* 62(5):777–95.

Allen, Douglas W. (1990). "An Inquiry into the State's Role in Marriage." *Journal of Economic Behavior and Organization* 13(2):171–91.

(1991a). "Homesteading and Property Rights; or, 'How the West Was Really Won'." *Journal of Law and Economics* 24(1):2–23.

(1991b). "What Are Transaction Costs?" *Research in Law and Economics* 14:1–18.

Alsberg, Carl L. (1926). "Protein Content: A Neglected Factor in Wheat Grades." *Wheat Studies* (Food Research Institute) 2:163–76.

Barzel, Yoram (1977). "An Economic Analysis of Slavery." *Journal of Law and Economics* 20:87–110.

(1982). "Measurement Cost and the Organization of Markets." *Journal of Law and Economics* 25:27–48.

(1997a). *Economic Analysis of Property Rights*, 2nd ed. Cambridge University Press. (Originally published 1989.)

(1997b). "Parliament as a Wealth Maximizing Institution: The Right to the Residual and the Right to Vote." *International Review of Law and Economics* 17:455–74.

(2000a). "Property Rights and the Evolution of the State." *Economics of Governance* 1(1).

(2000b). "The State and the Diversity of Third-Party Enforcers," in *Institutions, Contracts and Organizations*, ed. Claude Ménard, pp. 211–33. Cheltenham, UK: Edward Elgar.

(2000c). "Dispute and Its Resolution: Delineating the Economic Role of the Common Law." *American Law and Economics Review* 2:238–58.

Barzel, Yoram, and Tim R. Sass (1990). "The Allocation of Resources by Voting." *Quarterly Journal of Economics* 105:745–71.

References

Barzel, Yoram, and Wing Suen (1995). "Equity as a Guarantee: A Contribution to the Theory of the Firm." Mimeographed paper, University of Washington.

Becker, Gary S. (1985). "Public Policies, Pressure Groups, and Deadweight Costs." *Journal of Public Economics* 28:329–47.

Bernstein, Lisa (1992). "Opting Out of the Legal System: External Contractual Relations in the Diamond Industry." *Journal of Legal Studies* 21(11): 115–58.

(1996). "Merchant Law in a Merchant Court: Rethinking the Code's Search for Immanent Business Norms." *University of Pennsylvania Law Review* 144:1765–821.

Brown, Horatio F. (1895). *Venice, An Historical Sketch of the Republic.* London: Rivington, Percival.

Buchanan, James M., and Gordon Tullock (1962). *The Calculus of Consent.* Ann Arbor: University of Michigan Press.

Chai, Sun-Ki, and Michael Hechter (1998). "A Theory of the State and of Social Order," in *The Problem of Solidarity,* ed. Patrick Doreian and Thomas Fararo, pp. 33–60. New York: Gordon & Breach.

Cheung, Steven N. S. (1970). "The Structure of the Contract and the Theory of Non-exclusive Resources." *Journal of Law and Economics* 13:49–70.

(1974). "A Theory of Price Control." *Journal of Law and Economics* 17:53–72.

Crawford, Michael (1978). *The Roman Republic.* Atlantic Highlands, NJ: Harvester Press.

Dawkins, Richard (1989). *The Selfish Gene,* 2nd ed. Oxford University Press.

Demsetz, Harold (1967). "Toward a Theory of Property Rights." *American Economic Review* 57(2):347–59.

Dennett, Daniel C. (1995). *Darwin's Dangerous Idea.* New York: Simon & Schuster.

DeSoto, Hernando (1989). *The Other Path.* New York: Harper & Row. (Originally published, in Spanish, 1987.)

Dittmer, Timothy (1997). "Substitutes for the Sword: A Measurement Cost Explanation of Voting." Mimeographed paper.

Dollinger, Phillipe (1970). *The German Hansa.* Stanford, CA: Stanford University Press.

Durant, Will (1939). *The Life of Greece.* New York: Simon & Schuster.

Ellickson, Robert C. (1989). "Hypothesis of Wealth Maximizing Norms." *Journal of Law, Economics, & Organization* 5:83–97.

(1991). *Order Without Law.* Cambridge, MA. Harvard University Press.

(1993). "Property in Land." *Yale Law Journal* 102:1315–400.

Finer, S. E. (1997). *The History of Government from the Earliest Times.* Oxford University Press.

Friedman, David (1977). "A Theory of the Size and Shape of Nations." *Journal of Political Economy* 85:57–78.

Gambetta, Diego (1993). *The Sicilian Mafia.* Cambridge, MA: Harvard University Press.

Gould, John P. (1973). "The Economics of Legal Conflicts." *Journal of Legal Studies* 2:279–300.

Greif, Avner (1989). "Contract Enforceability and Economic Institutions in Early Trade: The Maghribi Traders." *Journal of Economic History* 44:857–82.

——— (1994). "On the Political Foundations of the Late Medieval Commercial Revolution: Genoa During the Twelfth and Thirteenth Centuries." *Journal of Economic History* 54(2):271–87.

——— (1999). "On the Social Foundation and Historical Development of Institutions that Facilitate Impersonal Exchange: From the Community Responsibility System to Individual Legal Responsibility in Pre-modern Europe," in *Communities and Markets in the Process of Economic Development*, ed. Aoki and Hayami.

Grossman, Sanford J., and Oliver D. Hart (1980). "Takeover Bias, the Free-Rider Problem, and the Theory of the Corporation." *Bell Journal of Economics* 11:42–64.

Hayek, Friedrich A. (1948). "The Meaning of Competition," in *Individualism and Economic Order*, pp. 92–106. University of Chicago Press.

Hechter, Michael (1987). *Principles of Group Solidarity.* Berkeley: University of California Press.

Hobbes, Thomas (1991). *Leviathan.* Cambridge University Press. (Originally published 1651.)

Holt, J. C. (1965). *Magna Carta.* Cambridge University Press.

Johnsen, D. Bruce (1986). "The Formation and Protection of Property Rights among the Southern Kwakiutl Indians." *Journal of Legal Studies* 15(1):43–67.

Klein, Benjamin, Robert Crawford, and Armen A. Alchian (1979). "Vertical Integration, Appropriable Rent, and the Competitive Contracting Process." *Journal of Law and Economics* 25:297–326.

Klein, Benjamin, and Keith B. Leffler (1981). "The Role of Market Forces in Assuring Contractual Performance." *Journal of Political Economy* 89:615–64.

Landes, William M. (1971). "An Economic Analysis of the Courts." *Journal of Law and Economics* 14:61–108.

Lane, Frederick C. (1973). *Venice: A Maritime Republic.* Baltimore: Johns Hopkins University Press.

——— (1977). "The First Infidelities of the Venetian Lire," in *The Medieval City*, ed. H. A. Mishinin, D. Herlihy, and A. L. Udovich, pp. 43–64. New Haven, CT: Yale University Press.

Levi, Margaret (1988). *Of Rule and Revenue.* Berkeley: University of California Press.

Lueck, Dean (1989). "The Economic Nature of Wildlife Law." *Journal of Legal Studies* 18(2):291–324.

Masten, Scott E. (1999). "Contractual Choice," in *Encyclopedia of Law and Economics*, ed. B. Boukaert and G. De Geest, Cheltenham, UK: Edward Elgar.

Mayers, David, and Clifford W. Smith, Jr. (1990). "The Corporate Demand for Insurance: Evidence from the Reinsurance Market." *Journal of Business* 63(1):19–39.

Milgrom, Paul R., Douglass C. North, and Barry Weingast (1990). "The Role of Institutions in the Revival of Trade: The Law Merchant, Private Judges and Champagne Fairs." *Economics and Politics* 2(1):1–24.

Moore, Ellen Wedemeyer (1985). *The Fairs of Medieval England.* Toronto: Pontifical Institute of Mediaeval Studies.

North, Douglass C. (1981). *Structure and Change in Economic History.* New York: Norton.

(1990). *Institutions, Institutional Change and Economic Performance.* Cambridge University Press.

Nozick, Robert (1974). *Anarchy, State, and Utopia.* New York: Basic Books.

Olson, Mancur (1965). *The Logic of Collective Action.* Cambridge, MA: Harvard University Press.

(1982). *The Rise and Decline of Nations.* New Haven, CT: Yale University Press.

(1993). "Dictatorship, Democracy and Development." *American Political Science Review* 87(3):567–76.

(2000). *Power and Prosperity.* New York: Basic Books.

Ostrom, Vincent (1971). *The Political Theory of a Compound Republic.* Blacksburg, VA: Public Choice.

Popper, Karl R. (1962). *The Open Society and Its Enemies,* 4th ed. London: Routledge & Kegan Paul.

Posner, Eric A. (1996). "The Regulation of Groups: The Influence of Legal and Nonlegal Sanctions on Collective Action." *University of Chicago Law Review* 63:133–97.

Priest, George L. (1980). "Selective Characteristics of Litigation." *Journal of Legal Studies* 9:399–422.

Riker, William H. (1976). "Comments on Vincent Ostrom's Paper." *Public Choice* 27:13–15.

(1987). *The Development of American Federalism.* Dordrecht: Kluwer.

Rousseau, Jean-Jacques (1761). *A Discourse upon the Origin and Foundation of the Inequality among Mankind.* London: Printed for R. and J. Dodsley.

Schwartz, Alan (1992). "Relational Contracts in the Courts: An Analysis of Incomplete Agreements and Judicial Strategies." *Journal of Legal Studies* 21(2):271–318.

Sened, Itai (1997). *The Political Institution of Private Property.* Cambridge University Press.

Shleifer, Andrei, and Vishny, R. W. (1993). "Corruption." *Quarterly Journal of Economics* 108(3):599–617.

Skogh, Goran, and Charles Stuart (1982). "A Contractarian Theory of Property Rights and Crime." *Scandinavian Journal of Economics* 84(1):27–40.

Taylor, Michael (1982). *Community, Anarchy and Liberty.* Cambridge University Press.

References

Telser, Lester G., and Harlow N. Higinbotham (1977). "Organized Futures Markets: Costs and Benefits." *Journal of Political Economy* 85(5): 969–1000.

Tirole, Jean (1988). *The Theory of Industrial Organization.* Cambridge, MA: MIT Press.

Tullock, Gordon (1994). *The New Federalist.* Vancouver: Fraser Institute.

Umbeck, John (1981). "Might Makes Right: A Theory of the Function and Initial Distribution of Property Rights." *Economic Inquiry* 19:38–59.

Waley, Daniel (1988). *The Italian City-Republic,* 3rd ed. London: Longman.

Weber, Max (1968). *Economy and Society.* Berkeley: University of California Press. (Originally published 1922.)

Weingast, Barry R. (1994). "Constructing Trust: The Political and Economic Roots of Ethnic and Regional Conflict." Mimeographed paper, Stanford University.

Williamson, Oliver E. (1975). *Markets and Hierarchies: Analysis of Anti-Trust Implications.* New York: Free Press.

(1983). "Credible Commitments: Using Hostages to Support Exchange." *American Economic Review* 73:519–40.

(1999). "Private and Public Bureaucracies: A Transaction Cost Economics Perspective." *Journal of Law, Economics, & Organization* 15:306–42.

Wittfogel, Karl A. (1957). *Oriental Despotism: A Comparative Study of Total Power.* New Haven, CT: Yale University Press.

Wykes, Alan (1964). *Gambling.* London: Spring Book.

Index

Index

protection specialists, 107, 238; of the state, 20, 238; third-party, 22, 42–3, 45–52, 103–4; threat of using, 239–40; and utility functions, 239–40; and vote allocation, 125, 127; and wealth, 238, 259. *See also* balance of power

precedents, 177

predictability of a country's behavior, 244–6

production: cost of, 210; lines, 204; vertical processes, 52–3

property: attributes of, 171–2; protection of, 160–1, 162–3, 199; protectors', 147; tax, for financing adjudication, 174–5; value of, 175; and vote allocation, 127–8

property rights, 186, 267

protection: abstention from, 201–2; and collective-action mechanisms, 5; cost of, 161–2; scale economies to, 138, 198–201, 239

protectors: balance of power between clients and, 46, 47, 60–1, 119–21, 151, 159, 241–2; becoming dictators, 6; clients of, 5–6; and collective-action mechanisms, 122, 268; common, 54–5, 199–200; and confiscation, 61, 115; constraining, 26–7, 33, 44–5, 261, 264, 268; emergence of, 267; as employees, 141–3; and legal rights, 165–6; organizational discretion of, 149; power of, 238; remuneration of, 141–3; as residual claimants, 141, 143, 149; restrictions on, 143–7, 149–50; and scale economies, 138, 198–201, 239; takeovers by, 120, 138, 268; tenure of, 145–6, 261; and theft, 162

public good, 127, 191, 270

punishment, in collective-action mechanisms, 116

quid pro quo condition, 169

rape, 178–9

rationing by congestion, 129

raw materials, 211

reassignment of futures contracts, 92

registration, delineation by, 169, 186–7

religious organizations, 29–30, 70–1, 107–8, 181, 196; jurisdiction of, 226–7. *See also* Catholic church

remuneration, 141–3, 147, 148

rent-seeking, 129–31, 272

reputation, 85; *versus* contract, 81–2; state loss of, 180

residual claimants: firms as, 153, 270;

individuals as, 247; partners as, 53; protectors as, 141, 143, 149; state as, 178, 270

resources for overthrowing dictators, 139–40

responsibility, assumption of, 97, 99

restrictions: on business enterprises, 151–2; on protectors, 143–7, 149–50

revolts, 262–3

revolutionary movements, 235

Riker, William H., 26, 131, 133, 196, 218, 219n2, 222n8

roads, 188–9

Rome, 189

Rousseau, Jean-Jacques, 13n1

rule-of-law states: balance of power in, 122; and collective action, 5, 113, 131–4; and contract trade, 212; *versus* dictatorships, 27, 256–8, 261–5, 270; evolution of, 5; *versus* firms, 260, 270; frequency of wars among, 245; institutions in, 257; mergers of, 135, 220–4; military forces in, 132; and rent-seeking, 272–3; stability of, 63; treaties between, 207

rulers, successors to, 133

Russia, 254, 255

Sass, Tim R., 126, 130, 152

scale economies: in adjudication, 173, 176; to contract trade, 95; and delineation of assets, 179, 181; to enforcement, 25; to protection, 138, 198–201, 239; to size of the state, 7; to standards, 194–6; territorial, 94–6; to use of power, 6–7, 239

self-enforcement, 36; of anonymous exchanges, 80; of cooperative ventures, 39–40; of relationships, 59–60, 66; between states, 244, 246

self-protection, of idiosyncratic assets, 167

Sened, Itai, 2n1

separability (of enforcement), 110, 111

separation of powers, 131

shipping, 81, 95

ships, 30

shirking, measures to reduce, 5

Shleifer, Andrei, 182n35

shocks, 6, 248; effects of, 250–4; random, 17

side effects, the burrden of, 230–1

simultaneity of actions, 114

Singapore, 258

Skogh, Goran, 239n1

slavery, 167–8, 248

Smith, Clifford W., Jr., 142n6

Index

socialization, 13–14
social mores, enforcement by, 56–7
society, early history of, 13–14
specifications in agreements, 88, 91–2, 95, 210
stability, 63, 176–7; and confiscation, 123–4; and frequency of wars, 245
Stalin, Joseph, 139n3
standardization: of commodities, 84–5, 88, 95, 190–3, 210, 269, 270; scale economies to, 194–6; of weights and measures, 204. *See also* uniformity
"state of nature," 2, 5
states: balance of power between criminal organizations and, 228, 235–6; contract enforcement, 202, 206, 231, 269; control of organizations, 108–9; criminal organizations as, 232; definition of, 4, 20–3, 28; domain, 104; enforceability of agreements between, 244–6; expansion of, 205–8, 209–13; *versus* firms, 150–4; involvement in disputes, 177–8; jurisdiction of, 104–5; legitimate *versus* illegitimate, 30; mergers of, 201; and power, 238; protection of idiosyncratic assets, 166–7; as residual claimants, 154, 178; restrictions on private exchange, 169–71; scope of, 23–4, 32, 33, 177, 264–5; size of, 198–201, 264–5; third-party enforcement, 23
Stuart, Charles, 239n1
substitutes to state enforcement, 69–76
Suen, Wing, 153n22
supermajority voting rules, 125
supervision, cost of, 147–8
Switzerland, 135–6, 222, 261

takeovers: by dictators, 6, 121–4; by protectors, 120, 138, 268
taxation, 160; for dispute adjudication, 174–5; by King John, 123; and mitigation of side effects, 230; for protection, 166; for transactions, 76–7, 192
Taylor, Michael, 23n21, 119n8, 201, 202, 259n13
team production, 74
Telser, Lester G., 89n15
tenure (of protectors), 145–6, 261
territorial continuity, 93, 94
territory, state, 22
theft: definition of, 35; of generic assets, 234; of generic *versus* idiosyncratic assets, 170–1, 179; insiders', 162–5; in merged states, 224; net return from prevention, 180; protection from, 53–5,

158–9; self-protection from, 162. *See also* capture
third parties, delineation by, 180–1
third-party enforcement, 269; and adjudication, 25; in city-states, 208; and collective-action mechanisms, 26–7; confiscation by, preventing, 43–5; and contract trade, 221; costs imposed by, 34–5, 38–9; diversity of, 39; fees for services, 103; and incentives, 37, 52–3; jurisdiction of, 55–6; and long-term relations, 25, 34, 40–1, 42–3, 68; market for services, 37–8; non-state, 28, 69–76, 182; power of, 22, 42–3, 45–52, 103–4; and protection from theft, 53–5; by social mores, 56–7; and states, 22; substitutes for state, 262–4; value of services, 45, 47
threats, 160
Tirole, Jean, 17n9
trade: anonymous, 269; of banned commodities, 231; in city-states, 208–9; costs of, 188–9; and jurisdictional overlap, 104–5; markets for, 189; reputation *versus* contract, 81–2; roads for, 188–9; and states, 6–7
trade organizations, 74–5
transactions: caveat-emptor, 79–80; caveat-emptor *versus* future-obligation, 83–5; enforcement of, 79; within firms, 72; future-obligation, 86–7; jurisdiction over, 110, 152; registration of, 169; and the state, 33
transferability, 32
transfers: and brand names, 82–3; and impartiality of legal system, 177; opportunities for, 272–3; preventing, 128–9; via voting, 126; within-firm, 98
treaties, 207, 218, 223–4
Trotsky, Leon, 264n19
Tullock, Gordon, 3n4, 109n7, 125n19, 226n15

Umbeck, John, 2, 3, 14n3, 238, 239
unanimity voting rules, 125, 126–7, 128
uncertainty (regarding power), 240–1
uniformity, 172, 193; of raw materials, 211. *See also* standardization
United States, 133
utility, 14, 239–40
utopia, 271

value: of agreements, 64; of individuals' holdings, 160–1; of interactions, 36; of long-term relations, 40–1; present, 126; of scope of the state, 23–4; taxation of, 77

Index

variability, 153
Venice, 124, 192n10, 261, 273–5
vertical integration, 71–4, 96–101;
definition of, 97; and local autonomy,
111; and scope of the state, 23–4. *See
also* firms
violence: in agreement enforcement, 3, 19,
22, 46; in contract enforcement, 231;
and cost imposition, 42; criminal
organizations' use of, 23, 231;
definition of, 35; in dictatorships, 41;
versus long-term relations, 19, 85; state
use of, 4, 33, 104; third party use of,
22, 38, 44, 66–7, 95
Vishny, R. W., 182n35
voting, 124–8, 242; enforcement of,
124–5

wages, 5, 37, 154, 268
Waley, Daniel, 126n21, 146, 147n16,
150n18
Wallis, John, 121n12

Walrasian model, 15n5, 80
war, 243–4, 246, 248; aftermath of,
247–9; civil, 253; among rule-of-law
regimes, 245; spoils of, 247–8
waste: in dictatorships, 130–1; and
rent-seeking, 129
water rights, 195
wealth: claimants to, 141; and power,
259; *versus* power, 238; protectors',
142; subjects', 139–40; transfers, 152,
153
weapons, 75, 107, 228, 230–1
Weber, Max, 20, 21n16
Weingast, Barry R., 3, 37n5,n6, 71n15,
114, 243
Williamson, Oliver E., 3, 37n4, 73n19,
100–1, 118
willingness to pay, 173
winning, cost of, 243
Wittfogel, Karl A., 21n17, 115n3, 260n14
writing, invention of, 203
Wykes, Alan, 233n6